The
IRISH
CIVIL WAR

T0158716

For David Enright

Seán Enright was called to the Bar at Middle Temple in 1982 and at the Four Courts in 1993. He practised at the Bar in London for many years and is now a Circuit Judge. He is the author of *The Trial of Civilians by Military Courts: Ireland 1921* (Irish Academic Press, 2012), *Easter Rising 1916: The Trials* (Merrion Press, 2014) and *After the Rising: Soldiers, Lawyers and Trials of the Irish Revolution* (Merrion Press, 2016).

The

IRISH
CIVIL WAR

Law, Execution and Atrocity

SEÁN ENRIGHT

MERRION
PRESS

First published in 2019 by
Merrion Press
10 George's Street
Newbridge
Co. Kildare
Ireland
www.merrionpress.ie

This edition published 2022
© Seán Enright, 2022

9781785371684 (Paper)
9781785372544 (Kindle)
9781785372551 (Epub)
9781785372568 (PDF)

A CIP catalogue record for this book is available from the British
Library.

Typeset in Minion Pro 10.5/14 pt

Front cover: Richard Mulcahy (left) and Chief of Staff Sean Mac Mahon
(right) inspecting the new National Army, autumn 1922.
(Courtesy of IMA)
Back cover: National Army troops fighting near Nelson's Pillar, June
1922. (Courtesy of NLI)

Merrion Press is a member of Publishing Ireland.

Contents

Acknowledgements

I acknowledge the patience and support of my wife, Lorna. Also, the Master and Fellows of Sidney Sussex where I was a visiting scholar: the facilities and library of the College made this book possible. In particular, I acknowledge the encouragement of Professor Eugenio Biagini.

I also acknowledge and thank Hugh Beckett of the Irish Military Archives and the kind assistance of the staff at the National Library of Ireland, the National Archives of Ireland and the United Kingdom and the library staff at Stamford, Middle Temple and the British Library. Also, a special thank you to Aoife Torpey at Kilmainham Gaol Museum for generous assistance with photographs.

My thanks also to Tom and Aideen Carroll for on-the-spot help in Dublin; Tim Horgan for a tour of the cliffs overlooking the Clashmealcon caves in Kerry and help with Ballyseedy; and Stephen Kelleghan for help with Cahersiveen. Also help from Seán Hogan (Tipperary), Fr J.J. Ó Ríordáin from Kiskeam and Michael Byrne of the Offaly Historical and Archaeological Society in respect of the executions of Cunningham, Kelly and Conroy. My thanks to Ian Kenneally (Athlone) in respect of Tony Lawlor and Tom Toomey from County Limerick. Pat McCarthy in Waterford for help with the executions of Fitzgerald and O'Reilly, and Kieran Glennon in respect of the Drumboe executions. A special mention for John Dorney, who gave assistance in respect of James O'Rourke, Grealy and Burke. To Maura O'Cronin and Dr John Cunningham from NUI Galway, Meda Ryan from west Cork and Peter Beirne of Clare County Library in respect of the Ennis executions. Also, Tommy Mahony from Kerry, Eoin Walsh in Kilkenny and Ellen D. Murphy for help generously given. A big thank you also to Amelia O'Connor, Davide Corbino, Charles Falk, Christian Jowett and Al Smith.

I acknowledge permission to use photographs given by the Irish Military Archives, National Library of Ireland and Kilmainham Gaol Museum.

Mistakes and omissions are my responsibility.

Key Events and
Main Protagonists

THE KEY EVENTS

July 1921. The Truce between Britain and Ireland came into effect and brought the War of Independence to an end.

December 1921. The Treaty was signed at Westminster. The contentious parts of the Treaty allowed the creation of an Irish Free State under the sovereignty of the British monarch and permitted the Unionist majority in Ulster the opportunity of opting out of the new state.

7 January 1922. After lengthy and bitter debate the Treaty was approved by the Dáil by a margin of 64–57. A provisional government was formed to govern until the Irish Free State could be brought into being.

The anti-Treaty Executive took over the Four Courts and plans were made to launch an attack on units of the British Army not yet evacuated and bounce the provisional government into a resumption of the war between Britain and Ireland.

16 June 1922. The general election in which the Treaty was the dominant issue. Fifty-eight pro-Treaty Sinn Féin candidates were returned and thirty-six anti-Treaty. Most of the other elected deputies were broadly pro-Treaty.[1] In total, about 78 per cent of those who voted favoured pro-Treaty candidates.[2]

22 June 1922. The assassination of Sir Henry Wilson in London by London-based IRA men. The government of Lloyd George blamed the anti-Treaty faction that had taken over the Four Courts and briefly considered direct military action.

28 June 1922. The National Army of the provisional government bombarded the Four Courts and the civil war began.

August 1922. The death of President Griffith and Michael Collins, Commander in Chief of the National Army.

28 September 1922. The Dáil passes the Army (Special Powers) Resolution creating military courts with the power to impose the death penalty for possession of arms and other specified offences.

17 November 1922. The first executions.

6 December 1922. The Irish Free State came into being. As expected, the Six Counties in the North opted out.

8 December 1922. The Mountjoy executions. Four anti-Treaty prisoners were executed without trial as a reprisal for the murder of Sean Hales TD.

10 April 1923. The death of Liam Lynch, Chief of Staff of the anti-Treaty faction. This effectively brought about the end of the civil war.

27 April 1923. Ceasefire order issued by Frank Aiken, the new Chief of Staff of the anti-Treaty faction, to take effect in seventy-two hours.

24 May 1923. Dump arms order issued by Frank Aiken, Chief of Staff of the anti-Treaty faction.

2 June 1923. The last executions. In total, eighty-three men were executed by firing squad.

THE FACTIONS

Pro-Treaty: this faction favoured the Treaty between Britain and Ireland. After the Dáil adopted the Treaty, their leaders formed a transitional administration known as the provisional government that lasted until the creation of the Irish Free State, which took place on 6 December 1922. Where possible they are referred to in this work as the provisional government or pro-Treaty and, after 6 December 1922, as the government of the Irish Free State.

Anti-Treaty: this faction was composed of those opposed to the Treaty terms agreed between Britain and the Dáil. This faction favoured complete independence from Britain and the Commonwealth, and were opposed to the partition of Ireland. During the civil war this faction was variously known as the IRA, Irregulars or Irreconcilables. 'Anti-Treaty' is a neutral term and that is how they are generally referred to in this work.

THE LEADERS

Michael Collins was a signatory of the Treaty and head of the IRB. He was commander in chief of the National Army and the de facto head of civilian government. He was killed in action in August 1922.

William T. Cosgrave had been a long-time member of the Dublin Corporation where he did much to alleviate poverty in the city. He was a junior officer in the Irish Volunteers in 1916. After the rebellion he was tried and narrowly escaped execution. During the War of Independence, he was minister for local government. He was a grocer by trade before his involvement in politics. A slightly built man with a big quiff and a fondness for morning dress. He became head of the provisional government after the death of Arthur Griffith and Michael Collins. Few thought Cosgrave had the mettle to lead the pro-Treaty faction through the civil war.

Richard Mulcahy was chief of staff of the National Army until the death of Michael Collins. Thereafter, commander in chief, chairman of the Army Council and minister for defence, then aged only 36. He had been a long-time member of the Volunteers and fought in 1916 under Thomas Ashe at Ashbourne, although it was he, not Ashe, who was the architect of the victory at Ashbourne. After the general surrender, he avoided court martial by a fluke and was interned in Wales until the general amnesty of 1917, when he returned to Ireland and became chief of staff of the reformed Volunteers. He was a careful, methodical man from a conservative, middle-class Waterford family, with an interest in promoting the Irish language and culture which remained with him throughout his public service.

Gearóid O'Sullivan was from west Cork where he had been an Irish teacher before becoming involved in the Volunteers. He served in the GPO in 1916 and was later interned in Wales where he and Collins established a close friendship. During the War of Independence, he became the right-hand man of Collins and lived in imminent danger of capture until the Truce. While on the run he was elected to the Dáil. In 1922 he became the first adjutant general of the National Army and a member of the Army Council at the age of 32. After the war he left the National Army and trained for the bar, where he built a successful practice before being re-elected as a TD in 1927.

Kevin O'Higgins was minister for home affairs including the justice portfolio during the civil war. He was then aged 30, a solicitor by training. He had spent the War of Independence years working in the ministry of local government set up by the first Dáil. He was one of an emerging brand of professional politicians. O'Higgins was highly articulate, forceful and histrionic. He was from a comfortable middle-class background and was intensely conservative and ambitious for himself. He was distrustful of the army and General Mulcahy. O'Higgins became the minister most closely associated with the execution policy and was assassinated in 1927 for that reason. As he lay bleeding on a pavement he joked: 'I was always a diehard.'

Joe McGrath was a 1916 veteran. He had served at Marrowbone Lane but, along with a handful of others, walked out just before the general surrender and avoided court martial. One of the junior officers under him (Con Colbert) was tried and shot. During the War of Independence, McGrath robbed banks for the cause and skimmed off some of the proceeds to live on. He was arrested and interned at Ballykinlar and escaped by walking out dressed as a British officer. During the civil war McGrath served briefly as minister for labour, director of intelligence and minister for trade and commerce. A taciturn man, still in his early thirties during the civil war, he supported the execution policy. He left government in 1924, somewhat disillusioned with the revolution. In later life he became a successful and quite shady businessman.

Desmond Fitzgerald was also a 1916 veteran. He was given ten years' penal servitude for his part in the defence of the GPO. A TD, he was minister for external affairs for most of the civil war. Like the other members of the government he was still in his early thirties. In his early days he was a free thinker and writer but quickly became very conservative in outlook. He supported the execution policy. After the civil war he became minister of defence and was famously punched by the army chief of staff in an argument over officers' pay.

Ernest Blythe was a northern Protestant and an Irish language enthusiast and also a long-time IRB member. He was a member of the Executive Council. He remains an enigmatic figure who was not attached to any clique within the government.

Eoin MacNeill. Formerly a professor of early Irish history. In 1916 he was chief of staff of the Irish Volunteers and famously signed the countermand when he became aware that the Volunteers had been jockeyed into rebellion by Pearse and his followers. He narrowly avoided execution after the Rising. In 1922 he became part of the Executive Council of the provisional government and held the education portfolio. He was a man of considerable intellect.

Tom Johnson. A Liverpool-born self-educated trade unionist. He was leader of the Irish Labour Party during the civil war and effectively head of the opposition. He was an eloquent critic of the execution policy.

George Gavan Duffy, a solicitor and a member of the Dáil, had made his reputation by representing Casement at his trial for treason and bringing a test case in the High Court in London to challenge the legality of the 1916 trials: *R v The Governor of Lewis Prison ex parte Doyle* [1917] 2 KB 254. He was briefly a member of the Executive Council of the provisional government where he was nicknamed 'sore toes'. After failing to achieve POW status for captured anti-Treaty prisoners, he left the government in the summer of 1922 and became one of the most vocal backbench critics of the execution policy. In later years he became a distinguished but reactionary justice of the Irish High Court.

Éamon de Valera narrowly avoided execution after the 1916 rising. He was later prime minister and president of the Dáil until January 1922. Tall and thin, his egotistical nature only really became apparent during the Treaty debates and he was blamed by many for allowing the civil war to come about. During the civil war he became the head of state of the anti-Treaty Republic but remained in hiding – a marginal figure. All the real power was exercised by Liam Lynch, chief of staff of the anti-Treaty army.

Liam Lynch, at only 29, was chief of staff of the anti-Treaty army. He had formerly been a divisional commander during the War of Independence. He kept the civil war going long after it had been lost. On 10 April 1923, during a National Army sweep across the Knockmealdown mountains, he was wounded and died later that day. This precipitated the end of the civil war.

The Lawyers

Sir Charles O'Connor, Master of the Rolls. During the War of Independence, he gave judgment against the British Army and in favour of the prisoners in a landmark case that brought executions to a halt in the martial law area: *Egan v Macready* [1921] IR 265. He was one of the judges kept on by the new provisional government after the Treaty. It was said, rather cynically, that he had 'acquired merit' in the eyes of the new administration. He also gave judgment in the case which resulted in the execution of Childers: *R (Childers) v the Adjutant General of the forces of the Irish Free State* [1923] 1 IR 5. He was a member of the O'Connor clan – a subject on which he would bore anyone who cared to listen.

Cahir Davitt. Son of the land leaguer, Davitt had been a judge of the Dáil courts in 1920–1. In the summer of 1922, he was recruited by Collins to be judge advocate general of the new National Army. He had a supervisory role in respect of all trials by military courts.

Thomas Francis Molony – a long-time home ruler. He was appointed chief justice of Ireland in 1918 and steered the law through the most difficult times. The courts over which he presided were partially supplanted during the War of Independence by the new Dáil courts and also by the martial law courts set up by the British Army to try those captured with arms. In this era he gave judgment in many of the leading cases, notably *R v Allen* [1921] 2 241. During the civil war the new Irish Army would also set up military courts to try civilians and once again the courts over which Molony presided were marginalised. It was not until after the civil war in the summer of 1923 that Molony was able to reassert the rule of law.

Michael Comyn, KC. Comyn was anti-Treaty. He used his legal skills to try to discredit the actions of the provisional government through a series of inquests into the deaths of men killed in the custody of the state.

Tim Healy, KC. A pro-Treatyite from west Cork. Healy was an author, journalist, barrister, MP. Small in build and red-haired, with a foul temper, he was a formidable defence advocate with a pungent wit. At an early stage in his career he was responsible for the Healy Clause in the Land Act of 1881 which meant that increases in rent could not be levied as a result of improvement to land made by a tenant. He helped bring down Parnell. He made his career as a constitutional nationalist politician, although there were long-standing suspicions that he was an IRB man and also a British spy. He was one of a handful of lawyers who helped shape the policy of the provisional government and the drafting of the Irish Constitution. He would become the first governor general of the Irish Free State in December 1922.

Author's Note

It was the worst possible start for a small state that had just secured a measure of independence. After the death of Collins, the new commander in chief of the National Army, General Mulcahy, urged his men not to retaliate, and, on the anti-Treaty side, Liam Lynch also urged his men to adhere to recognised standards of warfare. Both sides fell far short of this ideal.

The war was a complex and multi-layered event that cannot be recorded in a single volume and this book deals only with one dimension – deaths in custody of the state. By focussing on the execution policy and the fate of prisoners killed in custody, it should not be thought that the death and suffering of so many others is considered less important or not highly relevant to the context in which these events took place. One distinguished historian has argued that all that took place allowed the losing faction to assert 'victimhood' and the full context of all that took place should be acknowledged.[1] The anti-Treaty forces perpetrated killings that still shock. Not just civilians shot in the crossfire but during attacks on the National Army in Dublin that sometimes showed a reckless disregard for civilians. Others were killed in the flood of robberies that overtook the country, although not every robbery or even most robberies can be safely ascribed to the anti-Treaty faction.

The attacks on the railways also claimed the lives of civilians: the Liscahane train derailment is an example. At Ballyconnell, a column of anti-Treaty fighters killed two civilians, wounded a third and left a trail of arson and robbery in their wake before disappearing into the hills. There were also occasional killings of unarmed national soldiers on leave, like National Army Private

Denis McCarthy who was shot in the back as he was taking leave of his wife, and the assassination of Commandant Peter Doyle at Wexford Cathedral. In a final category was the occasional shooting of prominent or outspoken Free State supporters, like Old Doctor Higgins, the Coroner of King's County. This perhaps gives the flavour of events, but what follows is not a comparison of the conduct of both sides.

This book explores the execution policy and unauthorised killings in custody, which were closely connected. It examines how a climate emerged in which prisoners could be tried by rudimentary military courts and then executed, how so many other prisoners were killed without any trial and why so much of what took place was simply blanked out of the public consciousness.

Chapter 1

Jock McPeake

His name was Jock McPeake. He had been the machine-gunner on the armoured car Slievenamon on the day Michael Collins was killed.

A few months later, McPeake drove the Slievenamon out of the barracks and handed it over to anti-Treaty fighters. One cynical account implied that he was a good-looking young man with an eye for the ladies and had been suborned by a girl from a local Cumann. Others said that McPeake had become disillusioned with the civil war; he had taken part in some hard fighting in the summer of 1922.[1] He witnessed a landmine explosion in west Cork that killed seven National Army soldiers and afterwards watched as an anti-Treaty prisoner was put to death by officers of the Dublin Guard. Although McPeake had served in the British Army, he was still only 20. He had been recruited in Glasgow and seems to have realised, too late, that he had got himself involved in a war with few rules. McPeake made contact with anti-Treaty fighters and did a deal: in exchange for getting him out of Ireland he would hand over the Slievenamon. When the time came, he drove the Slievenamon out of Bandon barracks and delivered it to anti-Treaty fighters. McPeake was forgotten while the National Army tried to recover the armoured car.

The fate of the Slievenamon became tangled up in myth and legend. According to the judge advocate general (JAG) a team of officers from General Headquarters (GHQ) went down to Cork and quickly recaptured the armoured car and brought it back to

Portobello barracks, where they held a party in the officers' mess. Late that night, as the party was winding up, a gun was discharged and Bob, one of the mess orderlies was mortally wounded. The barracks chaplain rushed in, still in dressing gown and pyjamas, and was about to administer the last rites when Bob spoke his last words: 'Tell Father Concannon to go and fuck himself. I'm a Protestant.'

The account about Father Concannon is entirely true, but in fact more than one armoured car was captured during the war and the JAG seems to have mixed them up. The real story is that the Slievenamon was brought into action against the National Army again and again with telling effect.[2] Eventually, riddled with punctures and lacking spare parts, it was driven into the furze, where it gathered rust.

Jock McPeake hid out in the hills and took no further part in the war. In the summer of 1923 he escaped to Scotland in the hold of a cattle boat. After the civil war was over and at the request of the Free State government he was deported back to Ireland on a charge of larceny of the Slievenamon. McPeake appeared before the District Court in Cork. A slim young man in a blue suit, he gripped the rail of the dock and looked about for a friendly face as the district judge remanded him for seven days. When he next appeared before the court, he had acquired a young and quite inexperienced solicitor.[3]

State Prosecutor Captain Healy told the court that the witnesses were all soldiers and could not be traced and the state wanted to drop the case. McPeake's solicitor informed the district judge that his client would plead guilty. 'No,' said the state prosecutor, 'we are dropping the case.' McPeake's solicitor again urged the court to adjourn so the witnesses could be found and his client enter a guilty plea. The state prosecutor refused: 'We are not proceeding with the case. We cannot.' McPeake's solicitor insisted that the witnesses should be traced and that the case be adjourned to allow this to happen. District Judge Kelly was increasingly perplexed and turned to McPeake's solicitor: 'I don't see how your client can suffer by not being prosecuted.'

The lawyers did not enlighten him, but McPeake's fears were that his deportation for larceny was a ruse by the National Army to bring him into the jurisdiction in order to try him for treachery. In the autumn of the year before, dozens of National Army soldiers had deserted and gone over to the other side. Most had taken as many rifles and as much ammunition as they could carry, but McPeake had gone a step further and taken an armoured car, which had been used in action against the National Army. Most of the deserters were never traced, but at least one was killed fighting for the other side.[4] Some were recaptured but not identified and went off to internment camps. Six of the deserters were recognised and all were tried and executed. McPeake was reckoned to have done 'immense damage' to the government cause and he was now at risk of sharing their fate.[5]

McPeake was released by the district judge and set off to catch a ferry back to Scotland, but as he came down the steps of the court with his supporters he was arrested by a squad of National Army soldiers who had been lying in wait. Jock McPeake was taken to the barracks, a charge of treachery was laid against him and preparations for a trial by a military court began. His brother Frank, who had come over from Scotland to help him, was also picked up and held without charge. In a letter smuggled out of Keogh barracks some days later, the brother wrote that he had been badly beaten and was in fear for his life. McPeake's solicitor retained Michael Comyn, KC. A small wiry man with a black handlebar moustache, he had used his skills to challenge the legality of all that the Free State government had done during the war. Comyn sought a writ of habeas corpus at the High Court in Dublin.[6]

McPeake's case came before the only judge on duty during the long vacation; it happened to be Chief Justice Molony. In argument, Comyn accepted that on the face of the papers the deportation of McPeake for larceny was legal, but there was a more sinister dimension.[7] He argued that the charge of larceny had been used as a pretext to bring McPeake into the jurisdiction to allow the National Army to bring the charge of treachery and try him by military court. He could never have been deported to Ireland for treachery, Comyn argued. This was because McPeake deserted before the creation of the Irish Free State on 6 December 1922. Before that date the new state was not a legal entity and nor was the National Army. How, argued Comyn, could a prisoner be charged with treachery to an organisation that had never been an entity recognised by law?

Comyn's more fundamental argument was that the civil war was over and the power of the army to try civilians by military court had evaporated. In this respect, Comyn had correctly stated the law, but as a matter of fact trials by military court were still continuing.[8] He posed the question: was Ireland governed by the rule of law or the army? This was a question being asked by many. As the civil war had taken hold, the army had gradually become the most powerful institution in the country. In the Dáil, Kevin O'Higgins and many other deputies wanted to curb the power of the army and reassert the authority of the democratically elected government. Tension between ministers and General Mulcahy, the commander in chief of the National Army, had been an enduring issue throughout the civil war and culminated in Mulcahy and his staff submitting their resignations.[9] Their resignations were not accepted and they remained in post, subject to increased oversight by the cabinet.

Subsequent events suggest that Chief Justice Molony also had an agenda: to reassert the rule of law. Molony had steered the law through some difficult years when the authority of the courts had been usurped by the British Army, the Irish Volunteers and then the National Army during the civil war. In the summer of 1923, there were about 13,000 prisoners interned without trial in Ireland. Most were captured anti-Treaty fighters or those suspected of involvement in the anti-Treaty cause. Over 100 more had been unlawfully deported from England, but it was only a ruling of the House of Lords, not the Irish Courts, that resulted in them being set at liberty.[10] There were quite a number of other prisoners still in custody for no reason that would withstand scrutiny.[11] In June, anti-Treaty prisoners brought a series of habeas corpus actions against the army, arguing that the war was over and there was no longer any lawful power to hold them. In each case, the courts had accepted the argument put forward by the army: the country was at war and according to case law, the courts could not intervene *durrante bello*. But the civil war had fizzled out and McPeake's habeas corpus writ had exposed the tensions within government: the politicians wanted control, but the army seemed not ready to give up power. The minister for home affairs, the leading critic of the army, still needed a few more days grace to put in place emergency legislation legalising internment, and the Dáil was sitting overnight on the Bill. McPeake's case threatened to unravel the fragile status quo. Chief Justice Molony issued a conditional writ and the case was adjourned for both sides to be represented.

At the full hearing, Attorney General Hugh Kennedy, KC, appeared for the state and told the court it had all been a mis-understanding: the witnesses had been found and were now all available. McPeake was no longer in army custody; he was back in a prison run by the civil authorities and was to be sent for trial by jury on a charge of larceny.[12] The attorney general had avoided or at least delayed the great constitutional issue and the government had found some breathing space to get emergency legislation through the Dáil that would legitimise the internment of thousands of prisoners then in custody. The circumstances of McPeake's case hinted at unrecorded high-level discussions to avoid a habeas corpus ruling that might come before the government was ready. The application for a writ was withdrawn, but Chief Justice Molony awarded substantial costs against General Mulcahy – a slap on the wrist for the generals.[13]

It was in these circumstances that McPeake passed out of the control of the army and back into the hands of the civil authorities, and was sent for trial before the courts of justice. The charge was larceny not treachery: the death sentence had been avoided. In late October he was moved up from Cork prison to Mountjoy. McPeake's case was still a sensitive political issue and, by order of the minister for home affairs, the prison guard was reinforced by a convoy of soldiers. From Mountjoy he was brought to trial for the theft of the Slievenamon at the Green Street courthouse – the graceful neo-classical building that had seen so many of the most important criminal trials in the preceding century. Chief Justice Molony again presided.

There is no doubt that McPeake stole the Slievenamon, but like many criminal trials, what was true and what could be proved were two different things: the evidence in support of the charge was not overwhelming. While McPeake debated with his counsel the decision to fight or plead, events took another twist. McPeake confided in his counsel, Michael Comyn, that he was gravely worried about the emerging rumour that he killed Michael Collins.[14] The known facts were that at Béal na mBláth his Lewis gun had kept the anti-Treaty fighters' heads down, but then it had jammed and could not be fixed again that day. The rumours about McPeake focused on his antecedents: he was Scottish not Irish and he had previously served in the British Army. All these factors and his subsequent desertion with his armoured car had fuelled suspicions he had some involvement in the death of Michael Collins. Jock the Giant Killer was a nickname being bandied around by those who knew no better.[15]

'There is no such charge against you,' said Comyn. McPeake's fears about the danger to him were well grounded. The bodies of anti-Treaty supporters had been turning up around Dublin for many months: kidnapped, shot in the back of the head and dumped in quiet locations. The last was Noel Lemass, whose remains had been found in the Featherbed Mountains only ten days before. The inquest, which was widely reported, heard evidence that he had been kidnapped and killed by clandestine supporters of the government. The coroner said his body bore signs of torture that would 'shame the most primitive savage'.[16]

All this must have been in McPeake's mind; heightened by the knowledge that prosecuting counsel in his case was attended by a bevy of army officers who suspected him of involvement in the death of their old commander in chief. Collins had suffered a gaping wound to his head, which could have been caused by a handgun fired at close range. The army officers asked defence counsel: 'What about his revolver?'

Counsel went back down to the cells and relayed this to his client. McPeake agreed revolvers were standard issue, 'But I had no revolver.' This explanation was relayed to the army officers but did not satisfy them. Comyn went back down to the cells for another conference and advised McPeake that he might be acquitted but 'killed before nightfall'. Michael Comyn advised McPeake that prison was the safest option and he came up from the cells before Chief Justice Molony and pleaded guilty. The sentence was six years and McPeake went to prison.[17]

Over the preceding twelve months the government had delegated the suppression of the anti-Treaty faction to the National Army. The army brought in military courts to bring about the executions of people found in arms. Nearly 1,200 men were tried by the military courts and committees, and of these over 400 were sentenced to death. Eighty-three prisoners were shot by firing squad during the civil war.[18] Over 125 more were killed in the custody of the state: kidnapped and shot; shot after surrender; shot under interrogation; or tied to landmines and blown up. These men were killed because they were anti-Treaty fighters or because they were suspected of involvement or just being in sympathy. McPeake only narrowly avoided their fate.

During the civil war, the rule of law had just fallen by the wayside. To understand how it all came about it is necessary to wind the clock back twelve months.

Chapter 2

A State in Chaos

'We have no army, we have only an armed mob,' said Michael Collins, speaking just after the siege of the Four Courts.[1] Dozens of republican prisoners captured at the Four Courts had been allowed to escape from Portobello barracks by National Army men assigned to guard them. The doors of the holding area were left open and prisoners just swarmed over the barracks' walls and disappeared into the night.

Lack of discipline in the National Army had become a major issue; desertion and drunkenness were rife.[2] Some units were well run, but in many battalions officers went drinking with their men, making control of troops all but impossible. In Limerick there were reports of sentries falling drunk at their posts, and in Clonmel soldiers potted birds with handguns and leered intimidatingly at passers-by on street corners. In the months that followed, National Army soldiers would commit an astonishing number of criminal offences unrelated to the war.[3]

The cause of it all was that the National Army had been created in a tearing hurry. In the spring, the Irish Republican Army had parted company with the provisional government over the Treaty and this brought with it the first hint of civil war. To guard against this threat, the provisional government had created the National Army and many less than savoury men were recruited in the rush. 'We have put guns in the hands of criminals,' admitted Collins. Many other recruits had come from the British Army which was downsizing. Soldiers, demobbed in England, were brought over on the ferry and collected in lorries to be taken to Beggars Bush barracks and signed up.[4] In the summer of 1922, the National Army was still taking shape: ill-disciplined and short of guns, ammunition, uniforms, boots and bedding. Poor diet and late pay fuelled discontent out in the west.[5]

Lack of uniforms, boots and ammunition hampered operations against the anti-Treaty faction. In County Leitrim, dissatisfaction about pay and supplies led to a collapse of morale and the surrender of an army barracks.[6] At Riverstown in Sligo, dozens of National Army soldiers surrendered to a small anti-Treaty force. The defenders of the garrison were not inclined to fight 'for those who do not care for us'.[7] Discipline was one issue and divided loyalties were another: in Mayo and Cork, National Army soldiers sold guns or just gave them over to anti-Treaty men. In Limerick, many soldiers 'handed over arms wholesale to the enemy'.[8] In Kerry, soldiers sold ammunition to anti-Treaty fighters: the going rate for a full bandolier was 12s/6d.

The critical point that Collins had recognised was that he could not create an army without a legal process to impose discipline by court martial.[9] He hurriedly convened a meeting with a small group of men. One was a young lawyer, Cahir Davitt, son of the land leaguer. Davitt was then just 28 years old; he had established his ability by serving as a judge of the Dáil courts during the War of Independence. Also present was Gearóid O'Sullivan, the adjutant general, who had been Collins' right-hand man for some years.

Collins asked Davitt to become the first judge advocate general of the National Army to run the army legal department and oversee courts martial. 'Get into uniform as soon as possible,' said Collins. Davitt agreed to take the post and was given a small office at Portobello barracks.[10] Realising he knew nothing whatsoever about military law, he went out and bought a copy of the British Army Manual of Military Law and began to read up with a view to creating a legal service from scratch. The military court system that he brought into being would soon be utilised to try anti-Treaty prisoners captured in arms.

There were more immediate pressing problems for the embryonic legal service. Out in the west the National Army had been carrying out policing functions and occasionally trying civilians, and Cahir Davitt began to review their efforts. The first case involved a man who had stolen a pair of trousers. Had the trousers belonged to a common soldier it might have rested there, but the owner was a National Army colonel. The prisoner had been tried and sentenced to three years and twelve strokes of the 'cat' to be administered every three months. Davitt went off to see the adjutant general to point out the obvious: the army had no power to try civilians and the barbaric sentence was not a punishment known to law. It was a small victory for due process: the prisoner was released.

One Dublin case concerned an anti-Treaty spy. Suspicion arose that one of the civilian staff at National Army headquarters was passing information to the anti-Treaty forces and officers began to keep watch on James McGuinness from Offaly, who had a brother fighting on the other side.[11] McGuinness was given access to a confidential file and followed that night to a pub where he met his contact. Both were arrested and notes from the file were recovered from his contact, who turned out to be an anti-Treaty intelligence officer. McGuinness was taken to Wellington barracks and got a beating from which he never fully recovered. As he rested up in hospital, he learned that he had more serious difficulties to face. An order was made for his trial by court martial and the sentence on conviction was death. An acrimonious argument followed between Davitt and O'Sullivan. Davitt, the new JAG, questioned the legality of what was taking place. O'Sullivan, the adjutant general, simply maintained the man was a spy and had to be shot.

Only a year earlier, before the Truce with Britain, the IRA had routinely court-martialled suspected spies. These were often hurried night-time affairs and the result was very often inevitable.

The habits of the revolution were ingrained. The trial of James McGuinness went ahead and he was convicted and sentenced to death by firing squad. Davitt intervened again and pointed out that if the man were executed, then after the conflict was over, they might all face a murder charge. In this, he was speaking no more than the literal truth. The trial was not lawful and obeying orders would be no defence to a murder charge: the law was beyond doubt. O'Sullivan relented a shade: the sentence was commuted to life and the prisoner stayed inside until after the war.

This situation had come about because the country lacked a coherent justice system or even a police force worth the name. In the spring, the Royal Irish Constabulary (RIC) had been disbanded. The bulk of the British Army marched out and with them went the Black and Tans and the Auxiliaries. Dublin was still policed by the Dublin Metropolitan Police (DMP) – a legacy of the outgoing British regime.

The new police force, the Civic Guard, was still undergoing training, which had become a turbulent process. One night Dublin city centre echoed to the sound of 'terrific volleys' and a government minister, fearing the worst, asked an old man what the firing was about. 'It's them Civic Guards,' said the old man. 'They were paid last night.'[12] In the summer, the Civic Guard rebelled and chased their commanders out of camp and later handed over lorryloads of guns and ammunition to the anti-Treaty faction. In the weeks that followed, the Guards were disbanded and the process of starting a police force was begun again.

In the provinces, law and order of a sort was maintained by the two opposing armies that were already beginning to fight. The country was riven by crime – land grabs, stock driving and gunpoint robbery for personal gain – often on the pretext of defending the Republic. There were also shootings of ex-RIC men, attacks on the homes of Unionists and murder of a more domestic hue.[13]

The justice system was more problematic because there were now two competing court structures. In Dublin, the courts established under British rule was still functioning but so also were the Dáil courts. Out in the provinces, the only remnant of the British justice system was the coroner's jury. The remainder of the justice system had been substantially supplanted by the Dáil courts. This dual system was unsustainable and it all came to a head when the Four Courts siege was broken by an artillery bombardment by the National Army. One of the republican prisoners captured was George Plunkett, whose father, Count Plunkett brought an application for a writ of habeas corpus before a Dáil court. Judge Diarmuid Crowley issued the writ after hearing legal argument.[14] The writ required the release of George Plunkett and, if taken to a logical conclusion, all the hundreds of republican prisoners. Unsurprisingly, the prison governor declined to obey the writ and passed it to the National Army headquarters at Portobello. The status quo had changed very suddenly and the provisional government ordered Crowley's arrest. Judge Crowley was picked up late at night by an army officer, 'one of the intelligence crowd'. He was held at Wellington barracks and his abiding memory was the brutal interrogation of an anti-Treaty prisoner in the adjoining cell and the sound of mock executions.[15] Crowley got out some weeks later, but only after an intervention by Cahir Davitt.

The provisional government's formal response to the habeas corpus writ was even more robust. They retained the British justice system in Dublin and abolished with immediate effect all the Dáil courts except for the parish and district courts in the provinces.[16] Two more momentous events took place that summer. Arthur Griffith, president of the provisional government died suddenly. His health had been on the wane for some months and his death was keenly felt, but he was hardly a war leader and so the loss was managed. Twelve days later, Michael Collins was killed in an ambush and this was a critical event.[17]

Collins' body was brought up by sea to Dublin's North Wall, arriving long after midnight. In the darkness, the cabinet of the provisional government and many others stood in silence as the coffin was brought onto the quayside and loaded onto a horse-drawn carriage. The cortege crossed the city with just the sound of a piper, the rattle of the gun carriage and murmured prayers for the dead. A procession of ministers, soldiers and many others followed. The funeral took place later that week: huge silent crowds lined the streets for 6 miles on the road to Glasnevin cemetery. Collins had been the last pro-Treaty leader who had both the inclination and the ability to forge a peace.

After the deaths of Griffith and Collins, William Cosgrave emerged as the new head of the provisional government. A quietly spoken man of slight figure with a silvery blond quiff, he was a grocer by trade although he had an incongruous fondness for a top hat. Many of the anti-Treaty faction reckoned that Cosgrave had not the mettle for the coming fight. He had last handled a gun at the South Dublin Union in 1916 and afterwards made his reputation as minister for local government, but as a leader he did not initially inspire many on his own side. This new government teetered as the war intensified. The threat of assassination was very real and the inner core of the government camped out in offices on Upper Merrion Street with a heavy guard. Some slept on mattresses that were rolled up each morning so that the business of government could begin.

There was much more to all this than fighting the war: the public sector pay bill had to be met, schools needed to run, hospitals had to remain open, the post had to be delivered. They were running a small country without allies in the North or in Britain.[18] That summer and autumn one crisis followed another: the Four Courts siege, the death of two great leaders and a prison hunger strike – the prisoners were told they would be buried in unmarked graves. A postal workers' strike was beaten off and also a long-running industrial action by railwaymen. There were other pressing political issues to be dealt with. Not least bringing in a new constitution consistent with the terms of the Anglo-Irish Treaty and therefore acceptable to the British government but palatable to the Irish electorate. It was a heavy burden.[19] Not all of the ministers were weighed down by responsibility. Eoin MacNeill was writing what would become his most famous monograph on ancient Irish legal history: *Franchise or Law*. A big man with gold spectacles and a heavy grey beard, buried in Brehon law tracts, he occasionally waved away requests to go down to his office.

In the long evenings, ministers and their wives gathered in the main lounge, but the women became a source of friction and they were soon evicted, while the men smoked, talked, read newspapers or played endless games of bridge that MacNeill often won. The only senior figure absent was Mulcahy, the new commander in chief. Mulcahy kept long hours at GHQ Portobello and spent the rest of the time at his home next door and did not often attend cabinet meetings. Kevin O'Higgins distrusted the army and also General Mulcahy in equal measure. O'Higgins was right about the National Army – it was malleable, riven by cliques and honeycombed with IRB members who were now without their leader (Collins). O'Higgins' suspicions of General Mulcahy would prove to be entirely misplaced: the general, dark, wiry and a little intense, was driven by his work and, for the time being, was oblivious to the suspicions of his colleague.

It was still the war that dominated events. The casualties in the fighting grew on both sides and the National Army lost some of their best men – shot down in ambush or occasionally shot in the street or leaving church.[20] In the streets of Dublin, anti-Treaty fighters threw grenades and planted mines with a singular lack of regard for civilian casualties. In the face of all this, the government began to formulate the execution policy and while this was developing a new trend became apparent. There began a covert campaign of the kidnap and murder of men suspected or believed to be involved in the anti-Treaty cause. A review of inquests in the Dublin area alone shows that during the civil war thirteen suspected anti-Treaty men were kidnapped from their homes or workplaces and shot dead.[21] There were ten other cases where the evidence showed that prisoners were shot after surrender or while in custody.[22] These killings, never publicly disavowed by any government minister until the war was all but won, became part of the process by which victory was achieved.

One of the responses by the anti-Treaty side was a concerted legal challenge to the killing of prisoners. This could not be effected through the Dáil as it had been adjourned and when it finally reconvened it was boycotted by the anti-Treaty deputies. The press was heavily censored and so the focus of the challenge became the inquest system, which began with the inquest into the death of Cathal Brugha, who was shot down at the end of the Four Courts siege. He had already surrendered some said, but the coroner declined to allow witnesses to be brought to court.[23] A few weeks later, Harry Boland, another anti-Treaty deputy was killed.[24] Here again, the coroner refused to allow evidence to be called to show Boland had been killed after capture.

A series of inquests into the deaths of anti-Treaty fighters killed in custody followed. Usually there was no one left to tell the tale to the inquest jury, but in a handful of cases there was evidence of state involvement. The Yellow Lanes affair concerned the kidnap and shooting of two unarmed youths in broad daylight. One of the killers wore a National Army uniform and the case caused profound embarrassment to the government. Another inquest concerned Patrick Mannion, who was shot dead near Mount Street Bridge by a National Army patrol, but the evidence at the inquest showed that he was unarmed and in custody when he was shot. The jury returned a verdict of 'wilful murder by National Army soldiers'.[25] Journalists had their notebooks confiscated by plain-clothes men after the hearing and *The Irish Times* published a short report recording the verdict of 'wilful murder by men in uniform' and said little else.

In response to a letter of protest written by Count Plunkett, *The Irish Times* conceded the report had been 'summarised by order of the government censor'.[26] President Cosgrave told the Dáil the next day that the censor had intervened because the evidence was untrue and there the matter rested. What was done in Dublin was more easily done in isolated districts. Anti-Treaty prisoners in the custody of the National Army became particularly vulnerable. Three prisoners were killed in Kerry, six in Sligo, three in Cork and one each in Limerick, Tipperary and Mayo.[27] It is likely that there were many more, but usually there was no one left to recount what took place apart from the national soldiers who had fired the fatal shots.

One prisoner was Tim Kennefick from Coachford.[28] He was one of the many anti-Treaty fighters captured in early September as the National Army swarmed around Cork. The inquest jury viewed the body in the usual way and heard evidence that Kennefick was captured, badly beaten, shot in the head and dumped in a ditch. The inquest jury returned a verdict of 'wilful murder by National Army troops'. This cut no ice with the government. In the Dáil, General Mulcahy stated that 'the inquest was held under the auspices of Irregulars armed to the teeth, and before a jury that was apparently selected by Irregulars'. He announced that 'no action has been taken to bring the so-called guilty troops to justice'.[29] The local commander, Major General Dalton, issued a proclamation in Cork prohibiting further inquests without written permission.[30]

Another prisoner killed in custody was Jerry Buckley, after an ambush on the road from Macroom to Kerry. A National Army convoy stopped to defuse the landmine in the road and thought they had made it safe, but this was a 'trip mine' and the detonation mortally wounded Commandant Tom Keogh and killed six of his men.[31] Tom Keogh had been a long-time member of Collins' Squad during the War of Independence. In the aftermath of the explosion, a group of Dublin officers also from Collins' old Squad went looking for revenge. There had been extensive fighting around Macroom that day, but only a single man had been captured: 41-year-old Jerry Buckley, a no-rank prisoner.[32] Buckley was seized, shot and tossed into the crater made by the explosion.

The local National Army commander wrote to General Emmet Dalton at HQ: 'The shooting of a prisoner here in the operations has caused considerable contempt among the garrison here … They have paraded before me and gave me to understand that they would not go out on the hills anymore.' The incident, he told his commander, had resonated for fifteen miles in every direction and brought the National Army into disrepute with local people. Dalton wrote to Commander in Chief Mulcahy about the killing:

```
This shooting was the work of the Squad.
Now I personally approve of the action, but
the men I have in my command are of such a
temperament that they can look at seven of
their companions being blown to atoms by a
murderous trick without feeling annoyed, but
an enemy is found with a rifle and ammn. They
will mutiny if he is shot. On this account
I think it would be better if you kept the
'squad' out of my area.
```

It may be taken that General Mulcahy understood all of the nuances; he did not ask questions but replied: 'You are at perfect liberty to return here any officer you think well of so returning …'[33] Afterwards, Dalton returned all the officers responsible to Dublin.[34] No questions were asked by General Mulcahy about the identity of the killers or the steps taken to enforce discipline within the National Army.

That same week another letter arrived at National Army headquarters, sent by David Robinson, then a staff officer on the anti-Treaty side.[35] Robinson, from Wicklow, was an ex-British Army tank officer who had been much decorated during the Great War where he had lost an eye and almost his legs. Tall and lanky, 'Dead Eye' had taken part in the War of Independence and went with the anti-Treaty side after the split. He was still hanging onto an old-fashioned sense of decency and expecting others to do the same. He wrote to his counterpart in the National Army headquarters asking him to raise the question of the killing of prisoners: 'I cannot believe that Mulcahy would tolerate it for a moment.'[36] Robinson also raised a concern about another prisoner, 'a boy called Murphy', who had been killed after capture.

The 'boy called Murphy' was 17-year-old Bartholemew Murphy from Castleisland. The National Army later maintained that Murphy had been a prisoner on an army lorry and was fatally wounded in an anti-Treaty ambush at Brennan's Glen. He was in fact a prisoner of the National Army at their makeshift barracks at the Great Southern Hotel in Killarney, where he had been in custody for some days and had been used to clear barricades laid in the road. The day of his death there was an ambush at Brennan's Glen, where a Dublin Guard convoy lost three men. Afterwards, there was a commotion at the barracks and Murphy was picked on because he was from that area and was thought to know who might be responsible. He was thrown down the steps by an officer and shot to death with a revolver.[37] The allegations were specific, detailed and contemporaneous, and having regard to what is now known about the activities of the Dublin Guard there is no reason to doubt that this young man was put to death in custody. David Robinson wrote: 'The number of bullet wounds alone would make you suspicious.'

None of this came out at the inquest, which was held the next day under the County Coroner William O'Sullivan and a jury. The local National Army commander, Brigadier Paddy O'Daly, gave evidence in uniform: a man of compact build and of slightly more than average height, he had a curiously cherubic appearance. He looked across the room at the mother of the dead youth: Julia Murphy, a widow with two children who ran a dressmakers shop on the Main Street in Castleisland.[38] O'Daly related that her son had been killed while on a National Army lorry when the lorry had been ambushed and two soldiers were killed and nine others were wounded: 'under no circumstances do we permit our political prisoners to be ill-treated'. O'Daly looked across the court to the bereaved mother: 'I sympathise with you ... I really do.'[39] It may have been difficult for her to express a contrary view or to call witnesses. The Coroner's Court had been convened at army headquarters at the Great Southern Hotel in Killarney, the very place where her son had been killed. It became a pattern in Kerry. The Dublin Guard killed prisoners and Brigadier O'Daly would go to the inquest to cover up for his men or limit the fallout.[40]

David Robinson also raised the killing of another prisoner, Jack Galvin, who had been captured by National Army forces in an attack on Killorglin. It seems he was suspected of having killed a National Army Officer, Captain Burke, who had been a friend of the colonel of the First Westerns. At least one National Army officer recognised the threat to Galvin and placed him at the centre of a group of prisoners clearing trees. Galvin was unfit to work because of a broken arm and soon became separated from the prisoners and was found shot dead soon after. David Robinson finished his request with a comment that resonates through the ages: 'You may imagine what the result will be if this goes on.' The killing of Jack Galvin raised a bit of a storm among National Army troops and the colonel of the Kerry 1st Brigade wrote to General Mulcahy and threatened to resign unless a full inquiry took place to vindicate 'the honour' of the National Army. He added that if these incidents were allowed to continue, 'We would soon find ourselves in arms against a hostile population.'

The General Officer Commanding (GOC) in Kerry was W.R.E. Murphy. A photo of the time shows a tall scrawny officer with a small moustache. He was from Wexford, but like many of his generation, he had served with distinction in the British Army during the Great War and went back to his old career as a school teacher until he was recruited to the National Army. W.R.E. Murphy also wrote to Mulcahy about Galvin's death but advised against any inquiry: 'This scoundrel shot capt Burke. Signed a form and got out and took up arms again. He was the terror of the countryside.' Therefore, the GOC wrote: 'I will not sacrifice any officer or man of the 1st Western Division (a splendid lot of troops).'[41]

There was no army inquiry into the death of Galvin or Bertie Murphy, and their deaths became part of a pattern that was already taking shape. Sean Moriarty from Tralee was killed the month before. He had been removed from his home late at night by armed men. He and another man, Healy, were taken to waste ground outside Tralee where they were questioned about their involvement in attacks on National Army troops. Moriarty was shot dead and although Healy was riddled with bullets, he recovered consciousness and crawled off to get help. He later told the full story at the inquest into the death of his companion.[42] Some historians have described these events as part of 'a ruthless counter insurgency campaign.'[43] It is hardly an accurate description. Even in the extreme circumstances that existed, the law provided no special dispensation for soldiers or policemen.

There was one last organised effort to hold the government to account for killing suspects in custody. It was the inquest into the killing of three teenagers who had been posting anti-Treaty leaflets. The leaflets laid the blame for the recent spate of killings on CID officers attached to Oriel House and army intelligence and, in turn, incited the murder of those officers. These young men were picked up by National Army men late one night and the following morning the bodies of two were found dumped by the roadside near the village of Red Cow. The bodies were still warm and it seemed they had been killed around dawn. The trajectory of the bullet wounds suggested they had been shot while lying down. The third had run for his life and was discovered in the quarry, lying in a clump of nettles riddled with bullets.

Witnesses soon came forward identifying Charles Dalton, a National Army officer, as having arrested the youths the night before. Dalton lived a few streets away from where the young men were picked up. He was, on the surface, every inch an officer: a photo shows a singularly handsome young man in uniform, but that was not the full story. During the War of Independence, Dalton had been part of Collins' Squad and shooting opponents in cold blood had been part of their work.[44] In the run-up to the civil war, most of the Squad joined the new National Army. Dalton became part of the intelligence team that had grown up around Oriel House and Wellington barracks: the leafleting campaign had been directed against Dalton and that group of men.

The Red Cow inquest took place in the reading room at the Carnegie Library in Clondalkin, where tables were hurriedly pushed together for the lawyers and the coroner. The lawyers crammed in on one side of the table, the jury on the other, with the witnesses nearly in touching distance of both. The rest of this windowless, low-ceilinged room was packed with bereaved relatives and National Army men in an atmosphere that heaved with grief and anger.

The provisional government instructed John Byrne, a tall, thin, austere advocate who had great experience of defending hopeless cases. The killings had attracted nationwide publicity and there was no mechanism to dispense with inquest juries as was done in Cork. The evidence could not be suppressed as it was in the cases of Brugha or Boland, or censored as in the Mannion inquest, or explained away as in the case of the Yellow Lanes killings. It was going to come out in all its tawdry detail, but Byrne would play a subtle game distancing himself and the government from the accused officer and letting the other lawyers fight it out. Michael Comyn, KC, again appeared for the families. He was joined by two barristers representing the anti-Treaty GHQ. They squeezed in around the tables alongside their main opponent, Tim Healy, KC, who acted for the accused officer. Healy, a small, pugnacious, west Cork man, hated Michael Comyn and took every opportunity to let him know.

This was a case that was followed in the press by anyone who could read and raised issues that no one could ignore. Over the previous few months, Dublin had been assailed by ambushes; National Army soldiers shot in the back, at home or in the street. Landmines had been detonated and grenades hurled with little care for civilian life and there had been many casualties. The anti-Treaty faction now came to court to litigate the circumstances in which three of their own had been killed. All of this tended to obscure two important points: that these youths had been killed in the custody of the National Army and that it was part of a pattern which the state did not oppose or condemn, at least in public.

At the outset, the old coroner protested that he could not allow the anti-Treaty side to be represented, but it was pointed out to him that pending the creation of the Irish Free State, the provisional government had no legal status either. The duty of the coroner was to inquire into the cause of death and not allow the lawyers to pursue a political agenda, but like most coroners, he was not a lawyer, just a local doctor who carried out the occasional inquest after a car crash or a fatal accident at a farm. Out of his depth and intimidated, the coroner lost control of the lawyers, who began to fight it out for a verdict that would give comfort for their cause.[45] Tim Healy called witnesses to prove that Dalton had carried out four arrests that night and taken the prisoners to Wellington barracks, but none of this established a watertight alibi and just confirmed Dalton was on duty and in the vicinity looking for anti-Treaty suspects. The evidence showed that much later that night the young men were driven from the barracks by intelligence officers to a quiet spot and murdered. But which officers were involved? All at Wellington barracks and Oriel House remained silent.

Michael Comyn argued that this was murder, whether by Dalton or his colleagues, but the inquest did not go well for Comyn. During the inquest his home was raided by the National Army and he was briefly placed under arrest, and when he was at the inquest, Tim Healy, KC, was always ready with some withering put down. Comyn was heckled by a hostile gallery and questioned by exasperated jurors: 'Why is this taking so long?' one asked. It was not the function of the inquest jury to say whether Dalton was guilty or not, but it was part of their duty to send a suspect for trial before the criminal courts if there was a case to answer. The jury declined to indict him and perhaps that should not be surprising: Dublin was a small city and his reputation was well known. The jury did not even condemn the murders as was the custom at the time. The colourless verdicts simply recounted that the young men had died of 'gunshot wounds inflicted by person or persons unknown'.

Counsels' closing speeches in the Red Cow inquest received the widest publicity, and the failure of the jury to condemn the murders probably owed much to the advocacy of Tim Healy, KC. It was an open secret that he would soon be appointed governor general of the new Free State. His voice, in a very real sense, was that of the new establishment in Ireland and he delivered his closing remarks just before the official executions began. He argued that the inquest evidence could be ignored and that the rule of law could be abandoned. He asserted the war had been started by the anti-Treaty faction and as he put it: 'What man can place bounds on the march of extermination?'

Chapter 3

The Origins of the Execution Policy

The pro-Treaty side believed the war would be wound up in a few weeks and at first all went well. Anti-Treaty forces were driven out of most towns and villages with seaborne landings being a prelude to decisive offensives in Cork and Kerry. Large numbers of prisoners were taken and there were many arms seizures. Michael Collins privately intimated that modest punishments might be handed out for possession of arms and his Chief of Staff Mulcahy agreed.

But as the weeks wore on, the anti-Treaty campaign began to develop into guerrilla warfare. For the National Army, there were no bases to attack and no set-piece battles to be fought against an elusive enemy. In the weeks before his death, Collins' attitude began to shift. He went down to west Cork for a requiem mass for National Army soldiers killed in action and that night he wrote to his fiancée about the mothers and widows 'weeping and almost shrieking'.[1] The people were 'splendid' wrote Collins, but the country was also beset by the looters and carpet baggers that ride on the coat-tails of every revolution. A few days later, he wrote a memo to his director of intelligence that 'any man caught looting or destroying should be shot on sight'.[2] He still could not countenance summary executions of captured anti-Treaty fighters.

The hard fighting in Cork and Kerry was driving Collins onwards. Only two weeks before his death, Collins wrote to the provisional government in Dublin suggesting 'special punishments' for those found in arms in areas designated special military areas.[3] He did not stipulate the nature of the punishment, but no one was in any doubt what was implied. It was a poisoned chalice and it was batted back and forth in meetings and memos. In response to a note from Cosgrave, Collins wrote: 'I am against shooting down unarmed men.'[4] Such a decision, he told Cosgrave, was for the government not the army. In the emerging six county state in the North, possession of arms by anti-Treaty fighters was already being dealt with by lashes with the cat and a long term in prison.[5] South of the border, policy was developing more slowly but into a much more draconian response.

A pivotal event took place in late July. Just outside Abbeyleix, on a bend in the road, a National Army convoy was ambushed. Reinforcements soon arrived led by National Army Commandant Jack Collison and Divisional Commandant McCurtain: both officers died in a single volley. Very quickly their attackers threw up their hands and all twenty-eight were taken into custody.

The next day, at the old courthouse at Maryborough, the inquest jury heard evidence that the officers had been killed by expanding bullets. 'Wilful murder' was the verdict of the jury, who added a rider condemning the use of expanding bullets.[6] The funerals followed soon after and at the graveside Executive Council member Joe McGrath praised the survivors for the 'extraordinary forbearance they had shown after their much loved officers had been shot down'. In terms of how the conflict was fought, that quality of forbearance would soon dissipate and in the months that followed there were many well-grounded complaints of ill-treatment of prisoners.

For the provisional government, the ambush resonated of all that was wrong. Collison and McCurtain had fine records in the recent war and both were now dead, but the prisoners had gone off for internment without trial. They were mostly young – too young to have fought in the recent war but raised in an era when fighting for country was everything and there were many more like them still out there. Ernest Blythe seized the moment and suggested the surrender should not have been accepted. It was the first time the argument had been made in public and no one dissented.

August became the month of ambushes. The anti-Treaty fighters were still well organised and not at all short of ammunition, and the National Army suffered fifty-eight killed and many more wounded. A significant number of casualties were high-ranking National Army officers. Among these was Colonel Frank Thornton, who led a convoy out into Tipperary to make contact with the enemy with a view to negotiating a peace. Thornton's convoy was ambushed and only he survived, gravely wounded. His brother, Colonel Hugh Thornton, died at Clonakilty and Michael Collins was killed at Béal na mBláth and the attackers once again disappeared into the hinterland.

After the death of Collins, General Richard Mulcahy became commander in chief and was immediately under pressure from his generals to permit the execution of captured anti-Treaty fighters. In Cork, Major General Dalton was sustaining heavy casualties and wrote to Mulcahy at GHQ asking for permission 'to shoot without trial men caught in possession of arms'.[7] The request was echoed by General O'Duffy in Limerick. Permission was refused, but events were boiling over and the first execution by firing squad soon went ahead. National Army Private 'Barney' Winsley was a chimney sweep from Cork. After a spell in the British Army, he came back to Cork and ended up in the National Army: semi-literate, still living on his wits and the only breadwinner for his widowed mother. Like other National Army men in Cork, he was selling guns to the anti-Treaty forces and he was singled out for court martial. Major General Emmet Dalton had him shot by firing squad and that put an end to selling guns to the anti-Treaty faction, in Cork at least. Commander in Chief General Mulcahy was informed and replied: 'I approve.' All the while, however, there was the continuing guerrilla action and a tide of gunpoint robberies. On the Executive Council all ministers had now come round to the view that executions were necessary, but the final straw was unexpected and mundane: the economy.

The Economic Crisis

The strategy of the anti-Treaty faction had begun to morph into making the country ungovernable and seizing a republic from the wreckage. That policy was pursued by guerrilla action and also by degrading the transport and communications infrastructure: roads were trenched, bridges and railway lines torn up and engines destroyed. Telephone wires were cut and as soon as they were fixed, cut again. The big houses were burned out and the old ascendancy was forced out of the country by degrees and their money went with them.[8] The provisional government had been warned months before by Churchill, the minister in England with responsibility for implementing the Treaty: 'Capital is taking flight.'[9]

People were taking flight also: the Protestant exodus in 1920–2 had damaged the country financially and young people were still leaving Ireland as they always did when times were hard.[10] Economic migration was damaging the new state. The turning point in this growing crisis came in September when the institutions of the state began to pull in the same direction. In a habeas corpus motion brought by one of the thousands of anti-Treaty prisoners, the High Court upheld internment during the emergency.[11] From the pulpits, the bishops put out a strong message that had the approval of the government: 'stay and live in the land of your birth and work for the good of the country'.[12] Cosgrave's big cabinet shuffle and his address to the Dáil promised decisive action: 'life and property must be respected and the laws of the country must be obeyed.'

Cosgrave had financial experience as a minister for local government in the recent war and balancing the books quickly became the central plank of government policy. In his budget statement he told the deputies that revenue from taxes stood at £27 million but projected expenditure was £40 million. He attempted to calm speculation by adding that there was 'no immediate cause for concern'. Cosgrave was rather understating the position; he was one of a number of cabinet ministers not drawing pay. In Ireland, agriculture was the main source of revenue, but the country lacked any significant mineral resources and industry, fishing, forestry and tourism were all at an embryonic stage of development. There was also a growing urban population to sustain.

Unlike established states elsewhere, this new Ireland had no gold reserves, assets or bonds to fall back on in bad times. The provisional government was operating on a loan from Westminster that was fast running out because of the cost of fighting the war. In that year, the army bill exceeded seven million pounds: one quarter of government revenue. That figure would continue to rise sharply the following year.[13] The army and public-sector wage bill had to be paid or the new state would simply unravel. Everything depended on people paying taxes and doing so promptly. The anti-Treaty faction was alive to this weakness and would soon begin to try and drive the government into bankruptcy.

It was at this stage that the two prongs of government policy emerged. First, to rid the country of arms and second, to build the confidence of the business community. The financial cost of anti-Treaty action continued to grow: theft, damage and arson were becoming a heavy burden.[14] Cosgrave recognised that these claims had to be paid by his government or the business community might take their investment capital elsewhere. To meet this, the provisional government let it be known that compensation would be paid for damage occasioned by anti-Treaty action and an official announcement to this effect soon followed.[15]

The concept of a failed state is a modern one and remained unarticulated at that time, but this was the fear driving events: that the state would become bankrupt, ungovernable and would be plunged into chaos and that Britain might once again send in the troops. It was then, and in these circumstances, that the provisional government drew up plans to allow the army to use military courts to try prisoners captured in arms and carry out executions. These proposals were set out in the Army (Special Powers) Resolution in late September 1922.

The Army (Special Powers) Resolution

The Army (Special Powers) Resolution has been variously described as the Emergency Powers Act,[16] 'legislation',[17] 'legally dubious',[18] or as the Public Safety Bill.[19] It was none of these things. It had no legal standing and was simply a resolution passed by the Dáil. When the provisional government decided to take this drastic step a fundamental question arose: was there power to legislate before the Free State was brought into being in December? In the Dáil there was some muddled discussion on the legal position and eventually the Attorney General Hugh Kennedy advised the provisional government that the Anglo-Irish Treaty provided a legal power to legislate.

A further difficulty quickly emerged. The problem was that legislation required the consent of the King, which would in practice be given by the governor general. However, the provisional government was not yet able to create the new state, not least because the Irish Constitution was still a work in progress and a governor general had not yet been appointed. Hugh Kennedy wrote a supplemental opinion the same day and advised that, pending the creation of the Free State, legislation would require the personal consent of the King.[20] Kennedy anticipated the British government would object to legislation passed without royal assent and added 'this question may give rise to much difficulty'.

The provisional government saw the difficulty of legislating very differently. To seek the personal consent of an English king to execute anti-Treaty prisoners was not a step they were comfortable with and it would have played into the hands of the other side. It might also have been a step too far for many pro-Treaty deputies.[21] On 25 September, the cabinet met to discuss the draft proclamation creating military courts. As was so often the case, the minutes do not disclose what was said, but the law officers were asked to attend and the subject matter of the discussion may be inferred. The result of the discussions was soon made known: 'We will not ask for royal assent.' It was made to sound like a grand statement of principle, but the reality was the government chose not to legislate to create military courts because of political embarrassment. Instead, it was decided that the Dáil would simply pass a resolution asking that the National Army take steps to bring the emergency to an end.

Supporters of the provisional government were able to argue that it had simply taken a leaf out of British colonial jurisprudence where, in times gone by, rebellion might be overcome by bringing in the army. At this juncture in Ireland, the argument ran, the institutions of the state were not able to curb widespread and serious disorder and there was no choice but to call in the army. The weakness of this argument was that the provisional government had the opportunity of passing legislation but chose not to do so. Going ahead on the basis of resolution alone would expose the government and its supporters to the risk of prosecution after the war, but a pragmatic solution soon emerged: an act of indemnity would be passed after the crisis. Such a statute would not render lawful that which was unlawful, but it would provide a bar against any prosecution or litigation arising out of the war. The Army (Special Powers) Resolution invited the National Army to set up military courts and committees to try offenders for attacking the National Army, possession of arms or explosives, arson and destruction of property and looting.

The pro-Treaty deputies had been briefed in private before the debate and some were not enthusiastic, but the provisional government's task was made easier because half of all the elected deputies were not present at this crucial debate. Three anti-Treaty deputies were already dead: Boland and Brugha, and Seamus

Devins, who had been killed on Benbulben. An order had been issued for the arrest of anti-Treaty deputies who had taken up arms and two of them were now in custody.[22] One more had been expelled for suggesting the assembly was an illegal body that had usurped the authority of the Dáil.[23] This line of thinking had led Eamon de Valera to pursue an abstentionist policy, and in any event the rest of the anti-Treaty deputies were out leading the fighting against the provisional government. By this series of events the provisional government had found itself with a complete grip on the levers of power.

The brunt of the argument in the Dáil was carried by Mulcahy, who was now commander in chief and minister of defence. Mulcahy told the Dáil that the destruction of bridges, roads and the rail network in the south and west was choking the life out of the country. There was no machinery of justice to deal with the Irregulars and while the government established itself, the army needed to 'stand in the gap'. Internment of prisoners was not a sufficient deterrent: 'Life must be taken, if necessary and it is the responsibility of the government to say that it must be taken.'

Mulcahy also raised a fresh argument: that his soldiers out in the field were constantly exposed to ambush and did not regard internment of prisoners as a sufficient response to inflicting casualties on the army. He cited two examples: one near Ballina, where a Free State officer had struggled to prevent his men shooting prisoners who had laughed at the sight of a dead National Army soldier; the second, the Macroom landmine explosion that had claimed the lives of seven soldiers. The Dublin Guard had responded by killing a prisoner. The argument advanced by Mulcahy can be simply stated: our troops must know that we will execute where necessary or they will do so themselves.

Opposition to the measure was led by Tom Johnson, leader of the Labour Party, who favoured open justice carried out by criminal courts, although it was probably unrealistic to suggest that juries would convict in such cases. George Gavan Duffy also opposed the measure. He had defended military court trials under British rule and there had been many executions and he perhaps foresaw where all this might end up. He may also have had an eye on the wider picture. Europe was riven with small civil wars and the many atrocities that had been committed had caused the Red Cross to stipulate that captured fighters should be accorded prisoner-of-war status.[24] There was no support for these alternatives, but some amendments on matters of detail were made, and after an acrimonious debate and an overnight adjournment the Resolution was passed by 47 votes to 15. The judge advocate general had been finishing the regulations governing the trial by court martial of National Army soldiers. Even before the vote in the Dáil, he was asked to produce regulations to govern the summary trial of prisoners as a matter of urgency.[25]

The government signed off the military courts proclamation in early October and at the same meeting despatched a formal request to the bishops to intervene to halt 'the low moral standard prevailing throughout the country'.[26] There can be no doubt that the support of the Catholic Church had been canvassed in advance. The pressure on the government was mounting in other ways that may not have been obvious. Cosgrave's uncle was shot dead in a raid on his grocery shop: just one of a wave of revolver-point robberies blighting the country. An attempt was made to storm General Mulcahy's home in Rathmines: a grenade was thrown and a shoot-out followed before the raiding party was driven off, but the press rather unhelpfully published Mulcahy's address. The war was getting closer to home.

Preparations for military courts and firing squads were finalised and the National Army published a proclamation announcing the setting up of military courts with power to inflict the death penalty for 'proclaimed offences' committed on or after 15 October.[27] A second proclamation offered an amnesty to all those who surrendered arms and gave up the fight by the cut-off date. These proclamations went up on walls and fence posts all over the country. The support sought from the Church now materialised: the Bishops' Pastoral Letter was read out in every Catholic church in the country. The bishops framed their approach on the footing that the provisional government had won the elections decisively and called on their congregation to back that decision. They condemned those who fought against the government as 'guilty of grievous sins, which may not be absolved in confession if they persist' and denounced the killing of national soldiers as 'murder before God'.[28]

Regulations for trial were signed off by the judge advocate general. Three army officers would be assembled to carry out summary trials of prisoners for attacking national forces, looting or possession of arms and other specified offences.[29] The criminal courts would continue to sit, but in respect of 'proclaimed offences', would give up their jurisdiction to military courts.[30] Prisoners' rights were few. No prisoner could be tried within forty-eight hours of capture. The prisoner was entitled to see a charge sheet and summary of evidence no later than twenty-four hours before trial. The regulations stated prisoners could have the services of a lawyer but were silent on the issue of who paid. The core of the legal team headed by Cahir Davitt began to live in at army HQ at Portobello barracks in Dublin and there was a last-minute rush to recruit lawyers to ensure that every army command had a legal officer to oversee the trials.

Chapter 4

Military Courts and the First Executions

The first execution took place only a few days later and it was entirely unauthorised. It happened at the end of October in Ballyheigue, a single-street village on the edge of Kerry's Atlantic coast. On the hill overlooking the village stood the burned-out ruins of the Crosbie castle and a little further inland the square tower of the church of Saint James and its small graveyard filled with mausoleums and stone crosses where no one lingered long. There had been intense fighting in Ballyheigue parish for some days and the anti-Treaty fighters had been driven off by the First Western Division of the National Army. During the retreat two shotguns had been left hidden in the graveyard. That evening Jack Lawlor and another man came back under cover of darkness to retrieve the firearms. Lawlor was then aged 21, a big solid young man, a farm labourer, who lived with his widowed mother on the headland. When the split came many young men from the parish had gone with the anti-Treaty faction and Lawlor had been one of them.

Lawlor and his companion were seen and fired on by a National Army patrol. Both were captured but escaped in the darkness and the maze of mausoleums. Lawlor was wounded in the arm and both were soon recaptured. He was tried that night at McCarthy's shop, where the National Army had established their base in the village. The trial, if it can be called that, was presided

over by Colonel Commandant Michael Hogan from the First
Western Division. Lawlor was sentenced to death.[1] The National
Army had no barracks in Ballyheigue and so Lawlor was held
overnight in the old RIC station which was just a small terraced
house with a cell built onto the rear. In the morning he was taken
up to the graveyard on the hillside and shot in plain sight of the
village. Lawlor's body was left where he fell and a messenger was
sent to tell his mother.[2] This trial was not authorised by GHQ and
the rudimentary safeguards laid down in the regulations were not
followed.[3] The officially sanctioned trials by military court began
on 3 November and in Dublin and Kerry military courts convened
at once.

In Kerry, a National Army raid netted another arms find
and two more prisoners: Patrick O'Connor from Causeway and
Patrick Joseph O'Halloran from Ballyheigue.[4] They were tried
and convicted and went back into custody while sentence was
considered. In Donegal, a few days after military courts were
brought in, a National Army raid had resulted in the arrest
of two unlikely prisoners. The first was a formidable widow
farmer, 53-year-old Catherine Johnstone from Letterkenny. She
was charged with possession of bombs, detonators, ammunition
and part of a stolen wireless. Her 21-year-old daughter Georgie
was charged with possession of an automatic pistol. The widow
Johnstone was wealthy and immediately instructed her solicitor
to challenge the legality of the military courts by writs of habeas
corpus, and the case stalled while the lawyers prepared their case.

By mid-November only twelve cases had been tried, all for
possession of arms and only a single conviction had been confirmed: twelve months hard labour was ordered.[5] The Executive
Council had been pressing for executions, but the Army Council
delayed for many days and the sequence of events suggests that
the Council had already settled on four young men who had not
yet been tried. A prisoner at Wellington barracks later wrote that
the young men were brought out of their cells, tried and executed

the same night.[6] It was not so, but the facts are only a little less grim. On 8 November, these four young men were each tried by military court at Wellington barracks for the unauthorised possession of revolvers.[7] The evidence showed that each had been found in possession of a loaded revolver in a Dublin street. Their trials by military court were held in secret and lasted only minutes and all were sentenced to death. The prisoners were Dubliners: James Fisher, John Gaffney, Richard Twohig and Peter Cassidy. The oldest, Cassidy, was 21 and the youngest was 18. They were shot by firing squad on 17 November.

There were many prisoners in custody who might have been singled out for execution and the question is: why this four? It was their misfortune to be captured when the Executive Council was pressing General Mulcahy to commence the execution policy. A more important factor was that these men were suspected of taking part in an attack on Oriel House, which was the headquarters of the counter-insurgency operation in Dublin. The Criminal Investigation Department at Oriel House had been set up to combat the wave of armed robberies. That was a misnomer if there ever was one because it was swiftly redirected to counter the anti-Treaty forces and later amalgamated with another semi-vigilante outfit – the Citizens Defence Force. Oriel House quickly acquired a reputation for torturing and killing prisoners and for these reasons the anti-Treaty forces launched a series of attacks on the building. It was not an easy target: a substantial four-storey terrace on the corner of Westland Row and every assault was fought off.

The fighting in Dublin was now reaching a new pitch. Ernie O'Malley, the anti-Treaty deputy chief of staff, had been operating from a concealed compartment built onto the bedroom of a house in the suburbs. During a raid on the house, his hiding place was found. He fired through the door and in the frenetic shoot-out that followed one of the ladies in the house was wounded and a National Army soldier killed. O'Malley got out of the house, firing a rifle from his hip as he crossed the lawn and here he was shot down. A National Army soldier who tried to finish him off had his gun knocked away by another soldier. There were many attacks on the National Army that week; at Wellington barracks troops on parade were fired on from the rooftops on the other side of the canal. One National Army soldier was killed and seventeen wounded. The firing went on for some minutes and was watched by anti-Treaty prisoners from their cells overlooking the parade ground. As the attackers made off, some of the men on parade turned their guns on the prisoners.[8]

The following night there were attacks on both Portobello and Wellington barracks. At Portobello, the army legal team were playing poker and there was a scramble as they rushed to grab their guns and get out into the barrack square, where one of the lawyers tripped and fell into barbed wire. He was the only casualty inside the barracks. The streets resounded to the rattle of Lewis machine guns and it was described in the papers as 'twenty minutes of din', although it was rather more than that: two civilians were killed. This was the developing context of the fight in Dublin, but it seems that Oriel House was the big issue.

Kevin O'Higgins was the minister with responsibility for that unit. The day after the attack on Oriel House he assured deputies that action was being taken, confirming 'I have reports from Oriel House and the DMP and the Military … The situation was well in hand,' he said and invited deputies to a private briefing. Ostensibly, no one was ever charged with the attack on Oriel House, but the provisional government issued a directive to General Mulcahy to bring the suspects to trial immediately.[9] This directive has some significance because the trial regulations put control of the military courts entirely in the hands of the army, but it suggests that the usual separation of powers between those who tried criminal cases and the Executive had evaporated. The only delay was occasioned by the absence of the main witness, who had gone on leave without leaving a forwarding address. The men were tried and convicted on the day he returned.[10]

Mulcahy and his chief of staff reckoned the executions to be 'the most severe test on our troops'. It was feared soldiers might decline to fire on old comrades or might even mutiny.[11] After some tense discussion, it was decided to bring in the best available army unit and the prisoners were moved to Kilmainham for execution. It was an odd choice on the face of it, but it may have been selected because it was a small prison and the easiest to contain if events took a difficult turn. The night before the first executions, the provisional government briefed pro-Treaty deputies and there were tremors in the ranks. The minister who gave the briefing remembered the Deputy Speaker Pádraic Ó Máille's big face quivering 'like a blancmange'. Some deputies called for clemency, but the genie was out of the bottle: power now lay with General Mulcahy and the Army Council.

There were no last visits for prisoners: the sight of distressed relatives may have dented the resolve of the National Army recruits. All the prisoners were allowed access to a priest and that was the case in all the executions that followed. But the absence of last visits was keenly felt by the prisoners who all lived within walking distance of Kilmainham. James Fisher, aged 18, wrote home: 'Oh Mother, if I could just see you again.' None of the prisoners had any property to bequeath except Richard Twohig, who wrote to his parents: 'I send home the mouth organ to you for Paddy.' And so, these four young men were brought out for execution into the stone-breakers' yard. Buoyed up by words of comfort from the priest, these young men found new strength in the certainty of death. Ernie O'Malley later wrote: 'One had the butt of a cigarette; he took a few puffs, then he handed it to his friends, who in turn took a few jerks. "Shoot away, now."'[12]

Sean Mac Mahon, the chief of staff of the National Army had deployed his chosen company to undertake this duty, but the executions did not go according to plan, perhaps because the National Army was so new and because shooting by firing squad was not as straightforward as might be supposed. In this first group of executions, only three of the prisoners died instantaneously. The death certificate prepared by the army doctor hints at a different outcome for Peter Cassidy: 'shock and haemorrhage following gunshot wounds.'[13] A memoir written by the JAG recorded that Cassidy was rendered unconscious but did not die. In this scene of carnage, the young National Army officer in charge panicked and made to call an ambulance, but recovering his equilibrium, he drew his pistol and shot Cassidy dead.

Something could have been learned from the British Army's experience of firing squads, which was extensive. In the Boer War, the British Army had executed forty-nine men and in the Great War another 329 soldiers, rebels and spies had been shot by firing squad. It had been discovered that execution by firing squad was more complicated than might be thought, in part because the average Tommy hated this duty and soldiers were induced to participate by the promise of extra leave or rations of rum. Sometimes soldiers on firing squad duty missed the target because they were nervous or because they had closed their eyes and a few fired wide or did not fire at all. Therefore, British Army firing squads utilised certain safeguards such as the presence of a provost marshal to supervise the executions and an army doctor to certify death. The usual medical certificate read 'death was instantaneous' or 'practically instantaneous', which was the desired standard. Even these safeguards were sometimes insufficient.

The new National Army had no experience of executions and replicated only some of these procedures. Where a number of prisoners were due to go before a firing squad, the practice of the British Army was sequential executions. The National Army chose to carry out executions simultaneously using a single firing squad. This was intended to be merciful so that prisoners awaiting execution were spared the sound of other firing squads at work, but it was not often effective.

British Army firing squads usually numbered twelve per prisoner, but in Ireland the practice of simultaneous executions meant there were often as few as five men firing at each prisoner. In firing squads convened by the British Army, a single rifle was loaded with a blank and men were sometimes induced to take part in the hope of being the one to fire a blank. It became National Army practice to load a significant number of rifles with blanks, increasing the chances of a prisoner surviving the volley and this would happen again and again. These difficulties were made worse because many of the executions took place in different parts of the country, so no local command ever acquired the necessary degree of competence. In a significant number of civil war executions, the prisoner survived the firing squad and lay on the ground wounded and sometimes conscious. In a small number of cases, the prisoner survived the volley and in a desperate reflex got to his feet. The presence of an officer with a pistol to administer the coup de grâce was essential and soon the National Army was billing the state for whiskey for the firing squads.

After the executions, the families of the dead men were sent a typed pro forma notification. The note for the Cassidy family read as follows: 'I am to inform you that Peter Cassidy was tried by a military court on 8 November 1922. That he was found guilty of possession of a firearm without lawful authority and that he was sentenced to death. This sentence was executed on the morning of 17th November 1922.' This practice was challenged in the Dáil but continued throughout the civil war, and it became common for parents to learn that their son had been executed through a press release or a typed memo shoved through the letterbox.[14] In Dublin, the public and the Dáil learned of the first executions in the afternoon papers. Later that day there was an emergency debate in the Dáil and the decision to execute was hotly challenged by the Labour opposition and other deputies.

Mulcahy justified what was done by what he called the need 'to stem the tide' of lawlessness. 'These men', he told the Dáil, 'were found on the streets of Dublin at night carrying loaded revolvers and waiting to take the lives of other men.' They had certainly been tried and convicted of possessing loaded revolvers. It is a reasonable inference that they were not charged with the attack on Oriel House because it could not be proved against them. To be tried for one reason and executed for another would become a common scenario during the war.

In the Dáil, government ministers rallied to support Mulcahy. Nothing at all was said about the men being involved in an attack on Oriel House and O'Higgins argued that in order to deter others it was best to execute the rank and file: 'If you took as your first case some man who was outstandingly active or wicked in his activities the unfortunate dupes through the country might say, Oh he was killed because he was a leader or he was killed because he was an Englishman ... better to take the plain ordinary case.' Not all the deputies were satisfied with this and some argued against the government: 'I think they ought to have got a public trial'; and another argued that possession of a handgun could never merit the death sentence. Other deputies questioned whether the prisoners were represented by lawyers, and on behalf of the government Ernest Blythe reassured the Dáil that the prisoners had a 'full opportunity of employing legal aid and calling witnesses in their defence'. Blythe added that: 'Every person who will be tried under the Resolutions passed by the Dáil will have a full opportunity for conducting his defence.' This was certainly the undertaking given to the Dáil when the Army (Special Powers) Resolution was passed. Although it should be said that the trial regulations approved by the Dáil contained no provision for legal representation at public expense.[15] It does not seem that many prisoners had the money to pay for a lawyer and the trials were often carried out so swiftly and in such secrecy that the families of the prisoners had no chance to arrange a lawyer.

The provisional government survived the immediate crisis, but the deterrent effect of the execution policy remained uncertain and the daily round of shooting and killing continued. At Inchicore in the west of Dublin, four young men laying a road mine for National Army troops blew themselves to pieces. On the Monaghan border a mine detonated as a National Army lorry crossed a bridge. An officer lost an eye and five of his men were wounded.[16] The following day, the attention of the country turned to Erskine Childers who had just been tried at Portobello barracks for possession of a handgun.

There were at this time only a handful of senior ranking anti-Treaty officers captured in arms after the cut-off date. One was Ernie O'Malley, who was unfit for trial because of wounds and there was no enthusiasm to execute him on account of his record. Another was the burly Pax Whelan: a brigade commander in west Waterford who was captured in arms with two of his officers in a safe house.[17] Pax Whelan was a man with friends on the other side, perhaps. The only other ranking prisoner was Childers, who the provisional government blamed for fostering opposition to the Treaty and also believed (wrongly) that he had played a leading role in the fighting.

Chapter 5

Childers

He was not captured by chance: National Army intelligence officers had built a file on Childers and were actively looking for him. It had been known for some time that he was coming back to Ireland by ship: just before Michael Collins was killed he had directed that Childers be held as 'a stow-away', which, it was reckoned, would be sufficient to snuff out the threat. But Childers was an accomplished yachtsman and he got into the country undetected. He joined the anti-Treaty forces in Cork and after many weeks trying and failing to establish a role, he set off for Dublin on foot and got as far as Wicklow.[1]

The National Army got a tip-off as soon as he arrived at his cousin Robert Barton's home in Wicklow. The raiding party was led by an officer who himself had been a fugitive at the house during the War of Independence. He knew that the maid came out of a side door early every morning to get milk. Just after dawn, Captain Byrne and his men crept up behind the house and surprised the maid at the door and forced their way in. Coming up the stairs, Byrne was challenged by one of the Barton ladies for his warrant. 'This is no time to speak of warrants,' he replied and pushed her away with the butt of his gun. Childers emerged from a bedroom holding an automatic. He made no attempt to use it but passed along the hallway with the gun at his side and at last it was wrestled from his grip. At the time, it was suspected that he was on his way up to Dublin to act as secretary to de Valera, who had announced a new counter-state, but until Childers produced a gun there had been nothing to hang a capital charge on him. All that had now changed.[2]

Trial

Childers was brought up to Dublin and held at Portobello barracks. The JAG later wrote that Childers had been roughed up after capture: his watch and cufflinks had been stolen and he had been kicked so hard he was unable to lie down. He was put down for immediate trial and he asked for legal counsel. Under the trial regulations, a prisoner was entitled to a lawyer if it was practicable and Michael Comyn was telephoned.

Comyn was then appearing at the Red Cow inquest.[3] In the preceding months, he had appeared at many inquests, attempting to secure verdicts of murder against National Army forces, but jurors resisted efforts to make propaganda out of their verdicts and the Red Cow inquest was proving no different. Comyn left the inquest to his junior counsel and cadged a lift to Portobello in an army convoy. There he found his old friend chain-smoking and drinking tea from a tin mug. Childers was then aged 52; clever, thin and usually impassive but for the 'disdainful sniff' that infuriated opponents. A few weeks before, he had been with the anti-Treaty forces that had retreated from Clonmel in a tearing hurry. When the dust settled, Childers sat down and wrote a thank you note to the hotel where he had been staying and enclosed a cheque for bed and board.[4] Comyn had a brief conference with Childers. He was perfectly calm, Comyn recalled. Childers had been told that his trial was to take place in forty-eight hours and he had little to say to his counsel except: 'There is no defence in fact. I had a gun.'[5] He had already begun writing his last letter home to his wife Molly.

Comyn had defended many prisoners who lacked a defence and his most famous victory had been won in just such a case during the War of Independence.[6] In that case, it was Comyn's tactical acumen and his ability to spin the case out until the Truce that saved the lives of the prisoners and many others. Comyn also brought in Patrick Lynch, KC, another formidable advocate.[7] On the day of the first four executions, Childers was tried by military court at Portobello barracks on a charge of being in possession of an automatic without proper authority. The trial was conducted in private; the press and the public were never admitted to these hearings nor was any public notice given of the trial. No defence was advanced to the charge, but counsel submitted a list of legal objections to the jurisdiction of the army tribunal. The fundamental point was that it had been open to the Dáil to pass a statute permitting trials by military court; it had not done so and therefore the trial was unlawful.

Second, it was argued that the defendant was not a civilian, but a staff captain in the anti-Treaty forces and therefore there was no power to try him under the General Regulations as to the Trial of Civilians by Military Courts. Alternatively, the conflict did not generate a sufficient degree of necessity to justify martial law proceedings. The final significant argument was that there was legal power to try him for possession of arms under the Arms Act of 1920, which permitted penal servitude for life.[8] That was a lawful step, counsel argued, but trial by military court was not.[9]

Having made their submissions and disputed the authority of the court, counsel left and the case continued in their absence.[10] The evidence showed that Childers was arrested in the hallway of his family home with a loaded automatic. Childers took no part in the trial except to cross-examine to establish that he would have used the gun on the raiding party but for the presence of women. Unsurprisingly, he was convicted.

The Habeas Corpus Application
While the trial was still in progress, counsel began finalising a habeas corpus challenge. Childers had given his consent to a legal challenge because the case could be used to protect other prisoners who were either under sentence of death or awaiting

trial. The truth of the matter was that the anti-Treaty lawyers were determined to test the legality of the military courts: if Childers did not agree to a test case then it would be another prisoner.

Childers' solicitor chased round Dublin late that night trying to find someone in the government who would give an undertaking to put the execution on hold and to provide the names of the other men in custody. He was batted from one department to another until, at last, he secured an undertaking from Judge Advocate General Cahir Davitt that execution would not take place before the case could be heard in the High Court. That night, Michael Comyn and Patrick Lynch, KC, went to the home of Master of the Rolls Sir Charles O'Connor for an ex parte writ of habeas corpus, requiring the army to produce the prisoner at court and justify the legality of his detention. Sir Charles had come to public notice the year before when he granted a writ of habeas corpus in *Egan v Macready*, a martial law case. His decision, delivered just after the Truce, put a stop to the British Army policy of executing prisoners found in arms in the martial law area. When General Macready, the GOC of the forces in Ireland, had refused to produce the prisoner, Sir Charles had issued a writ for the arrest of Macready and his commanders. This absurd situation was resolved when the British government gave way and released the prisoner. Sir Charles was one of the few judges kept on by the new revolutionary government and it was said, rather cynically, that he had 'acquired merit' in the eyes of the Dáil.

It was for these reasons that Patrick Lynch and Michael Comyn called on Sir Charles at his home late one Friday night. Sir Charles, a small figure in a smoking jacket, received them in his drawing room. He was a man easily flattered. His proudest boast was membership of the O'Connor clan: a subject on which he would bore anyone who would listen. But that night he was frosty and brusque and the lawyers were ordered to apply to the court 'on notice' to the other side after the weekend. The lawyers returned to his home late on Sunday with information that the

National Army would no longer honour the undertaking given by the JAG. Sir Charles declined to make any order.

On the other side of the city, members of the provisional government shared their fears that Childers might get free because 'some cracked judge might order his release'. The crisis was grave: if the court ruled against the army, then it meant that the whole military court scheme was unlawful and that the four prisoners already executed had been unlawfully done to death and that in every such case, prisoners under sentence or awaiting trial would have to be released. There were tense discussions about what should happen if the judge should 'abuse his position'– that is, rule against the government. A minority of ministers argued that if the court granted the writ, the prisoner should be brought out and shot straight away. This view did not prevail and curiously it was General Mulcahy who opposed it most strongly. Other cabinet ministers favoured simply shutting down what remained of the courts.[11] There was an echo here of the imprisonment of Judge Crowley earlier that year and the abolition of Dáil courts in Dublin.[12] Meanwhile, out in the provinces the Dáil courts were being replaced with district judges of a more reliable political hue.[13]

The Childers case was coming to a conclusion, but the chaotic nature of the Irish legal system meant that there were now two cases on the legality of military courts being heard by different judges on the same day. The other case was being brought by Catherine Johnstone, the redoubtable widow farmer, and her daughter Georgie, who were in custody for possession of arms. That case was heard in the Kings Bench before Chief Justice Molony. Childers' case was heard in the Chancery Division at King's Inns because the Four Courts was still in ruins. The provisional government was represented by Hugh Kennedy who relied on an affidavit sworn by Adjutant General O'Sullivan which recounted the state of the country:

```
They have by force of arms robbed banks of
large sums of money, and plundered public
and private property. They shoot from house
tops, and throw bombs in the public streets
... demolishing bridges, tearing up railway
lines, cutting the wires and blocking the
roads. These things they continue to do from
day to day for the purpose of terrorising
their fellow-countrymen ... an armed rebellion
is being carried on throughout the country
against the Parliament of the people and the
Government which has the allegiance of the
vast majority of the people.
```

Hugh Kennedy cogently identified the inconsistency in the arguments advanced for Childers: 'one said that there was no war and another said that he had been taken as a prisoner of war'.[14] The attorney general contended that if a state of war existed then the courts could not intervene. Comyn took the lead for Childers and argued the case he had presented to the military court. The central argument was that the Dáil had the means and the power to pass laws to bring in military courts but had elected not to do so. Applying the logic of recent case law, he argued that the military courts were unlawful. After many hours of argument, Comyn protested that he was too exhausted to continue. He asked for another adjournment and it was refused. Sir Charles delivered his judgment by candlelight in the great hall at King's Inns. In his judgment he recounted the state of the country:

```
I am sitting here in this temporary make-
shift for a Court of Justice. Why? Because
one of the noblest buildings in this country,
which was erected for the accommodation of
the Kings Courts and was the home of justice
```

```
for over a hundred years, is now a mass of
crumbling ruins, the work of revolutionaries,
who proclaim themselves the soldiers of an
Irish Republic.
```

Sir Charles said little about the loss of life but lamented the explosion at the Four Courts and the destruction of the Public Record Office – 'reduced to ashes' in an explosion that had sent a huge cloud of smoke hundreds of feet into the air. The Record Office had been left in ruins with the Four Courts gravely damaged and for hours afterwards papers had rained down over the city. That same day, the government had put out a proclamation asking people to hand in whatever they found, however damaged or charred. When the dust settled, the Great Seal of Ireland was found in the ashes, but most of the paperwork had been destroyed and the loss to the heritage of the country was incalculable. Sir Charles blamed it on 'the irreconcilables' of which the prisoner was one.

The failure of the Dáil to pass legislation was dismissed by Sir Charles as an argument without merit – 'this gets rid of a technical point' said Sir Charles with breathtaking simplicity. Finally, said Sir Charles: '*Suprema lex, salus populi* must be the guiding principle when the civil law has failed. Force then becomes the only remedy, and to those whom the task is committed must be the sole judges of how it should be exercised … the salvation of the country depends upon it.' The prisoner, said the judge, 'comes to this civil court for protection, but its answer must be that its jurisdiction is ousted by the state of war which he himself has helped to produce'. After the hearing, Sir Charles was asked to consider the cases of the eight unnamed prisoners also in custody on capital charges. 'I cannot do it,' replied Sir Charles. Having found in the Childers application that the court had no jurisdiction, he declined to say anything more about the other eight prisoners.[15]

The weight of academic opinion is that the legal reasoning of the Master of the Rolls was poor and that he had strained to find in favour of the National Army and that an appeal would have raised arguments of substance.[16] Michael Comyn gave notice of an appeal but crucially did not ask for a stay of execution. In the other habeas corpus case concerning Mrs Johnstone and her daughter, Chief Justice Molony had just given a similar judgment.[17] Chief Justice Molony's judgment was short and pragmatic: 'a state of war does exist in County Donegal which justifies the application of Martial Law'. The court declined to intervene and Mrs Johnstone and her daughter remained in custody awaiting trial.[18]

Execution

At Beggars Bush Childers finished his last letter to his wife: 'It all seems perfectly simple and inevitable like lying down after a long days' work.'[19] He had already smuggled out a short statement setting out his explanation for his involvement in the civil war: 'I was bound by honour, conscience and principle to oppose the treaty by speech, writing and action, both in peace and, when it came to the disastrous point, in war.'[20]

Childers was brought out into the square at Beggars Bush before dawn and taken to a shed used for a firing range where a coffin had been laid out. It was later said that the National Army had got wind of an attempt to rescue Childers from Beggars Bush and decided to bring forward the execution and this may explain one final twist. Childers pointed that it was standard practice for an army doctor to be present at executions and it was still too dark for a firing party to do the job properly. He was awkward and stubborn to the last. The execution was deferred 'Till morning's beam should rise and give him light to die.'[21] While they waited for dawn Childers chatted with the Dean of Kildare and shared cigarettes with the firing party until at last the sun came up. He was blindfolded against his wishes and as the firing squad came to order, he spoke his final words: 'Take a step forward lads. It will be easier that way.' The firing party consisted of twenty men; fifteen of the rifles were loaded with blanks. Childers was blown off his feet and when he was examined he seemed dead, but his body remained entirely stiff and the medical officer declined to certify him dead. After a hurried conference, an officer fired a revolver into the body. Another junior officer, probably overwrought and perhaps misunderstanding what was taking place, rushed up and fired a round into the dead man's face.[22] Such was the hatred that had been whipped up against Childers.

He had been a sailor, gun-runner, pilot, bestselling novelist and a clerk to the House of Commons at Westminster before becoming involved in the Irish War of Independence as a propagandist against the British.[23] There may have been a number of reasons for Childers to come up to Dublin on his last journey. A plan had been laid by an anti-Treaty column at Leixlip to capture the Baldonnel airfield, seize the Free State's tiny air force and carry out a daylight bombing raid on Leinster House. Childers had combat experience as a pilot during the Great War and so 'Childers was coming up for Baldonnel' became part of the legend.[24]

His lawyers learned of the execution later that morning while they were still trying to get his case listed before the Court of Appeal.[25] Did the publicity attached to Childers prejudice his trial? On conviction – no. The evidence was beyond doubt and he made no defence. Setting aside the substantial question of the legality of the proceedings which affected all such trials: even on his own case he had no factual defence to the charge. A number of objections have since been made on his behalf. First that the gun was 'a tiny automatic, little more than a toy'.[26] In fact, it was a .32 automatic – a lethal weapon – it was loaded and its size made it easy to conceal. Second, it was pointed out that the gun was not fired. The evidence, however, showed that Childers drew the gun when the raid took place and he did not dispute this. It was also said that the gun was a present from Collins.[27] This may have been so, but it was not carried as a memento, it was carried with hostile intent. It was pointed out by Gavan Duffy and other opponents of the government that the offence was committed on private premises – his cousin's home. This was perhaps the most risible objection. Childers' counsel had told the court that he was a staff captain in the anti-Treaty army on active service, although they wisely did not disclose the nature of his mission.

It has become popular for historians to berate O'Higgins about Childers and to claim that the provisional government had demonised him and prejudiced his trial.[28] That does not quite state the position. Childers was blamed by many for starting the civil war: he had agitated against the draft treaty while part of the Irish delegation in London and later during the debates in Dublin. By the autumn of 1922, he had become a hate figure for the Executive Council in the same way as de Valera, but Childers, being English and not a hero of 1916, was rather easier to vilify in the press. O'Higgins described him as 'bent on the complete breakdown ... of the country ...', but in reality this was no more than a description of the emerging anti-Treaty policy to make the country ungovernable and seize a republic from the ruins. Press reports had wrongly identified him taking a leading role in the fighting. Although he was nominally a staff captain, he had done little more than print posters and drag his printing press on a donkey-drawn cart from one place to another.[29] After the retreat from Clonmel, he had kicked his heels for weeks while others fought.

The propaganda war was waged by both sides and neither held back. During this war of words, O'Higgins and his emerging clique imputed to Childers influence that he did not enjoy. Until Childers was unexpectedly captured and brought forward for trial, members of the provisional government were free to say what they wished about him. After the arrest of Childers and while he was about to be tried, O'Higgins made a very public and unwise reference to the execution of an Englishman. One ugly criticism has always endured: that Childers was executed because the Executive Council, and O'Higgins in particular, detested him. As a matter of fact, responsibility for the decision to execute lay with the five-man Army Council: the regulations adopted by the Dáil stipulated this much.[30] Mulcahy was in control of the execution process, but in the days before Childers was captured, the correspondence between ministers suggests that the Executive Council was anxious that executions should take place soon and were pressing for a start: 'your business is first on the agenda,' Cosgrave wrote irritably to Mulcahy.

Mulcahy chaired the Army Council and also held the post of minister of defence which gave him complete control over what was done. It seems likely, however, that he shared the decision-making process with the Executive Council as he did with other critical events during the war.[31] An obvious indicator is that although there were many pleas for clemency for Childers, the Executive Council minutes are silent about the executions taking place that week. It all resonates very much of discussions not recorded.[32]

The Fate of the Remaining Prisoners

Two weeks later, Mrs Johnstone and her daughter Georgie got their case before the Court of Appeal, where they lost by a margin of 2–1. After a review of the evidence against them, the National Army ordered their release.[33] The remaining prisoners included a handful of Dubliners charged with possession of handguns[34] alongside two prisoners from Newtowncashel.[35] All received prison terms bar one who was acquitted.

An unexpected hiccup in the execution policy now began to emerge: some National Army commanders did not favour executions and resisted their implementation. In the new National Army, some commanders held rank at least in part on account of their reputation and the loyalty of their men derived from shared pre-Truce service as well as familial and county connections. They could not easily be sacked. At Nenagh, Brigadier Liam Hoolan would not sanction executions and none would take place there during the civil war and the same was true in Tipperary Town.[36]

In Cork, Major General Emmet Dalton had been the first to resort to firing squads: he had Private Barney Winsley shot two months previously for selling guns to anti-Treaty fighters. Now Dalton wrote to GHQ to inform Mulcahy that he had the events under control and 'in the present state of affairs in the area no trials of civilians are to be held'.[37] It is likely that General Mulcahy did not welcome this show of independence and Emmet Dalton resigned his commission soon after, although it cannot be asserted this was the reason or, at least, the only reason. There were other straws in the wind, however. Dalton's deputy, Tom Ennis, also opposed the execution policy and let that be known at GHQ. Ennis, a redoubtable frontline commander who was much respected by his troops, was recalled in December and given an administrative post. It seems that this was the response by GHQ to dissent in the senior ranks. GHQ was getting its way, although there is anecdotal evidence that a few senior officers were discreetly non-compliant to the extent that they felt able.[38]

In Kerry, the GOC was W.R.E. Murphy, formerly a British Army officer and a veteran of the Western Front.[39] In his custody were prisoners who had been tried or were awaiting trial, including Patrick O'Connor and Patrick Joseph O'Halloran, who had been captured in a National Army raid in Ballyheigue just after the cut-off date.[40] When offered the chance to join the Childers case, Patrick O'Connor had declined to seek the protection of the court, but the solicitor had added him on the habeas corpus action. W.R.E. Murphy sentenced these two men to five years' imprisonment and this did not please the hardliners in the Executive Council: 'We could not induce him to execute anyone,' wrote Blythe. In due course, Murphy also would be recalled and it might have been sooner, but he avoided confrontation with GHQ. Instead, he argued that he had the Irregulars on the run in Kerry and that too many executions might prove counter-productive. Possession of arms only, Murphy argued, was not a reason to execute at that time. That was the reasoning that underpinned his decision not to execute O'Halloran and O'Connor, and since the regulations did not permit the Army Council to alter a prison term to a death sentence, the government was stuck with this outcome.

Also fortunate to escape immediate execution were four more Kerry prisoners who had been sentenced to death for attacking National Army troops and possession of a rifle and bandolier: Mathew Moroney, Thomas Devane, Cornelius Casey and Dermot O'Connor. Con Casey had led the others in an ambush on a Free State cycle patrol near Knockane in Kerry. The Free State patrol proved too strong and pursued Casey's men up the hillside despite the rifle fire from the fleeing men. 'They still kept coming,' remembered Con Casey and at last they were surrounded and taken prisoner. They were tried and convicted the day before Childers was executed. After Childers' execution there was an unexplained delay in carrying out the executions of these four Kerry men and this was probably due to the obduracy of W.R.E. Murphy, whose strategic arguments with GHQ barely masked his reluctance to execute anyone. The case of these prisoners was looked at again, but the new five-man Army Council was split on the issue of whether the executions should go ahead: some argued that if the prisoners were to be executed, then it should be done swiftly.[41] The fate of these men continued to hang in the balance.

Chapter 6

Spooner, Farrelly,
Murphy and Mallin

Less than a week after Childers was shot, four more men were ordered for execution in Dublin. Spooner, Farrelly, Murphy and Mallin were convicted of proclaimed offences. Spooner had a revolver, Farrelly had a bomb and Murphy two bombs (grenades) when captured. James Mallin was in possession of a revolver. The judge advocate general later recalled that the men were captured after an ambush on an army convoy on the south circular: bombs had been thrown and handguns fired, but no casualties were caused. These men were picked up in that vicinity and were suspected of involvement in that attack.[1]

These men were young Dubliners who held no rank in the anti-Treaty faction. None of the men were older than 21, but Mallin was the youngest: 18 and a student at UCD. The judge advocate general argued for a reprieve in his case and he was questioned as to his reasons by the Army Council. Sentence on James Mallin was commuted to five years' penal servitude, although it seems that the only argument that counted with the Army Council was that he was the son of Michael Mallin.[2] It is entirely unclear if this decision was driven by sentiment for an old comrade or by recognition that the late Michael Mallin had many friends and this would be an unpopular act.

A question arises: why were these three executed yet others were not? It was plainly not the policy of the National Army to execute every single prisoner captured in arms. At this time, a trade union official was arrested with a revolver, but closer inquiry revealed that he was taking strike funds to the bank and felt in need of protection, and he was soon released without charge. The system was not completely rigid. Also tried in late November were a handful of anti-Treaty fighters, who were for the most part convicted of attacking National Army forces. Curiously none were executed. One was Michael Burke from Windgap in Kilkenny, who was convicted of taking part in an ambush on national forces and possessing a rifle. He was sentenced to penal servitude for life.[3] Peter O'Connell from Annascaul was convicted of attacking National Army forces in ambush. He was initially sentenced to death, but the sentence was commuted to penal servitude.[4] The reluctance of the GOC in Kerry to execute may have been a factor in his case. Gerald Mulhern and Michael Hearty from Dundalk were surprised at a safe house – Mrs McGrane's farm at Monsacreebe near Dungooley. They ran out firing on National Army soldiers but surrendered when they realised they were completely surrounded. They were in possession of revolvers and in the farmhouse a large arms cache was found. There does not seem to have been any doubt about their involvement, but they were not convicted and the court simply made a recommendation for two years' detention with hard labour. This course of action might be explained if they were quite young, but there is no firm information on this point. Two other prisoners from Dundalk were given seven years for possessing a handgun.[5] Four more Dublin prisoners were all convicted of attacking National Army forces and possession of arms; six years was ordered in respect of each.[6]

There is a curious disparity between these most serious cases and those of Spooner, Farrelly and Murphy, who were themselves executed for arms offences only. It may be inferred that the gravity of the offence was not the only matter that weighed in the balance, although the destruction of trial records makes a full evaluation impossible. Another issue that begins to emerge is that officers conducting trials for arms offences were not required to make findings about the intent with which a weapon had been carried; proof of possession was sufficient and this put the prisoner's life in the hands of the Army Council, which decided if execution would follow. Once a case went before the Army Council, execution might be ordered because of matters that could not be proved in court, intelligence about the prisoner or some other extraneous reason that was never publicly disclosed.

The secrecy surrounding the trials troubled many deputies and on the day of this latest round of executions Deputy Thomas Johnson pressed the government for information: 'they are tried by the military authority and they are executed by the military authority and the announcement of their executions is made by the military authority … and no public person outside that military authority knows anything about it'. It was, he argued, 'anarchy – lynch law once removed'. There were some deputies who agreed, even in the government benches. Deputy Thomas Johnson focused on how the men were singled out for execution: 'Is the method of selection choice or chance? Is it by lot? Is it by the enormity of the crime …?'

The tenor of the Dáil debate that followed suggests that some deputies would not have supported execution on the basis of the possession of arms alone or any act falling short of murder. General Mulcahy, however, avoided the question of what the men had actually done and read instead a captured document written by an anti-Treaty officer: a dramatic account of the attack on Oriel House using landmines. Only one of the landmines had gone off. A cool-headed National Army officer had plucked the fuse out of another and but for that Oriel House would have been completely destroyed with potentially very many casualties. Mulcahy never stated that the executed men were involved in that attack, but his answer seems to have settled the disquiet of some deputies and the attack on the government failed.[7]

This round of executions would have profound repercussions. Just before the firing squad convened, the speaker of the Dáil received a letter from Liam Lynch, chief of staff of the anti-Treaty faction, warning that unless the rules of warfare were observed: 'we shall adopt very drastic measures to protect our forces'. It had become a war with few rules, but Lynch had railed against the ill-treatment and killing of prisoners, and he regarded the execution policy as an extension of those actions. Lynch claimed prisoner-of-war status for his men, but the provisional government framed the conflict in terms of suppressing disorder that threatened to overwhelm the new state. In public at least, the government did not distinguish between anti-Treaty fighters and those involved in armed robbery. The letter was put to one side. Lynch, perhaps anticipating a rebuff issued an order permitting captured prisoners to employ solicitors and counsel to contest proceedings before military courts.[8] It is now known that on the day of the latest executions another order was issued by Lynch that listed categories of people to be 'shot at sight', including TDs who had voted for what he termed 'the Enemy Murder Bill'.[9] The order also encouraged burning the homes of government supporters.

Chapter 7

The Creation of the Irish Free State and the Mountjoy Executions

On 6 December, the Irish Free State came into being with the enactment of the new constitution. Messages of good wishes came in from the King and the British prime minister as the government of the new Free State assembled at Leinster House to take the loyal oath. Cosgrave took the oath followed by O'Higgins, Mulcahy and Gearóid O'Sullivan, in army uniform. In turn, they swore: 'I will be faithful to H.M. King George V, his heirs and successors by law in virtue of the common citizenship of Ireland and the United Kingdom ...' Only eighteen months before these men had been fighting tooth and nail against the armies of King George and now they were swearing an oath of allegiance. A reporter in the gallery overlooking the oak-panelled room noted no lack of propriety but observed that 'they did not kiss the book' as was the custom at the time. There had been a reception just before the House convened, but a muted one. Perhaps the great event had been tarnished by the death of Collins and so many others.

Cosgrave announced his Executive Council almost immediately, but it was not a happy band. O'Higgins was the coming man and he barely disguised his desire to take Cosgrave's job. Cosgrave could not do without O'Higgins but kept him in check by excluding his ally (Patrick Hogan) from the Executive Council. General Mulcahy detested O'Higgins, Hogan and their privately educated clique – their second language was French not Irish and they had little regard for the cultural aspects of the revolution. It was Mulcahy who had built up the Irish Volunteers after 1918 and lived in constant danger of capture, and now these professional politicians who had never fired a shot were telling him how to run the army. Blythe, the only Protestant and northerner in the cabinet, remained aloof and without allies on the Executive Council. The personal antagonisms swirling around the cabinet table also touched Joe McGrath, but he was more guarded in what he said. Only MacNeill seemed impervious to the tensions.[1] The names of the senators who would take their place in the new Senate were also read out and it was a list that reached out to include all sections of society. It included luminaries of the rebellion like Madame Wyse Power, W.B. Yeats and Sir Bryan McMahon, formerly commander of the Irish 10th Division. There was also the surgeon, Oliver St John Gogarty, and a handful of businessmen and baronets of the old ascendancy class.

That day Ulster opted out of the Free State as expected, but Tim Healy, the new governor-general spoke warmly about building a common future with the North. A new Free State stamp priced 2d went on sale and there was a quiet air of optimism as life in the city moved on much as usual. The grand jury assembled at the old courthouse on Green Street to hear a case of selling methylated spirits for public consumption and a handful of a new class of motor car manslaughter cases were dealt with. It was not all business as usual because the grand jury heard that robbery in the city and county of Dublin had become endemic: hundreds of revolver-point robberies in less than two months and very few offenders had been arrested. The grand jury recommended that the lash be brought back in.

The following afternoon, two deputies, Sean Hales and Pádraic Ó Máille, came out of the Ormonde Hotel and jumped into an open-topped horse-drawn taxi cab on the north quays. Hales had become a well-known figure during the Treaty debates: a giant of a man, in the distinctive green Volunteer uniform and slouch hat. During the debates he had said: 'I have travelled a rocky road and now I want a rest.' An open-topped car pulled up alongside Hales and a group of men stood. Chief among these was Owen Donnelly, a slightly built, fair-haired young man. Donnelly and the others poured revolver fire into the stationary cab containing Hales and Ó Máille.[2] The jarvey was unhurt and flicked the reins, rushing straight to hospital, but Hales was dead on arrival. It was said rather unkindly by some that Ó Máille had been saved by his sheer bulk.

The news was brought to Leinster House within minutes and Cosgrave rose: 'I have just been informed that Deputy Sean Hales has been shot dead and that Deputy Ó Maille has been wounded.' Cosgrave offered no hint of any government response, but the Executive Council of the Free State government met that evening. Ernest Blythe, arriving late and in a hurry, heard the names of four prisoners read out: Mellows, Barrett, O'Connor and McKelvey. They had all been members of the Four Courts Executive during the siege earlier that summer and they were to be executed as a reprisal for the killing of Hales. The initiative on this step had been taken by General Mulcahy, although it is inconceivable that he did so without the prompting or the backing of the Army Council. Mulcahy sought the agreement of the Executive Council and did so perhaps because it was an extreme measure and in the hope that the sharing of responsibility might head off later retribution. None of the ministers dissented except O'Higgins, who asked: 'Is there no alternative?' It was the only occasion in the war when O'Higgins's desire for extreme action was out-matched by the army. Mellows was well known to all and six months previously, one of the prisoners, Rory O'Connor, had been best man for Kevin O'Higgins. But no cabinet minister raised the question of old friendships. O'Higgins relented after a short discussion: 'Take them out and shoot them.'

Just before dawn, the prisoners were woken and taken to a holding area. O'Connor had thought he might be deported and in his coat he had sewed two gold guineas given to him by O'Higgins at his wedding. Liam Mellows was first to find out the truth. He was given a typed note: 'You, Liam Mellowes [*sic*] are hereby notified that being a person taken in arms against the government, you will be executed at 8am 8th December as a reprisal for the assassination of Brigadier Sean Hales, TD, in Dublin.' The prisoners were given access to a priest who declined to give absolution unless the prisoners accepted the correctness of the Bishop's Pastoral Letter. Mellows would not back down and was determined to go to his death without absolution and sat down and penned a letter home:

> My dearest mother,
> The time is short and much that I would like to say must go unsaid. But you will understand; in such moments heart speaks to heart ...[3]

The other prisoners also began writing hurried last letters home as the time for execution approached. After mass the prisoners were brought out into the yard blindfolded but not restrained. Dick Barrett sang, but the other prisoners were silent. They were lined up against a wall in front of a twenty-man firing squad: five men for each prisoner. There were no sounds but for the murmuring of the priest and Mellows scraping his boots against the gravel to get a solid footing. A handkerchief was dropped by the officer and the squad fired a single volley. The priest who attended later wrote that McKelvey raised himself up slightly:

> 'Give me another ...'
> A shot was fired into him.
> 'And another ...'
> The officer stepped forward and fired another bullet.[4]

An account by another witness related that many of the squad fired on O'Connor, who fell dead, flames flickered here and there on his coat. Mellows, Barrett and McKelvey all fell to the ground mortally wounded and an officer fired a series of revolver shots to finish them off. It is not possible to corroborate this account although the women prisoners who were held close to the execution yard recalled the volley and afterwards counted nine single shots. Soon after, a squad of soldiers passed through the prison with a group of workmen who avoided the gaze of the watching prisoners.[5] There was silence but for the tramp of boots and one of the prisoners called to mind Oscar Wilde's lines:

> 'But we knew the work they had been at,
> By the quicklime on their boots.'

Outside the prison, the business of the country continued as usual. An inquest jury was convened and heard that Hales had sustained wounds to his temple, throat, lung and thigh. It was, said the foreman, 'wilful murder'. Back at Leinster House the deputies gathered and the question of the executions was raised by the Labour leader when Cosgrave opened the business of the day. Cosgrave seemed surprised and observed: 'I do not know that there is any necessity for making any statement on the subject … Is there not business on the agenda?' Something needed to be said. The government had shot dead four prisoners without trial and many of the deputies wanted answers. Who had authorised the executions? Were other executions expected?

There were other dimensions to all that had taken place. From a legal perspective, these men were executed without trial for acts committed by others. Since the policy of assassinating TDs had not been in the contemplation of the anti-Treaty forces when these men were taken prisoner in the summer, it cannot be said that legal or moral responsibility for the death of Hales could be laid at the door of these men. The new state was barely two days old and the constitution guaranteed life, liberty, freedom of conscience and due process, or at least trial by military court 'in time of war, or armed rebellion'.[6] The question was being asked: what is our constitution for – if not for this? It had already been recognised under international law that an army might take belligerent reprisals against an opponent who departed from recognised standards of war, but this had never extended to killing prisoners.[7]

The debate in the Dáil was restrained and eloquent. The charge was led by Deputy Thomas Johnson, the leader of the opposition: 'I am forced to say you have killed the new state at its birth ...' Thomas Johnson referred to the abandonment of due process in favour of military courts that sat in secret away from the gaze of the public and the press, and remarked how quickly the government had moved on to execution without any trial: 'We felt it necessary that we should raise a protest and a warning against secret trials. We feared the possibility that secrecy in the guise of legality would lead to secrecy without legality.' One of the backbench critics of the government was Gavan Duffy, who had parted company with Cosgrave's government earlier that summer over the treatment of prisoners. Gavan Duffy would, many years later, be a distinguished but reactionary Judge of the Irish Free State. Gavan Duffy likened the shootings to a Corsican Vendetta: 'When will it stop?'

The Executive Council members put aside their many personal antagonisms and rivalries and rallied behind a single point in rebuttal: necessity. Cosgrave observed that it was a psychological question of meeting terror with terror. O'Higgins told the Dáil: 'The safety and preservation of the people is the highest law.' He was supported by Eoin MacNeill, who spoke about the nature of threat faced by the new state and the killing of Hales, which he described as: 'A carefully laid plan to annihilate this government, this form of government in which we are taking part ... the killing of Deputy Hales yesterday was the entry of that plan on a new phase, and the object of that act was to annihilate the power of this assembly.' The government weathered the crisis, although there was some regret in the Executive Council about the wording of the official press release, describing the executions as a 'reprisal' which exposed the government to criticism. After this, all press releases on executions were scrutinised with some care.

Some have argued that the effect of the Bishop's Pastoral Letter was to give Mulcahy and Cosgrave, both devoted Catholics, the moral certainty to act as they did.[8] Some of the bishops were now privately drawing back from the execution policy but said nothing in public. Their silence was deafening. The JAG later argued that the shootings were entirely justified and the effect of the reprisal was complete and effective. It was not quite so. A few days later, an attempt was made to kill another TD and a lone anti-Treaty fighter took a pot shot at General Mulcahy's car on the way to the Dáil. After this, though, there were no more assassinations or attempts to kill TDs. There was, it seems, even in the most bitter anti-Treaty fighters, no enthusiasm for killing TDs.

Some anti-Treaty supporters tried to distance themselves from the killing of Hales, perhaps because the existence of the 'shoot at sight' order issued by Lynch was not then widely known. Generations later, some republican apologists were still doing so. One wrote that the shooting of Hales was 'never claimed and never sanctioned' by the anti-Treaty faction.[9] That was not so. The shooting of Hales and Ó Máille was the first step to put the order issued by Lynch into effect. Hales held the rank of brigadier in the National Army, but there is no doubt that he was killed because he was a TD.[10] Before the day was out the policy of Mulcahy and the Army Council would take a more a draconian turn.

Chapter 8

Trial by Army Committee

Even before the Mountjoy executions were carried out, the military courts' trial process had changed fundamentally. The Army Council had seen the order issued by Liam Lynch identifying categories of people to be 'shot at sight' including TDs who had voted for the Army (Special Powers) Resolution, senators and National Army legal staff officers.[1] The killing of Hales was the first step in putting that order into effect. It may be inferred that the Army Council perceived the shooting of Hales as the beginning of a greater crisis and a draconian response was prepared. While the condemned men were being singled out, Mulcahy called the judge advocate general and informed him it had been decided to set up a committee system to deal with possession of arms cases where there was no factual dispute. Trial by military court would be reserved only for cases where there was a dispute. Mulcahy asked Judge Advocate General Cahir Davitt to draft regulations with a view to a proclamation being issued the next day.

Davitt, according to his own account, said that no regulations would be necessary given the nature of the inquiry, which was effectively a drumhead court martial. He asked that he and his department be excused involvement in the trial by committee process and Mulcahy agreed. Davitt advised that in order to keep within the terms of the Dáil Resolution, the Army Council should insist on a legal officer and if a legal officer was required then he should be 'requisitioned' to sit on the committee. The judge advocate general's decision to absolve himself and his department from involvement is inexplicable and there is more than a hint of tension between General Mulcahy and his JAG over this development. General Mulcahy issued the new proclamation the same evening. It decreed that any person found in possession of a gun, ammunition, explosive or bomb would be tried by a committee of officers. For these offences, trial by military court was a thing of the past.[2] The punishments set out in the proclamation were 'to suffer death or such other punishment' as seen fit. It was intended that this new committee procedure be reserved for cases where there was no factual dispute, but the new proclamation did not say that. It simply related that this new procedure was in force. There was a subsidiary difficulty: the decision that there was no factual dispute was made by army lawyers and this essentially pre-judged the whole trial.

The General Regulations as to the Trial of Civilians by Military Courts had only been laid before the Dáil for approval a few weeks before and were now being swept aside. Those Regulations contained certain basic protections for the accused. Under the trial by committee scheme there were no such protections for an accused person, no procedural safeguards, no rules of evidence and not even a lawyer.[3] The position was exacerbated by the fact that the judge advocate general had excused himself of responsibility for supplying legal officers for committee duty or reviewing their decisions.

As part of this new process, Mulcahy issued a directive widening the definition of possession to include 'circumstances which point to possession'. This directive addressed a belief in the minds of many anti-Treaty fighters and National Army officers that if a prisoner was not captured holding a gun he could not be convicted of an offence of possession of arms under the regulations. This was certainly an evidential difficulty in some trials. One of the cases which brought this issue to the fore concerned Tom Maguire TD from Mayo. Maguire was captured without a weapon, but some distance away a handgun was found.

The legal officer who took the summary of evidence reported that 'the evidence would be insufficient to convict the prisoner on a charge of unlawful possession of firearms.'[4] The GOC in Athlone referred the matter upward to Mulcahy.

General Mulcahy now defined possession in a wider way so that possession could be equated with knowledge and control over weapons which might have been discarded, buried or otherwise hidden. This new definition cannot be criticised, but in the coming months, army committees would infer possession of hidden arms and ammunition in circumstances where the link to the prisoner was uncertain. Tom Maguire was tried a few weeks later in the detention barracks at Athlone and his was such a case. Like many, he had no prior notice of his trial and was simply brought into a room where he found a group of officers 'all in civvies'. The trial took a few minutes and he was convicted of possession of a gun that had been found some distance from the scene of his capture. He was sentenced to death. It cannot now be said if the committee reached the wrong factual conclusion in that case, but it is an example of how the system had becoming increasingly vulnerable to the risk of error. The new system of trial by committee was brought in immediately and the very first case concerned a group of prisoners captured at Rathbride in Kildare.

Chapter 9

The Rathbride Prisoners

Moore's Bridge was a single arch over the Grand Canal on the edge of the Curragh Plains. Nearby were a small house and three acres farmed by the Moore family and it was here that the Rathbride column had made their base under the leadership of Bryan Moore, a 28-year-old labourer.[1] Under the house a dugout had been fashioned to hide the men. All over southern Ireland there were cramped dugouts like this: filled with men who emerged at night to conduct a guerrilla campaign.

The Rathbride column was composed mostly of former railway workers who had been living in their dugout for some months, occasionally coming out to relieve local shopkeepers of groceries and clothing. They had disrupted rail services in and around Kildare by tearing up railway sleepers and smashing points, and they were becoming more ambitious and proficient. They had ambushed a National Army convoy in late November and inflicted casualties before disappearing into the night. Just before their capture they had removed two engines from the sidings at Kildare and despatched them down the railway tracks where they collided with logs jammed on the line. Both engines derailed. The terrain, however, was not suitable for a guerrilla campaign. The land was flat with little natural cover and there were major National Army barracks at the Curragh and the towns of Naas, Newbridge and Kildare, which made the position of the Rathbride men delicate. It was only a matter of time before someone, perhaps an irate shopkeeper, made the connection with the farm at Moore's Bridge.

One of the men was Tom Behan, who had an intelligence role. He got hold of his senior officers and told them the column was in imminent danger of capture, but no help was forthcoming.[2]

On 12 December, National Army forces, acting on a tip-off, raided the farmhouse and inside they found the farmer's daughter, 26-year-old Annie Moore, with a loaded revolver. She was arrested, but they found nothing else. They searched again and this time found the dugout built below the house. The National Army officer called down to the men to surrender and threatened to throw grenades into the dugout. The National Army report shows that ten prisoners emerged from the dugout. Also seized were ten rifles, some detonators and exploders. Many years later, Annie Moore wrote that the raiding party were 'an unruly mob' who 'ate and drank everything in the house', took up the floor and tore out ceilings. After two days, they left, 'stealing everything they could carry away'.

Among the ten prisoners was Tom Behan. The story soon got about that Behan had his arm broken by a rifle butt and being unable to climb into the lorry with the others, he was beaten to death. The official version released to the press related that Behan had tried to escape from the Curragh where the prisoners were being held in a military detention unit known as the Glasshouse.[3] The account related that he had tried to climb out of a narrow window in the upper storey and was warned to desist by a sentry before he was 'fired on and fatally wounded'.[4] It was later suggested by other prisoners that this was written to disguise the truth: why would the prisoner try something so desperate? The simple answer may be that Behan realised he had to escape or face a firing squad. There is support for the official report in a last letter home by James O'Connor who wrote that Behan had been shot dead 'the night we were all arrested'.[5]

The remaining men were investigated by a committee convened by the army. This was the first trial by committee and it was not a trial as we know it in that there were no rules of evidence or procedure. The men had no lawyers or any chance to make a case if they had one. Of the nine men still in custody, all were sentenced to death, but two were reprieved. One was Pat Moore, the brother of Bryan, the leader. The other was Jim White, younger brother of Stephen, who was himself just 18. The National Army press release suggested that these two men were part of the column. The inference is that they were spared for compassionate reasons.[6] White was under 18 and no prisoners below that age were executed in the civil war. A review of cases suggests that where two brothers were on trial for a capital offence, the National Army never executed both and this was probably why Patrick Moore was spared. The other seven prisoners were sent for execution.

Men awaiting execution were always given access to a priest and this was the greatest source of consolation for the prisoners and for their families. The official position adopted by the bishops was to urge their clergy to shun anti-Treaty fighters and many were denied confession, communion and in some instances even burial on sacred ground.[7] There were, however, some priests who favoured the anti-Treaty cause and made themselves available to condemned men. Stephen White, aged 18, wrote home to tell his widowed father of his impending execution. Of his brother Jim, who was to be spared, he wrote: 'Thank God it is me instead of him that was to go. He will be more use to you than I.' A close reading of the last letters home resonate of things that could not be written down. James O'Connor also gave a broader hint that his family should see Father Donnelly: 'I told him all.'

The following morning, 19 December, the seven prisoners were executed at the military detention barracks at the Curragh. Barely a week had passed between capture and execution. This event marked the beginning of the local execution policy. The executions were announced in the press and given wide publicity along with the arms seizures and an Aladdin's cave of stolen clothing and food.[8] It was through this press announcement that the families of the men learned of the executions. The two male prisoners who were spared were sent for internment. Annie Moore was not tried; it was not politic to try women. The records that still exist suggest that no women were tried by military court or committee, but many were interned without trial. Annie Moore was sent to Mountjoy, where she would learn of the execution of her brother and her fiancée.[9] With the breadwinners of the family dead or in custody, her elderly father sold off most of his three-acre smallholding to pay bills. He died soon after, leaving his widow in poverty.

Chapter 10

The Leixlip Prisoners

The Rathbride case was the first to be tried by an army committee, but there was still a backlog of men waiting for trial by military court. One of these cases concerned twenty-two prisoners captured in early December at Leixlip. The Leixlip column operated a campaign for several months and the landscape became scarred with blown-up bridges and trenched roads. At the heart of this affair was Patrick Mullaney, a national school teacher from County Mayo. He had fought in the recent war against the British. When the civil war broke out Mullaney went with the anti-Treaty faction and was briefly imprisoned at the Curragh but sawed his way through the bars of a kitchen window and returned to Kildare, where he led what became known as the Leixlip column.

From August of 1922, Mullaney and his men began tearing up railway lines, cutting telephone wires and ambushing National Army convoys. In the autumn, Mullaney made contact with a number of disaffected National Army soldiers who were on guard duty at Baldonnel airfield – the main base of the tiny National Army air force. These men included two corporals: Sylvester Healy and Leo Dowling; and three privates: Terence Brady, Laurence Sheehy and Anthony O'Reilly. They were persuaded to allow Mullaney to get into the base, capture large quantities of arms and burn the aeroplanes. One or two of the planes were to be spared for a daylight bombing raid on Leinster House.[1] It was later said that Childers, who had combat experience with the Royal Fleet Air Arm was 'coming up for Baldonnel'.[2] A number of attempts to put the plan into operation failed and eventually Healy and his men deserted and went on the run with Mullaney.

All of this came to a head on 1 December when Mullaney's men took over a house near Collinstown and captured the crew of a lorry that had broken down nearby. Mullaney failed to realise that one soldier had escaped and had raised the alarm. A lorry load of National Army soldiers arrived from the Curragh within an hour and spread out, walking cross country until they were fired on from the house. Inexplicably, Mullaney and his men remained in the house and exchanged fire and soon more National Army units from Dublin arrived. At this juncture, Mullaney and his men made a dash into open country and they fought a running retreat until the arrival of an armoured car made further resistance impossible.

National Army casualties included one soldier killed and two wounded. The twenty-two prisoners were taken back to Dublin for interrogation. All the prisoners had been living rough and they were unkempt and unshaven, but a few were wearing the remnants of National Army uniform and questioning focused on this issue. Five prisoners were identified as National Army deserters. They were entitled to a general court martial with all the protection and safeguards that carried, but in another way, they were very unfortunate. In the early days of the civil war many young men deserted and some were encouraged to do so if they could not support the Treaty. Just before the Four Courts siege Paddy O'Daly had addressed his men and told them 'no animosity would be shown against anyone who left.'[3] There were many deserters and some of them joined the anti-Treaty forces.

The Leixlip Five deserted in November and were captured when the civil war was approaching the most bitter stage. These five men were tried at Kilmainham gaol on 11 December. They were charged with treachery in that they assisted others in an armed attack on national troops. They were also charged with 'treacherously consorting and communicating others' on the occasion of the fight. They were all convicted and sentenced to death. They might have been executed a day or two later, but at this point something quite extraordinary took place. The leader of the column, Mullaney, and the other sixteen men who were captured at Leixlip were tried by military court for attacking a National Army unit and for the unauthorised possession of arms.[4] They were also convicted and sentenced to death. The case papers went to the Judge Advocate General Cahir Davitt as part of the process of confirmation and there was something of a shock in store for him.[5]

All seventeen had been represented by Edward Swayne, KC, who had told the military court that his clients saw no defence and he entered a guilty plea himself on behalf of all seventeen prisoners. This was a significant breach of procedure because the regulations required a prisoner to enter his plea personally because of the ramifications of that step. Put simply, the rule ensured that it could not later be said by a prisoner that the decision to plead guilty was not his or that it had been entered as part of a deal between the lawyers.[6] There followed a three-way row between Davitt, the legal officer, who had conduct of the trial, and the officer who had prosecuted. The officers pointed out that the accused had been represented by an able and experienced senior counsel and they wanted to plead guilty. Years later, Davitt speculated that the legal officer had simply fallen in to a trap laid by the defence counsel.[7]

The entire military court system depended on a handful of legal officers implementing a system that was still only eight weeks old. There had been difficulties recruiting lawyers of ability because there was no incentive for successful barristers to enter the army legal service in wartime. Joe Mooney was the most error-prone legal officer. Mooney was 28, a portly young Dubliner who had only been called to the bar a few years previously. He had given up trying to get his practice on its feet and had signed up with the National Army in late October. He had at once been sent out to act as legal officer for the whole of 2nd Southern Command – an area that extended from Kilkenny to Waterford. His list of requests came in thick and fast: 'send me a copy of Roscoe's Criminal Law' and 'send me a typewriter'.

Even in mid-November he still had no uniform and though he wanted to get up to Dublin to the outfitters for 'a try on', the roads were not safe because of a resurgence of the anti-Treaty cause in his area. He had other complaints that his legal assistant, Captain Fred Lidwell, was 'incompetent' and, more poignantly, that 'I have not yet been paid.' He recounted other difficulties about getting officers of the correct rank to serve on trials because they were all on 'double duty'.[8] His caseload had slipped further and further behind. This was the task facing all the legal officers outside Dublin and perhaps some were more resilient than others. Davitt had offered Mooney a transfer to Donegal, which was quiet and there was little to do, but Mooney refused. As events would soon show, a tragedy might have been avoided if he had gone. Davitt, no doubt pressed by his own heavy workload, signed off his advice on the Leixlip prisoners to the Army Council. He advised that the death sentence should not be carried out on Mullaney and his sixteen men. The fate of these prisoners hung in the balance and would not be known for some weeks.

Chapter 11

Christmas and New Year

Suspended Death Sentences

In mid-December a National Army proclamation was issued in Kerry suspending the executions of four men who had been under sentence of death for weeks. The four men had been held while lawyers argued over Childers and the legality of the military courts. Even after that W.R.E. Murphy, the National Army commander in Kerry, had proved unwilling to execute, despite pressure from government ministers. There followed some debate in the Army Council as to whether it was humane to execute the prisoners after such a delay. W.R.E. Murphy still argued he had won the war in Kerry and that executions might be counterproductive: 'much shooting could have the reverse effect'.[1] It was in these circumstances that the notion of suspended death sentences evolved.

The proposal went from the Army Council to Judge Advocate General Cahir Davitt for legal advice. There was hardly any law on this issue because the Regulations approved by the Dáil had all but been swept away. Davitt advised that the General Regulations as to the Trial of Civilians by Military Courts made provision for suspended sentences to ensure the good conduct of a convicted prisoner, but this new proposal was very different: punishing one man for what was done by others. Davitt advised that the concept was 'foreign to all ideas of fair play and humanity' but conceded that necessity might require such a step to bring the conflict to an end. He added almost as an afterthought that it was better than shooting prisoners who had not been tried. It was in these circumstances that the Army Council directed that the death sentences on the four prisoners be suspended. A National Army proclamation was issued in Kerry warning that 'If there are ambushes of troops or interference with railways or private property then executions would be carried out forthwith.'[2] The four Kerry prisoners remained in a state of uncertainty over the new year and there were many others in the same situation, like Patrick Mullaney, his sixteen men and the five deserters captured at Leixlip.

One of the other little-known prisoners was James Lillis from Muine Bheag, who had been convicted of taking part in an ambush of a National Army convoy. Now every time the cell door opened he feared it might bring news of his execution. In a letter home, he wrote: 'It would be better for everyone if it was all over.' Also awaiting trial was Ernie O'Malley, the highest-ranking prisoner in captivity. A few weeks before he had been riddled with bullets while trying to shoot his way out of a safe house. Now he was a pale, gaunt figure with eight bullet fragments floating around in his body. He was served with his court-martial papers and informed that his trial would take place in three days' time. Like many he put on a brave face and wrote: 'Another bit of lead won't do me any harm.'[3] The doctor at Mountjoy refused to sign him off as fit for trial and for him the days continued to pass in tedium and dread.

Not all the prisoners had to wait until the new year. There were two more executions before the year was out: John Phelan and John Murphy were shot by firing squad in Kilkenny. The prisoners were both no-rankers from County Kilkenny.[4] They were tried on charges of possession of firearms without proper authority and taking part in an armed robbery and sentenced to death. The judge advocate general was called on to perform his standard review of the case and found that the legal officer, Joseph Mooney, had failed to constitute the court with officers of the required rank. Davitt advised that the death sentences should not stand. Taking stock, Davitt realised that he had declined to recommend confirmation in any single one of Mooney's cases where conviction had resulted.

Meanwhile, Mooney's caseload had fallen behind lamentably. The first case assigned to him had concerned a private charged with sodomy, but months had passed and the prisoner was still in custody awaiting trial.[5] There was worse news to come as Davitt would now discover. Something happened in the course of the trial of Phelan and Murphy that had disturbed Mooney's placid outlook and he was 'much upset'. On the night the prisoners were convicted, Mooney had gone out on a drinking spree and it had finished late that night in the officers' mess. Mooney had become 'fractious and difficult' and had to be escorted to the guard room. A runner was sent to get Mooney's assistant, Fred Lidwell, about whom Mooney had often complained. Captain Fred Lidwell arrived and was helping Mooney get back to his room when a scuffle took place: the guard's gun went off and Lidwell was shot dead.[6] Mooney was censured by the board of inquiry into Lidwell's death. This was the nadir of Mooney's legal career.[7]

Despite all this, the Army Council was not persuaded that anything had happened which cast doubt on the safety of the convictions. They rejected the advice of the JAG and just before New Year's Eve the prisoners were bought out into the yard of the old barracks in Kilkenny, put against the wall and shot. The bullets that were fired still remain lodged in the wall: relics of a savage time. A question arises as to why these men were shot. Their arrest in mid-December coincided with an anti-Treaty surge in county Kilkenny – the area held by the 2nd Southern Command of the National Army. The surge had resulted in the capture of three barrack towns by subterfuge.[8] The 2nd Southern Command had become the butt of pub jokes and some cabinet members pressed for the removal of General Prout, the local commander.[9]

Phelan was from Thomastown and Murphy lived close by. It

was at Thomastown a few weeks earlier that the barracks had been briefly captured by anti-Treaty raiders; many rifles and ammunition were seized and nine army soldiers went over to the other side. There does not seem to be any other reason why these two no-rankers should be shot. It has been asserted that General Prout ordered the executions in a desperate bid to restore his credibility with GHQ: 'He needed to show his bosses he was capable of taking tough decisions.'[10] In fact, General Prout emerges as a steady commander who was popular with his men and accorded grudging respect by anti-Treaty fighters after the war. The idea that Prout had two men shot to save his job is unsupported by evidence. In any event, this theory can be laid to rest because the decision to execute lay entirely with the Army Council not the local commander.[11] It is possible at this point to discern developing Army Council policy on executions. First, the trend of local executions to deter those who might join the anti-Treaty faction. Second, to hit out at those still fighting by executing prisoners most closely associated with those responsible for the latest attack.

There was another killing on the day when Phelan and Murphy were shot. Francis Lalor, an anti-Treaty suspect was abducted from his lodgings in Dublin. The inquest jury heard evidence that he was visited by two men late at night. He demanded to know who they were and they replied: 'the authorities'. He clung to the grandfather clock in the hallway but was dragged out into the street and into a waiting car. The following day, his body was found at Milltown golf course liberally laced with bullets.[12] The death was noted in the minutes of the Executive Council, but as was so often the case, the detail of the discussion was reckoned to be too sensitive to be written down.

The End of the Year and the State of the War

The conventional military phase of the civil war had been won by the National Army the summer before. After that, the resistance to the government had morphed into a campaign aimed at making the country ungovernable and driving the state into bankruptcy in the hope that a Republic would emerge from the wreckage. As part of that campaign, income tax officers, the mail and the railways were all targeted and the anti-Treaty faction came close to achieving their aim. The government financial position had become acute: the loan from Westminster had run out and emergency credit had to be negotiated with the banks.

The military position was far better. By the turn of the new year, the insurgency in Dublin had all but been extinguished. The people were 'hostile', wrote Ernie O'Malley, as they were in many counties.[13] The command structure of the anti-Treaty faction had been broken: most were dead, interned or on the run. Dublin was still a small city of less than half a million and the net was closing on those still at large. Shortages of weaponry was another difficulty and the revolver and grenade attacks on the National Army diminished. Out in the provinces the civil war was pursued by small groups of men living in safe houses or in dugouts; short of ammunition and sometimes without food or winter clothing.

The campaign of arson

The arson campaign foreshadowed in Liam Lynch's 'shoot at sight' order began. In the days and weeks that followed, many homes were burned. President Cosgrave's home went up in smoke as well as that of State Solicitor Michael Corrigan. Sean McGarry TD also had his home burned out: his young son Emmet died in the blaze.[14]

The attack on the railways infrastructure

Short of men and arms, the anti-Treaty faction focused on the rail network which acted as the means for moving troops and supplies. Train tracks were torn up and railway bridges were destroyed. The month before, stations were damaged or burned out in Clare, Waterford, Tipperary, Wexford, Kerry, Mayo and Sligo. By the end of the war, 291 bridges and 3 viaducts would be damaged or destroyed, 103 signal cabins burned out, 419 carriages destroyed or rendered unusable, 86 engines damaged and three destroyed. The usual method was to set fire to the engine and dispatch it down the line at speed.[15] This tactic was used in Kerry, Carlow, Tullamore, Waterford, Kildare and Sligo, where seven engines were sent hurtling into the goods yard wrecking rolling stock. One engine smashed through the wall and toppled slowly into the harbour. And at Foynes in Limerick, the engine was derailed and sank into the river. In Kerry, the attacks were becoming frequent and well organised.

In response to this threat, the government formed the Railway Protection Repair and Maintenance Corps, which would eventually number 5,000 combat engineers. They were armed and also equipped with armoured cars converted for use on railway lines. Not every railway station and every remote train line could be protected and it was an impossible task. Kerry continued to be one of the most disturbed areas and just after the new year another ambush took place close to Castlegregory on the Dingle peninsula. Two National Army men were shot dead.[16] W.R.E. Murphy, the National Army commander in Kerry, continued to refrain from executions probably because a counter-proclamation had been issued by the leader of the local anti-Treaty faction that named eight prominent Free State supporters who would be killed if executions were carried out.[17] The National Army experiment with suspended death sentences had failed. W.R.E. Murphy was removed from his command in Kerry and the next step was now being considered.

Chapter 12

January

The Executions in January

January was the month of executions with a total of thirty-four across Dublin, Carlow, Dundalk, Roscrea, Limerick, Birr, Kerry, Waterford, Athlone and Portlaoise. The evidence suggests that the executions fall into two categories. In the first group were those which were already in contemplation as a result of trials that had taken place before Christmas. In these cases the gravity of the charges would probably have been decisive. The second group of executions arose out of a growing feeling in the Executive Council that the prosecution of the war had stalled.

The result of this perception was a joint conference between the Army Council and government ministers on 10 January. Some of the briefing memos survived and the sense of urgency is palpable. Time to 'win out' wrote one minister. Although some parts of the country had been barely touched by the civil war, O'Higgins scribbled an untidy note arguing for 'executions in every county'. This seems to have reflected his view that agrarian crime or gun-point robbery were as much a concern as the war itself. O'Higgins was supported by his confidante Hogan, who called for executions with 'machine gun like regularity'.[1] Cosgrave and Blythe were also hardliners and the consensus among ministers seems to have favoured a draconian use of executions to end the war quickly. After the meeting, O'Higgins wrote Mulcahy a slightly craven letter of thanks noting 'certain lines of policy provisionally agreed on'.[2] The new strategy would focus on local executions, the creation of many more capital offences and a major debasement of the trial system. The executions can be further divided into sub-groups which make the policy clear.

The deserters who had gone over to the other side
The five deserters captured at Leixlip were shot by firing squad at Kilmainham. In the autumn there had been a spate of desertions and defections in Cork and Kilkenny. The Leixlip men had the misfortune to be captured at a crucial time in the war. A bland press communiqué announced the executions and the message to National Army men who were thinking of swopping sides was clear.

Those convicted of attacking National Army troops
As to the rest of the Leixlip prisoners, Mullaney, the charismatic leader who had suborned the young National Army men, was not executed. Nor were any of his sixteen men. They remained in prison and hidden among their number was another deserter who had never been spotted: Sergeant Thomas McCann from Dundalk. It cannot now be established if the Army Council followed advice from the JAG about the deficiencies in their trial or whether it was thought unnecessary to execute so many from a single locality. The date of commutation of sentence in the trial register coincides with the end of the war and this rather suggests that these prisoners remained at risk of the firing squad until then.[3] They had become part of a bank of prisoners that might be drawn upon if the need arose for further executions.

There had been a flurry of trials in Carlow before Christmas and of these prisoners James Lillis from Muine Bheag was ordered for execution for his part in an ambush on a National Army convoy. He had been tried at Kilmainham and sent back to Carlow where he was shot in the coal yard of the military barracks.[4] He was 22, a mill worker in peace time. In his last letter home he left a ring to a girl called Lizzie. The same day, three more men were executed at Roscrea Castle in Tipperary. Frederick Burke, Martin

O'Shea and Patrick Russell were tried by an army committee for attacking National Army forces and for robbery. They had robbed a mail van on the Nenagh road and afterwards had taken shelter at Ross Cottage where they were found by a National Army unit. A gun battle continued all afternoon before the men surrendered. In a last letter home one of the prisoners wrote: 'They shelled the roof in on top of us with guns, rifles, bombs …'

According to one account there were difficulties finding clergy to see them. A few months earlier the bishops had issued the Pastoral Letter which had paved the way for executions, but now some of the clergy wanted to call a halt. The bishop of Cashel withdrew the services of his clergy in an effort to prevent executions, but the prisoners were moved to Roscrea which was pro-Treaty. A plan by anti-Treaty fighters to snipe at the firing squad from a nearby church tower fizzled out and the executions went ahead. Perhaps the message of these executions was that firing on the National Army was likely to result in a death sentence even where no casualties were caused.

Those convicted of attacking the railway network

Attacks on the railway infrastructure had become widespread. The rail network covered many remote areas and it was impossible to defend it all. In these circumstances, the Army Council resorted to executions. Two men were executed at Limerick for possession of a small amount of ammunition and for being concerned in the destruction of Ard Sollus railway station. It was later asserted by the National Army that they came upon a dugout where a number of unarmed men were hiding. During the raid Patrick Hennessy was wounded. One of the other men, Sean Darcy, made a run for it and was also wounded and made prisoner. After a protracted search of the area, the military found fifty-two rounds of rifle ammunition in a haystack.

The prisoners were taken to Limerick gaol where their names were entered in the book in red and they were kept separate from the 'No charge' prisoners. It transpired that Darcy's wounds were serious and he was sent to see the camp medical officer in the main compound. Knowing that he had been marked out for execution, the other prisoners hid Darcy in a clothes press where he remained. Hennessy had been a notable hurler until the year before: a serious, dark-haired young man with the heavy moustache that was fashionable at the time. He was 28, the son of John and Ann and the eldest of eight children. He had been secretary of the Clare GAA, which itself had been split in two by the war. Patrick Hennessy's last letter to his sister describes his trial: 'We were tried at midnight on Wednesday night, called from our cells where we were asleep, got no chance to defend ourselves.' Hennessy described the evidence against him: 'When arrested there was nothing on us, but afterwards the military found some stuff in a cock of hay and charged us with it, but we are innocent.'[5] To his friends in the prison, Hennessy wrote that the evidence on which he had been convicted was 'frivolous'. And 'Our lives are sworn away.' In his letter to his sister, he wrote 'no one will miss us but our own'. By the time Hennessy's letters home were smuggled out of the prison he was already dead.

It is perhaps Hennessy's comment about his trial at 'midnight' which is most revealing because it suggests a degree of haste that was remarkable even by the standards of the civil war. On 20 January, eleven prisoners were executed in different National Army commands. This required a degree of coordination and it may reasonably be surmised that Limerick Command acted in haste to provide two candidates for execution at short notice. Those two men were Hennessy and McMahon. McMahon's younger brother was spared.[6] Sean Darcy remained hidden in the clothes press at grave risk of discovery and his fate would not be known for some time.

Those convicted of arms offences

At Roscrea Castle, Patrick McNamara was executed for possession of a rifle. McNamara, from Killary, was a veteran of the War of

Independence and a simple young man who only a few months earlier had considered joining the new Civic Guard before doing an about face and siding with the anti-Treaty faction.[7] His last letter to his stepmother reads: 'There are three more to be shot with me from the Ragg, get Tuesday's paper, it will be worth 2d.'

In Dundalk, Thomas McKeown was shot by firing squad. He was a no-rank prisoner captured at Hackballs Cross just after the new year and tried for possession of a handgun and ammunition. His execution, like so many others, was poorly handled. Some days later, a letter was published in the press by McKeown's brother asserting that he had been innocent and although a gun and a small amount of ammunition had been seized, it was a multi-occupancy home. The family continued to agitate and a few weeks later General Mulcahy announced the prisoner had not denied the charge and he had accepted sole responsibility for the weapon.[8] This did not satisfy the family and the secrecy of the trial could only have reinforced their mistrust.

John McNulty and Thomas Murray were also captured at Hackballs Cross a few days after McKeown. Both were tried by military committee and each found guilty of possession of a revolver and ammunition. Confirmation quickly followed. Little is known about these men save that in the summer before Thomas Murray had been in the National Army, but when war became inevitable he started supplying arms to the anti-Treaty faction. He was briefly imprisoned at Dundalk but escaped in July after a bomb was detonated against the prison wall while the men were on exercise. Dozens of anti-Treaty prisoners got away and although most were quickly caught, Murray was at large for months. For McNulty and Murray, the process of capture, trial and execution took just five days.

On the evening of 19 January, at Custume barracks in Athlone six prisoners were separated out for execution. All had been convicted of possession of arms. The following morning, five of the six were executed. The sixth prisoner was Commandant General

Tom Maguire TD, who was returned to the holding area without explanation. Of the five executed men, all held junior officer rank save one who was a foot soldier. Four of the executed men were from Galway[9] and one was from Athlone.[10] The prisoner from Athlone town was 20-year-old Thomas Hughes, whose home was a few miles from the barracks. After the executions, the names of the executed men were posted on the barracks wall. That morning, his 43-year-old mother, Mary, had walked to the marketplace by the barrack walls. She would have heard the firing squads. Having done her shopping, she was struggling back home when she was overtaken and told that her son's name was one of those posted on the barracks wall. A little while later a letter arrived from her dead son: 'Do not fret for me … try and bear up mother …' The practice of refusing last visits and notifying next of kin after execution was challenged in the Dáil, but General Mulcahy refused to give way.[11]

On 22 January, three more men were executed in Dundalk. One was Joseph Ferguson, who was a trawlerman working out of the quays. A few weeks before he had been offered a boat to Liverpool with onward passage to America, but he declined to go. Another was Thomas Lennon aged 19. They were all local men tried and executed for possession of arms: offences committed only two weeks previously.

In Kerry, Major General O'Daly had taken over from W.R.E. Murphy. O'Daly's promotion to GOC in Kerry coincided with the failure of the suspended sentence initiative and the widespread assaults on the railway infrastructure. At Liscahane, a train derailment resulted in the driver being crushed to death and his fireman dying of scalding injuries.[12] One of O'Daly's first acts was to wire GHQ asking General Mulcahy to sanction the execution of prisoners: 'I am trying three exceptionally bad cases caught with arms.'[13] It appears the request to execute was sent before the prisoners were convicted.

The attacks on the railway infrastructure in Kerry probably weighed heavily with General O'Daly, but there was nothing exceptional about the three men being tried. James Daly had been captured just before Christmas running out of a safe house with a rifle. Michael Brosnan from Ballinadora and John Clifford from Mount Luke had been captured in a dugout in the new year. A revolver and 'military equipment' were found some distance away and this may be one of the new cases where possession of arms was imputed to the men.[14] Sanction was given for the execution of these three men. Also James Hanlon, a no-ranker captured near Causeway with a rifle some months before and held until it became expedient to order execution.[15] He was from north Kerry and the other three prisoners were from each of the other corners of the county. That seems to be why they were chosen for execution.

The following morning, Daly, Clifford, Brosnan and Hanlon were brought out into the yard at Ballymullen barracks at Tralee and made to stand beside their coffins in front of the firing party. The men were not blindfolded or pinioned, and while they waited at least two tried out their coffins for size and then swapped and chalked their names on the coffin lids. Some time passed before the officer in charge, Captain Edward Flood, arrived and brought the squad to readiness. According to a National Army eyewitness, one of the prisoners died at this point, probably of heart failure. The firing squad, some young and some tearful, failed to kill the remaining three prisoners cleanly.[16] This marked the end of the policy of suspended death sentences in Kerry.

On 25 January, two more men were executed in Waterford. These were Michael Fitzgerald and Patrick O'Reilly, both from Youghal.[17] They were convicted of possession of arms and ammunition at Ballinaclash. O'Reilly and Fitzgerald had rowed over the Blackwater from Youghal to visit friends and family when a Free State patrol appeared. The men ran and hid in the reeds on the banks of the river where they were found. They were tried and convicted and although a petition for a reprieve was got up and reached 2,000 signatures, they were shot. Curiously, the local brigade commander, Pax Whelan, and his staff officers had been captured in arms a few weeks before but had not been tried and this generated a conspiracy theory. It was said the executed men had been involved in the bombing of the Hampshire Regimental Band during the War of Independence. It was an event which had caused much revulsion and it was later said that the British government had insisted on the execution of these two men because of their role in that affair. There is no evidence that this was so and the theory was probably put about to embarrass the new Free State government.[18] Two others from County Waterford were tried at this time. Sentence on one was commuted and in the case of Patrick Cuddihy from Tramore, his case papers went astray and it may be this that saved him from execution.[19]

Two more executions followed on 28 January at what was then Maryborough. Patrick Geraghty and Joseph Byrne were both convicted of possessing a handgun in Offaly some months before. Geraghty died cleanly, but Byrne did not.[20] This case is significant because the arms were found near the scene of capture and it is likely the prisoners would not have been convicted but for General Mulcahy's direction encouraging officers to impute possession to the accused in such circumstances.

Those convicted of robbery

At Birr Castle in Offaly, William Conroy, Patrick Cunningham and Colum Kelly were executed for possession of arms and robbery at Tullamore. The prisoners had been part of an anti-Treaty unit, but Kelly had been sent home on account of his youth. Conroy and Cunningham had also been sent home for reasons which are unclear.[21] Finding themselves without money or even 'a smoke' they had carried out casual burglaries and gun-point robberies of local farmers going home after the market. They got away with a silver watch and about eighteen shillings but were soon picked up and identified. A local historian has suggested their executions were all to do with suppressing criminality in Offaly and nothing to do with the war.[22] Between them, they had a single handgun – 'a useless weapon, I think', wrote Father Gaynor, who attended the executions. On the morning of their execution they were invited to make a last request. Two of the youths asked for lemonade and one for a bottle of stout. Their composure so moved Father Pat that he later wrote: 'My own great fear was that I might break down and cry like a child.' He later recalled the young men remained completely unafraid as they were brought out into the Castle yard and told to sit in chairs to which they were to be tied. 'The tallest boy without any air of bravado asked to face the firing squad standing. There was not even a tremor in his voice …'[23] The executions followed the usual pattern: one firing squad was assembled for all three men; some of the soldiers were issued with live rounds and some with blanks. The officer stood to one side and dropped a hankie as a signal and the firing party delivered their volley: two died instantly. The third toppled from his chair and lay groaning on the ground. Three officers stepped up and fired a shot into the head of each prisoner.

Conclusions on the January executions

The destruction of the trial records makes a full evaluation impossible, but some trends are evident. The purpose of the new execution policy was to drive home the message at local level. Oddly, the origins of this policy lie with Thomas Johnson, the leader of the opposition who had argued against the execution policy in November. He had posed the question: if the executions were meant to deter then why were they only taking place in Dublin? The point was quickly adopted by O'Higgins and by the Army Council. Nearly all of those executed held little or no rank and it appears that this was a deliberate strategy. In a significant number of cases prisoners were not found in physical possession of arms, but possession was imputed in accordance with General Mulcahy's recent direction. To what extent this resulted in unjust convictions is difficult to evaluate. A notable feature of the arms cases is that trial and execution had started to follow very swiftly after capture: a matter of days in some instances. In other cases, the pattern shows prisoners were held for many weeks before a decision was taken that deterrence or retribution in a particular locality required execution by way of a response.

The suspended sentence policy that had been tried in Kerry had been abandoned and was never again mentioned in public. The reality, however, was that the Free State Army was building up a body of prisoners to secure the good conduct of others. An example was the Drumboe prisoners in Donegal. As early as November of the previous year nine men were captured in a safe house in a remote hamlet near Gweedore in Donegal. There was no apparent reason to delay the trial since the men were caught red-handed, but no trial took place until 18 January when four of these men – the officers – were tried and convicted of possession of three rifles, one revolver and 'a German egg bomb'. They were not executed. Donegal was largely quiet and it soon became apparent that the prisoners were hostages for the good conduct of the county.

The Development of Military Courts and Tribunal System
There were two other significant developments that emanated from the joint planning conference in early January: the first was the creation of new capital offences. The second was a major extension of the jurisdiction of military committees.

The creation of new capital offences
A new National Army proclamation was published on 20 January: The Stand Clear Order. The purpose was to split the anti-Treaty fighters from those who supported them. The proclamation stated that those who held command posts in the anti-Treaty ranks or who encouraged or assisted the fighters would be exposed to trial by military court and death by firing squad where the charge was proved. In addition, anyone who gave food, intelligence or supplies

would suffer the same fate. In the Dáil, a small group of deputies mounted a challenge to the order. General Mulcahy defended the proposal: 'stand clear' was the message, he said. If it was necessary for executions for 'technical offences' which would not ordinarily carry the death penalty, then so be it. The motion in the Dáil was comfortably defeated and the order came into effect.[24]

Extending the jurisdiction of trial by army committee

Trial by army committee had been introduced the previous month to deal with 'straight forward' arms cases where there was no factual dispute, but it was now widened to encompass a range of offences where the facts were in dispute. A new proclamation permitted trial by committee for attacking national forces, damaging property, possession of firearms, bombs and explosives and murder or conspiracy to murder.[25]

An internal order issued by Mulcahy the very same day instructed subordinate officers to proceed to trial by army committee in all cases.[26] The hastily and badly drafted instructions for trial by army committee ran to just under two pages. All the provisions of the General Regulations as to the Trial of Civilians by Military Courts were now completely swept away and with them the few protections for prisoners. The new instructions required cases to be handled with the utmost expedition – the same day if possible. The prisoner was not entitled to a lawyer, time to prepare his defence or assistance to bring defence witnesses to court.

The Anti-Treaty Response to the Executions

The homes and pubs used by many TDs were known to anti-Treaty fighters, yet no more TDs were killed or even shot at, despite the order issued by Liam Lynch. A fresh response to the flood of executions was slow in coming, but in the last week of January Liam Lynch issued an order that the homes of Free State senators be burned and that senators be shot by way of reprisal for the executions.[27] There was rather more appetite for burning out the big houses of the old ascendency. The homes of Sir Horace Plunkett and Sir John Keane were soon burned and also the house of senator John Bagwell, where irreplaceable historical records were lost to the nation. In the course of the next two months the homes of twenty-one senators were burned alongside others who were supporters of the government or simply part of the old ascendency class.

The attention of the anti-Treaty faction had already turned to the Senate. Sir William Hutcheson Poë, a 74-year-old one-legged senator had been briefly kidnapped over the Christmas holiday and he had left Ireland soon after. This was the beginning of a campaign to dismantle the Senate by terror. Senator John Bagwell was next. Bagwell was bundled into a car near his home at Howth by armed men to be held at an isolated farmhouse. General Mulcahy issued a proclamation stating that if Bagwell was not released within forty-eight hours then 'punitive action would be taken against seven associates in this conspiracy now in custody or otherwise'. Everyone knew that this meant more executions of unconvicted prisoners. The proclamation was unsuccessfully challenged in the Dáil the same day. The government had found a new slogan, *suprema lex salus populi*: the safety of the people is the supreme law.[28] It had been quoted in a legal argument during the Childers habeas corpus action and had become the government mantra.

Even while the Dáil debate was taking place, General Dan Hogan had rounded up prisoners from different prisons.[29] The news quickly spread that executions were imminent.[30] Bagwell escaped through a window of the cottage where he was being held.[31] President Cosgrave got news that Bagwell had turned up filthy and dishevelled at his club, and Cosgrave went straight round to steady him, but Bagwell followed Senator Poë into exile. Senator Oliver Gogarty was also kidnapped but escaped and swam the Liffey to safety and he too took some time abroad.

Not all the senators were inclined to await events: two had

already resigned.[32] With the Senate in danger of disintegrating, Cosgrave arranged for TDs and senators under threat to be housed and guarded day and night in Buswell's Hotel just across the road from Leinster House. Those who did not come willingly were cajoled. One was forcibly reminded that leaving the government in the lurch was not an option: Frank Bulfin TD was threatened by Cosgrave's bodyguards and given a broad hint that he had better not desert the government.

After the Bagwell kidnap was resolved, General Mulcahy directed his commanders 'to stop at once' the kidnapping campaign. The approach was refined a little: if a kidnap took place then a proclamation would be issued requiring the return of the person seized within forty-eight hours. Where necessary, prisoners captured after the cut-off date in October would have their trials by army committee expedited to allow the execution of one or more prisoners not later than six hours after the deadline. A failure to release the kidnapped victim would result in a further proclamation requiring the release within forty-eight hours. Failure to comply would result in double the number of executions.[33] The kidnapping of senators ceased.

As January came to a close it seemed that the spiral of killing and burning would go on unchecked. O'Higgins was still not satisfied and soon wrote another letter to General Mulcahy arguing that the prisoners captured in arms should be 'summarily shot without the option of being taken prisoner.'[34] The proposal was forwarded to the Army Council for consideration.

Handover of Beggars Bush, January 1922. (Courtesy of IMA)

Best of friends – de Valera, O'Higgins and Rory O'Connor, spring 1922.
(Courtesy of Kilmainham Gaol Museum)

Getting ready to shell the Four Courts, June 1922. (Courtesy of IMA)

Holding Dublin to ransom, June 1922. (Courtesy of Kilmainham Gaol Museum)

A National Army armoured car in action at the Four Courts, July 1922.
(Courtesy of IMA)

Blowing up the Four Courts and the Public Record Office, June 1922. (Courtesy of NLI)

After the bombardment of the Four Courts, July 1922. (Courtesy of IMA)

National Army troops fighting near Nelson's Pillar, June 1922.
(Courtesy of NLI)

Right: National Army forces attack the Hammam Hotel, July 1922. (Courtesy of Kilmainham Gaol Museum)

Below: National Army patrol ready to deal with an ambush, summer 1922. (Courtesy of NLI)

Anti-Treaty fighters captured in Cork being taken to the docks en route to Dublin and imprisonment, summer 1922. (Courtesy of NLI)

The anti-Treaty fighters waged war on the railways to prevent the deployment of troops by the National Army. Armoured trains were part of the response. (Courtesy of IMA)

Commander in Chief Michael Collins and Chief of Staff Richard Mulcahy leading the mourners at the funeral of President Griffith, August 1922. Less than two weeks later, Collins was killed in an ambush. (Courtesy of NLI)

An unhappy team – the Executive Council of the provisional government in the summer of 1922. From left to right: Desmond Fitzgerald, Attorney General Hugh Kennedy, Joe McGrath, W. T. Cosgrave, Ernest Blythe, Kevin O'Higgins and General Richard Mulcahy. (Courtesy of Kilmainham Gaol Museum)

Commander in Chief Richard Mulcahy (*left*) and Chief of Staff Sean Mac Mahon (*right*) inspecting the new National Army, autumn 1922. (Courtesy of IMA)

The Destruction Order. Cosgrave's government destroyed all records relating to trials by military tribunals just before de Valera came to power in 1932. (Courtesy of IMA)

CD. 334

ROINN COSANTA
(Department of Defence).
BAILE ÁTHA CLIATH
(Dublin).

The Secretary.

(a) Intelligence Reports - including Reports and particulars supplied by Agents and other persons.

(b) Secret Service Vouchers, etc.

(c) Proceedings of Military Courts, including Committee of Officers. Reports on and details of Executions 1922 - 1923 period.

As the above-mentioned documents contain information which may lead - if disclosed to unauthorised persons - to loss of life, you are hereby ordered to destroy same by fire, extracting therefrom previous to such destruction such particulars as you consider might be required hereafter in the conduct of the business of the Department of Defence.

MINISTER FOR JUSTICE.

7th. March, 1932.

Chapter 13

The Pause in the Executions: February to 13 March

It seemed that there would be no let-up in the executions, but the end of January saw a pause. Barring one case involving a National Army deserter who had gone over to the other side, no more prisoners would be executed until mid-March. This pause came about because the Army Council saw a chance to end the war. During a raid on a remote farmhouse, a man was found asleep in bed. The suspect, who was in poor shape, gave a false name and a revolver was found under his pillow. He seemed to be just another no-ranker and he was taken to Clonmel barracks for interrogation. His real identity then emerged: he was Liam Deasy, the general officer commanding the Southern Division of the anti-Treaty forces. He was tried by committee the following day and sentenced to death. Deasy later recalled: 'Very little was said apart from the reading of the charges by the prosecuting officer who asked for the maximum penalty. I remained silent.'[1] The finding was transmitted to GHQ by 'the special wireless telephone system' and confirmation of sentence came back within a few hours. At this point, Deasy asked for a stay of execution in order to persuade other members of the anti-Treaty Executive to call off the war. His request was 'wired' to General Mulcahy at Portobello and a response came back demanding his unconditional surrender as the price of a stay of execution. A few hours before his execution, Deasy agreed to sign an unconditional surrender on his own behalf. He had fought at Crossbarry and dozens of other encounters in the War of Independence and no one on either side ever suggested that he had been motivated by cowardice.[2] He later said that he had been resigned to death and when the news of his reprieve came through 'the fellows on the execution squad were more relieved than I was'.[3] He wrote that he had been fighting a war that had no prospect of victory but for which he bore moral responsibility. There were very many on the anti-Treaty side who privately shared his view.

Deasy was moved to Arbour Hill prison in Dublin, where a typed surrender note was put in front of him: 'I promise that I will not use arms against the Parliament elected by the Irish people or the government ... and I will not support in any way such action. Nor will I interfere with the property or persons of others.' Over the previous six months hundreds of men had signed this note and many had secured their release by doing so.[4] Some prisoners facing a capital charge had been persuaded to sign to avoid the death sentence and having done so found themselves 'half in disgrace' with the hardliners who refused to sign.[5] Deasy signed and he later wrote: 'I have never regretted the decision.' He also wrote an appeal to the other members of the Executive. There were no more executions while his letter was delivered by courier.

There were other dynamics at work. A peace campaign led by a loose coalition of neutrals, clergy and county councillors tried to broker a deal. Cosgrave's government treated the neutrals with hostility and O'Higgins damned them for moral weakness: 'the issue is scarcely one that admits neutrality'. Ultimately, the neutrals were rebuffed by Cosgrave, who stipulated that surrender must be unconditional and must respect the Treaty and the authority of the Free State government. The pause in executions went on, however, as the efforts of the peace campaigners were adopted by many prisoners.

On 9 February, the Army Council increased the pressure by issuing a proclamation offering amnesty to all those who surrendered in the following ten days. The proclamations went up in shops and post office windows, and in towns and villages people gathered to read about the prospect of peace. Some anti-Treaty fighters just went home and others surrendered their arms and were allowed to go free. The Army Council decided to press their advantage: 'If men surrender with arms even now, they probably should be released without delay.'[6] Two columns that had been active in north Kerry surrendered. One was led by Tom O'Driscoll from Kilmoyley, who had been responsible for much damage to the railways and the death of a train driver and his guard at Liscahane. O'Driscoll surrendered with eleven others, handed over their weapons and signed the surrender document. They were allowed to go home. The officer who released them sent a despatch to the GOC, noting that the publication of what had taken place had caused the surrendering men much embarrassment. Another column of sixteen led by Michael Pierce from Ballyheigue also handed in their guns and signed the surrender. Pierce and his men were released and went home.

There were other prisoners in Kerry still at risk of execution. One was Paddy Cahill TD. Cahill's column had been traced by a spotter plane and was surrounded and captured near Derrymore. The GOC in Kerry, O'Daly, wrote to Mulcahy about the effect of the amnesty on pending cases: 'In view of Pierce's surrender I would strongly recommend that death sentences be not carried out.'[7] There were different ways to bring in those still fighting. An emerging tactic was to let the word go out that a certain prisoner might be executed unless his brother or cousin surrendered. This tactic was used effectively in Cork and Kerry. When some of the Dalkey column were captured, the others still at large were induced to surrender by a promise that they and their comrades in prison would not suffer death.[8]

The pause in the executions continued. It was a moment when the National Army provided a way out to the anti-Treaty fighters and there were many who wanted to take up the offer. Prisoners in Tralee, Limerick, Clonmel and elsewhere joined the clamour for an end to hostilities. A note written on behalf of the prisoners in Limerick gaol asked that some be released to help bring about a surrender. The Army Council refused the request, but the letter and others in a similar vein were published, further exploiting the divisions in the anti-Treaty faction.

The evidence does not suggest that the Army Council anticipated the fighting would simply evaporate at this stage. At a planning meeting in mid-February the Army Council considered a range of options, including a suggestion by O'Higgins that prisoners captured in arms be shot on the spot. Mulcahy floated the suggestion in the agenda: 'Should we deal with prisoners as suggested in the circulated memorandum?'[9] The proposal was not taken up, but other draconian measures were agreed. It decided that after the amnesty had expired, 'no clemency will be shown in any case'. Speed was now the driving imperative: 'All cases … must be dealt with within one week.' To bring this about military courts would be phased out in favour of trial by 'committees of officers'.

The committee system had been brought in only weeks before to deal with cases where there was no defence, but the distinction between trial by military court and committee had become blurred. The policy of immediate retribution was discussed and refined: 'in every case of outrage in any battalion area, three men will be executed'.[10] The practical effect of this policy soon became apparent. If an ambush took place, the National Army would identify prisoners from the same unit as the attackers and send them for execution.

The anti-Treaty response was slow to materialise, but eventually the peace overture by Deasy was rebuffed by Liam Lynch. In a memo to all ranks, Lynch described the Deasy letter as an act of indiscipline: 'a calamity on the eve of victory'.[11] Lynch also disowned peace moves by some of his senior commanders still in the field. He still hoped for a big consignment of arms from the continent that would never arrive. Many never received Lynch's directive because they had signed the form, handed in their weapons and gone home. Lynch issued an order to stem the tide: men who surrendered or handed over arms were liable to court martial and if convicted faced death by firing squad.[12] The order was one of a number of increasingly unrealistic missives that would be sent out in the weeks that followed. Another fundraising order required dogs to be licenced. Five shillings a dog: pay up or we shoot your dog was the message. There were pro-formas to be filled in by guerrilla fighters who were being hunted by the National Army.[13]

In reality, the anti-Treaty faction was now close to defeat. Most of their active men were in captivity and the rest were hiding out in dugouts and safe houses. Many were short of ammunition, weapons and even food. The National Army was in the ascendant at last, carrying out large cross-country sweeps and raiding dugouts. Dinny Lacey was killed in a sweep of the Glen of Aherlow on the last day of the amnesty. Lacey had often escaped capture during the War of Independence, but hiding places were scarce now and Lacey and his men were run to earth at a safe house. This encounter presented a microcosm of the civil war: Lacey was killed with one of his men and eleven more were captured. Three National Army men and a child who had run into the field of fire were also killed. While these local dramas were being played out, the new trial by committee system was in full force. Trials and convictions followed fast. February became a very busy month for trials by committee.

One of the prisoners tried in February was Major General Michael Kilroy: a wiry 38-year-old blacksmith with a distinctive heavy black moustache. He had been a brigade commander in Mayo in the closing stages of the War of Independence. Charismatic, religious and teetotal, he was a man with an unbending outlook who was unlikely to abandon his oath and it was hardly surprising that he sided with the anti-Treaty faction. In the summer and autumn of 1922, he had led a series of successful attacks on National Army troops in Mayo and won fights at Newport, Clifden, Ballina and Glenamoy. In late November the National Army launched an attack on Newport. Kilroy was with the outlying anti-Treaty units and took the brunt of the attack as a National Army troop encircled his position. During the retreat a rifle bullet pierced Kilroy's back and emerged from his chest. He was captured and not expected to live.

Kilroy was held at Custume barracks in Athlone. Here the barracks had been spilt between Pump Square, where the internees were held, and a dedicated cell complex known as the detention barracks, which, under British rule, had been used to house military prisoners. Here the National Army held prisoners under sentence of death or awaiting trial on capital charges. Kilroy remained there until February when he was moved up to Mountjoy to be tried on two charges of attacking National Army troops and possession of arms. His case was now expedited. Kilroy received his charge sheet on 8 February and was listed to be tried a few days later. He declined legal representation, but Liam Lynch issued an order that he defend himself and the instruction was smuggled into Mountjoy. His counsel was Conor Maguire, then a little-known barrister who would later become chief justice. Maguire did not see Kilroy until the morning of his trial and on this brief acquaintance the trial began. Kilroy was convicted the same day and sentenced to be shot. He joined the growing bank of prisoners under sentence of death.

Dublin had become the administrative hub of the National Army and the major trial centre for military courts and committees. Prisoners were now being brought up from different parts of Ireland to be tried. This perhaps was the Army Council's response to those local commanders who had been less than cooperative about executions in their areas. It also allowed GHQ to assemble a panel of reliable officers to try these cases. A legal point of some importance now emerged as it became apparent that the new Free

State constitution limited the jurisdiction of military courts and committees: 'Such jurisdiction shall not be exercised in any area in which all civil courts are open or capable of being held …'[14] In the Dáil, Gavan Duffy pointed out that the civil courts in Dublin were open and the continuance of military trials was therefore inconsistent with the constitution. When challenged about this, General Mulcahy simply said these cases could not 'suitably' be tried by the civil courts.[15]

The prisons overflowed with men under sentence of death, serving long terms or imprisoned without trial. The total number of prisoners now ran to about 13,000 and most Irish towns became pockmarked with makeshift internment camps.[16] There was, however, only a single execution in February and it arose out of two apparently unconnected trials.

The Murder of Dr Thomas Higgins

He died in a pool of blood on the floor of his living room in front of his wife and daughters. He was 65 and the father of sixteen children. He was the coroner for King's County and a dispensary doctor who had tended to the poor for many years. His brother-in-law was the governor general and his son was Minister for Home Affairs Kevin O'Higgins. It was not the first time the old doctor had been targeted because of his son's political activities: during the War of Independence, he had been interned by the British Army. It was entirely typical of the doctor that he had assumed the role of medical officer for the prisoners. On 11 February, a group of young men arrived at the doctor's farm near Stradbally. The anti-Treaty arson campaign was in full flow: they had come to burn the haystack and the house also. They were invited in and during an exchange of words in the lounge, one of the men shot the old doctor. 'Wilful murder by persons unknown' was the verdict of the inquest jury.

Kevin O'Higgins arrived for the funeral a few days later escorted by a whippet armoured car with a machine gunner up top. The funeral, in driving winter rain, was the largest seen in Stradbally for many years and many tears were shed for the 'upright and honourable man' who had done so much for his community. A local youth, Martin Byrne, from Luggacurren was picked up and sent for trial by the army.[17] His case was dealt with by an army committee who convicted him and recommended a sentence of death. The Army Council confirmed the sentence and Byrne was brought up to Portobello to be shot the following Monday morning. While awaiting execution at Portobello, the prisoner asked one of the gaolers to smuggle a letter out of the barracks. The gaoler agreed but took the letter to an officer instead: it was to a friend asking for help to gather alibi witnesses. It was, of course, too late because Byrne was under sentence of death. By chance, the letter came to the attention of Cahir Davitt, the JAG, who had an office at Portobello.

With the execution less than forty-eight hours away, a small, whiskery old solicitor with a heavy briefcase turned up at Portobello barracks. He was Horace Turpin, a solicitor from Stradbally who was more used to dealing with wills and probate than murder. He had with him a bundle of sworn affidavits providing an alibi for the prisoner. Turpin told Davitt that he had been refused an interview with Adjutant General Gearóid O'Sullivan and feared his client would be shot for a crime he did not commit.

Barely two months before, Davitt had advised General Mulcahy on setting up the new army committee system for straightforward cases of possession of arms where there was no dispute. A few weeks later the army, pleased with the experiment, extended the remit of the committee system to murder charges and a wide range of other offences.[18] When 18-year-old Martin Byrne was picked up for the murder of Doctor Higgins, the army determined that he was not entitled to a lawyer or even the chance to call witnesses in his defence. Cahir Davitt started to stir himself at last and went to see the adjutant general and there followed 'quite a session'. He argued that the committee system had been set up to deal with cases where there was no factual dispute. The adjutant general was unimpressed: Doctor Higgins had been a good man who had been killed in cold blood in his own home. Davitt changed tack and pointed out that the case rested on a single identification by the dead man's daughter. He argued that visual identification was an inherently fallible form of evidence which had played a part in most known miscarriages of justice. In this case the only evidence was an identification which was disputed by the prisoner who claimed to have alibi witnesses. Reluctantly, the adjutant general agreed to a trial.

Turpin only had a few days to find a barrister to take the case and he briefed his nephew T.C. Kingsmill-Moore. At a time when the Irish bar was crammed with highly individual men, Kingsmill-Moore was up there with the best of them.[19] 'T. C.' had held a commission in the Royal Flying Corps until the end of the Great War and then came back to Dublin where he was called to the bar at King's Inns. As the years went by, he would become an authority on fly fishing and eventually a judge of the Supreme Court, but in 1923 he was still a raw beginner. He was probably briefed because of the family connection with Turpin. Dublin had become a dangerous place and it may be that most barristers would not have wanted this brief.

The trial took place at Portobello. As it turned out, the officers trying the case were not impressed with the alibi witnesses, but they were also not satisfied with the identification and acquitted.[20] Martin Byrne walked out a free man having escaped with his life by the merest chance. Adjutant General O'Sullivan bitterly regretted his decision to allow a trial which he regarded as a miscarriage in favour of the prisoner. Tellingly, other evidence later came to light which suggested the prisoner had been wrongly identified.[21] There were lessons to be learned from this case, but the army committee system remained in place, establishing itself as the usual form of trial.

The Trial of Tom Gibson

Tom Gibson was a National Army corporal who deserted in November, taking with him five rifles and a grenade.[22] Gibson had deserted and changed sides when it was already clear that the anti-Treaty faction was losing and why he made that choice has never been explained. The only point of significance is the date he deserted: he walked out of barracks when the news filtered through that the National Army had carried out the first executions. He was captured a few weeks later, asleep in a safe house with two other armed men who were described in the National Army press release as 'prominent irregulars'.[23] They were not executed and nothing else is known about them. Gibson was charged with treachery and sent for trial at Roscrea Castle. Because he was a soldier he was tried by a general court martial with all the usual protections, but he had no defence and was found guilty and sentenced to death on 18 January. Curiously, he was not executed until the end of February.

The press release put out by the Army Council stated that he was a deserter and a turncoat and he had been executed for that reason. This had been the fate of the five deserters captured at Leixlip the previous month and Gibson's case seemed no different. There was probably rather more to this. It may reasonably be surmised that Gibson's case was linked to the murder of Doctor Higgins and the acquittal of Martin Byrne a few days before. The hasty trial of Martin Byrne for the murder of the doctor had ended in an acquittal much to the chagrin of the adjutant general. The army had no culprit and therefore no execution to mark the murder of an old man who had important family connections. Gibson was not shot until 27 February 1923, nearly six weeks after conviction, and he was not informed that he was to be executed until the night before and this suggests a decision taken belatedly.[24]

There was an Army Council meeting at the Curragh in late February and it seems likely that this was when Gibson's fate was decided. He had deserted from Portlaoise barracks and he was from Cloneygowan: both close to the old doctor's family home. This was the Army Council's riposte to those who had killed Doctor Higgins.

Tom Gibson was sent for execution the next morning. Watching through the window of the prison hospital was a patient who later related that the rifle volley had knocked the prisoner to the ground. Gibson rose to his feet again and an officer walked up and shot him in the head with a pistol. This was the only execution that month, but the possibility of peace was receding. The government had maintained a united front and declined to enter negotiations that might weaken their hand. The position of the government was summed up by O'Higgins: 'It will not be a draw with a replay in the autumn.'

Chapter 14

The Kerry Landmine Massacres and the Resumption of Executions

In the first days of March a new dynamic was emerging in Kerry. There were no official executions, but it was the bloodiest time of the civil war. The landmine had become part of the anti-Treaty weaponry. Left on lonely bridges and culverts and detonated from a safe distance, the landmine wreaked devastation. The technology was later developed to include trip mines: when a searcher moved a heavy stone a hidden trigger detonated the mine.

The most vicious aspect of the civil war started with a grudge settled by a landmine. In Kerry, Lieutenant Pat O'Connor became a target for the anti-Treaty fighters because he had started ill-treating suspects, and a plot was laid to lure him to a remote cave where a trigger mine had been laid.[1] The cave was found and the mine detonated killing O'Connor, Captains Stapleton and Dunne of the Dublin Guard and two private soldiers.[2] Stapleton had been carrying a Lewis gun which was 'atomised' and there were body parts strewn in all directions. Major General O'Daly wrote to General Mulcahy the next morning with some feeling about his officers, Stapleton and Dunne, who had 'brilliant pre-truce records'.

O'Daly issued an order the same day, stipulating that officers who encountered stone barricades and dugouts should go at once to the nearest detention barracks and collect Irregular prisoners to clear the obstacle: 'The tragedy of Knocknagoshel must not be repeated.' O'Daly stipulated that the order was not to be regarded as a reprisal but the 'only alternative to us to prevent the wholesale slaughter of our men'. This reiterated the existing practice of using anti-Treaty prisoners to carry out road clearances, but subsequent events raises a question about the true purpose of the order. Whether by chance or design, General O'Daly went to Killarney that evening and events took a shocking turn. In the early hours of the following morning, twelve prisoners died in explosions at Ballyseedy Cross near Tralee and Countess Bridge at Killarney. Near Scartaglin an attempt to kill prisoners ended when a National Army officer removed the firing pin from a mine placed in a road barricade.[3]

The Aftermath

A National Army press release was issued to explain what took place at Ballyseedy and Countess Bridge:

```
A party of troops proceeding from Tralee to
Killorglin last night came across a barricade
of stones built on the roadway at Ballyseedy
bridge. The troops returned to Tralee and
brought out a number of prisoners to clear
the obstruction.

While engaged in this work a trigger mine
(which was concealed in the structure) ex-
ploded, wounding captain Edward Breslin,
Lieutenant Joseph Murragh and Sergeant Ennis
and killing eight of the prisoners.

On another bridge troops found a barricade
similar to that at Ballyseedy Bridge erec-
ted across the roadway. While the obstruction
was being removed, a trigger mine exploded,
```

```
wounding two of the troops and killing four
irregular prisoners who had been removing the
barricade.⁴
```

Internal army reports show that the incident at Ballyseedy took place long after midnight and the Countess Bridge incident took place some hours later.[5] The press release disguised the fact that both the explosions had taken place within hours of each other and invited the conclusion that these extraordinary events were coincidental. The next day, the National Army released the remains of the Ballyseedy prisoners from Ballymullen to the families that had gathered at the barrack gates in horse-drawn carts loaded with coffins.[6] The *Cork Examiner*, writing in the restrained language of the censored press, signalled concern by alluding to 'remarkable scenes' outside Ballymullen barracks. A military band played Ragtime as the families removed the remains from the coffins provided by the army and began the process of identification. One mother came to the scene because she was told of the body of a young man with black curly hair. Knowing that her son had been a prisoner at Ballymullen, she ran to the barracks and found his body lying in the street.[7] The remains of the dead men were placed on the pavements and transferred into new coffins: 'It was a painful process,' wrote the *Cork Examiner*. A riot developed outside the barracks and the army coffins 'were smashed and strewn about the road'.

O'Daly seems to have decided to get his account in first and informed Mulcahy that every facility had been given to the relatives to bury the prisoners killed at Ballyseedy, but the handover of coffins have been attended by 'disgraceful scenes'.[8] A despatch written by Humphrey Murphy, the leader of the anti-Treaty fighters, now surfaced, alleging a massacre and announcing there had been a survivor. Humphrey Murphy's despatch related the slaughter in a breathless rush and told that the survivor was 'practically demented'.[9] Something of this was learned by

O'Daly, who wrote to General Mulcahy at GHQ that a prisoner had escaped the blast at Ballyseedy, but 'he had gone insane'. In fact, the prisoner who was demented was Tadhg Coffey, who had survived the Countess Bridge blast.[10] There was also a survivor of the Ballyseedy massacre: Stephen Fuller had been thrown clear and was being hidden in the hinterland and this soon became widely known. The National Army in Kerry became locked into a search for the survivors.

O'Daly issued an order that prisoners who were killed in military custody would be interred on the base where they died. There would be no repetition of the fiasco outside Ballymullen barracks. O'Daly came up to Dublin for the funerals of his officers killed at Knocknagoshel. The funerals were grand affairs with President Cosgrave and most of the Executive Council attending with a large army presence. Within hours, another massacre had taken place.

In the early hours of the morning five prisoners were brought out of the workhouse near Cahersiveen and marched off to clear a barricade on the road. It was later announced by the National Army that the prisoners had been killed by a mine that had detonated during the clearance. There were no survivors, but the National Army soldiers had stayed in the hotel in Cahersiveen where the bomb had been put together and some had been indiscreet.[11] The officer in charge of the workhouse let it be known that the prisoners had been killed by officers of the Dublin Guard before resigning his commission.[12]

While O'Daly was in Dublin for the funerals he met his commander in chief, Mulcahy, but there is no record of what passed between these two men. It is well known that Mulcahy thought highly of O'Daly and it is not likely he suspected him of any impropriety. A review of Army Council minutes hints that O'Daly wrote letters of explanation, but these have not survived.[13] Minutes of Army Council meetings always refer obliquely to sensitive issues and it is plain the Kerry massacres were so regarded. There is no record of what was discussed, but the notion that a batch of prisoners from each of the three anti-Treaty brigades in Kerry had been killed in identical circumstances just a few days apart may have seemed too far-fetched. It is reasonable to surmise that the Army Council concluded that some National Army men in Kerry were out of control. The next step taken by the Army Council was entirely unexpected.

The Recommencement of Executions

Eleven men were executed in the space of twenty-four hours for offences committed mainly over the previous six weeks. Three were executed in Wexford at the old county hall: it had once been a grim old prison, then a home for alcoholics, and, after being burned out during the civil war, it had become the local barracks for the National Army. James Parle, John Creane and Patrick Hogan were part of a group of five who had been hiding out at the home of Major Lakins, the crusty old master of the Wexford hunt.[14]

The Major, a remnant of the ascendancy, had spent years steering a careful path between the warring factions in Wexford. It was not him who had given them shelter or turned them in. One of the servant girls had hidden the men in the loft, but 'the leggings of one' were seen by a Free State soldier visiting the house and they were surprised in the loft. Three of the five men were chosen to face the firing squad. The men were executed together as was the practice in the civil war and once again the firing squad did not perform well. Hogan died instantly, but the others did not. Wexford had been disturbed for much of the civil war and the Kyle column had been active in the vicinity of Wexford town. Parle (25) was believed to be second in command of the Kyle column and Creane (18) and Hogan (19) were also believed to be members.[15] It may be inferred that Army Council policy formulated the previous month was now being put into effect. The executions were retribution against the column to deter further ambushes. It may also be an example of how the executions were sometimes driven by intelligence about the prisoner rather than what had been proved in court. In Dublin, James O'Rourke was executed for his part in a spate of attacks on government income tax offices. The raid had been part of the strategy to undermine the ability of the government to raise revenue. As the attack on Jury's Hotel stalled, National Army troops arrived and fought it out in the street with the attackers. O'Rourke, aged 19, was wounded in the head, but his revolver, if he ever had one, could not be found at the scene. According to a National Army report, he declined to say what had become of his gun. O'Rourke was nursed back to health until he was fit for trial.[16]

Also, on the same day, William Healy was executed in Cork gaol. Healy, a 24-year-old farmer's son from Lackabane, had been convicted of conspiracy to murder, arson and aiding and abetting an attack on National Army troops. He had been one of a group of men who took over a house at Blarney Street in Cork. They sprinkled it with petrol and lay in wait for their target, Commandant Scott, who was a regular visitor. When Scott arrived, the door was opened and he was shot down and badly wounded. In the fracas that followed the attackers made off in a car, but somehow Healy had been left stranded at the scene. Although the offences took place in Cork, the prisoner was tried in Dublin. What happened to William Healy became an established pattern in the civil war: tried in Dublin – no doubt before a reliable tribunal – then despatched back to his home town to be shot as a deterrent to others.

More executions took place the following day at Mullingar, where Luke Burke and Michael Greely were shot. They had driven into Oldcastle and robbed the Northern Bank at gunpoint before going on in a leisurely way to empty the coffers of the Royal Hibernian. No one was killed or injured and they were caught with the £386 they had plundered. Luke Burke had given a false name. He was the 26-year-old youngest son of Catherine and

Francis Burke, smallholders from Keady in Armagh. Faced with the prospect that his mother and father might never discover his fate or even his grave, he gave his real name at the eleventh hour. Most historians relate that these men were not part of the anti-Treaty faction, although contemporary reports contradict that.[17] When captured, the prisoners maintained that they had kept up the fight because of pressure by their leaders and asked to be allowed to sign the surrender document and repudiate the anti-Treaty campaign. They were executed, although it is hard to see why: Mullingar was quiet and they had not been convicted of attacking the National Army. No other prisoner who asked to sign the surrender note and denounce their leaders was ever executed.[18]

Four anti-Treaty fighters were executed in Donegal: Charlie Daly, Dan Enright, Tim O'Sullivan and Sean Larkin were shot in the woods outside Drumboe Castle. These men and five followers had been captured in early November of the previous year in a remote hamlet near Gweedore. They had been part of the northern offensive organised by Collins before his death. After the split, they had gone with the anti-Treaty faction. Donegal was solidly pro-Treaty and there were no safe houses and this dwindling group of men lacked shelter, food and ammunition. When they were captured on their way south, the signs of privation were plain enough. They were not tried until 18 January and it does not seem there was any operational reason for the delay.[19] It is an inference that it had become desirable to try them in case deterrence made their execution necessary.

Events in Donegal came to a head with the killing of a Free State Army Captain Bernard Cannon, at Creeslough military barracks on 10 March. According to the account given at the inquest, shots were fired at the barracks and Cannon had unwisely opened a door and was shot dead. The doctor who examined the body found a single bullet wound in his chest with a large exit wound to his back. The story swiftly circulated that he had been killed in a row with some of his men.[20] This theory cannot be discounted because the National Army command log shows there was no anti-Treaty military activity in the county in the weeks preceding the attack. The idea of an attack by anti-Treaty fighters was viewed with scepticism by the National Army Commander Joe Sweeney, who knew better than anyone that the local anti-Treaty fighters were all in custody or had gone south. Sweeney conducted his own reconstruction which reinforced his suspicions, but if he communicated this to his commander in chief, no record of that can be traced. The incident was reported by a wireless message to GHQ at Portobello, but it recounted only the bare facts: 'Captain Cannon killed in attack on Creeslough post last night.'[21]

The Executive Council minutes, which are terse, show that the government received a plea for clemency on behalf of 'some people from Raphoe'. In fact, there was opposition to executions from pro-Treaty people in Donegal and urgent representations to the government began.[22] Bishop O'Donnell of Raphoe declined to permit last sacraments to the men in the hope that the executions would be deferred. The bishop knew General Mulcahy personally and believed he might influence him against execution, but the National Army made other arrangements for the last sacraments. The order for executions stood.

According to one account the men were invited to follow the example of Liam Deasy and other prisoners and sign a surrender note. Charles Daly and Sean Larkin held high rank in the anti-Treaty faction and although they had long since ceased to command large bodies of men, their surrender might have finished off the civil war entirely. They declined to sign and the executions went ahead. The senior National Army officer in Donegal was Joe Sweeney, a long-time friend of one of the prisoners, Charlie Daly. It was Sweeney's job to convene the firing squad, and he later said: 'to make sure there was no foul up, the firing party were all picked men, and they were told to put them out of pain as quickly as possible.'[23] In this, his last act of fellowship, he was successful. These executions may be seen as a product of the policy formulated by the Army Council the previous month. The other men captured with the Drumboe prisoners declined to sign a note of surrender. Four of them wrote a restrained letter which was smuggled out to the press: 'We think it not fair to hold us responsible for the actions of those we disclaim.'[24] They would have a long and anxious wait until their fate was known.

Why Were the Executions Resumed?

It has been suggested that the end of the war was in sight and there were fears of a backlash against National Army officers who had taken part in the execution policy. This prescient anticipation of an army mutiny gave rise to a view that the more senior officers who had blood on their hands the less likely any retribution from within their own ranks. It remains simply a theory. It is most likely that the executions resumed because Mulcahy and Cosgrave believed executions would stamp out the war. Cosgrave had written to Mulcahy only a few weeks before, urging him to withhold clemency 'until the irregulars crave it.'[25]

It is difficult to avoid the conclusion that some of the eleven prisoners were executed, not because they were perceived as being particularly culpable, but simply to achieve a satisfactory geographical spread in the interests of deterrence. It has also been suggested that the restart of the executions was driven by the Kerry landmine massacres.[26] This theory rests on an assumption that Mulcahy disbelieved the account put out by the National Army in Kerry and there would certainly have been good reason to do so. The timing of the resumption of executions is also odd. The execution policy recommenced within twenty-four hours of the last landmine massacre. It might be remembered that during the previous autumn Mulcahy had argued for the introduction of the death penalty partly on the grounds that it kept unauthorised killings in check. A final odd feature of the resumption of executions is that, although resistance to the National Army was harder in Kerry than anywhere else, Mulcahy did not order any executions in that county. There is a hint here that he thought the National Army had done quite enough in Kerry.

In any event, the immediate impact of the Kerry landmines massacre was to widen the gulf between the army and the government. Years later, Ernest Blythe wrote that some ministers were privately suspicious about the National Army account of the landmine massacres.[27] The notion that the army was no longer accountable had been gaining currency in the Executive Council for some time. Certainly, the tension between the government and Mulcahy can be traced back to the previous autumn. At this juncture, with the end of the war at hand, General Mulcahy and his staff resigned *en bloc* without any public explanation. Their resignations were refused and no one involved ever spoke publicly about it, beyond hinting that General Mulcahy had too much power and kept the Executive Council largely in the dark.[28]

The Anti-Treaty Response to the Resumption of Executions

The anti-Treaty response to the executions was a series of local attacks more driven by revenge than strategy. Four unarmed National Army soldiers were lured to a pub near Wexford. One was grievously wounded and the others dragged off to a remote townland where they were machine gunned to death. In west Cork, 16-year-old Ben McCarthy from Bantry was dragged from his home and shot dead. A note attached to the body announced he was a 'convicted spy' and shot in reprisal for the executions. It is sometimes difficult to say why men were shot and the apparent reason for this killing might be treated with caution. In Donegal, Bishop O'Donnell's well-intentioned instruction to his clergy not to give last rites to the Drumboe prisoners was misunderstood. The bishop's home was burned out as a reprisal and his brother, who had been ill, died a few days later.[29]

On the national front, Liam Lynch decreed that the nation had entered a time of national mourning for the executed men.

He ordered that organised sport cease and theatres and cinemas shut as a mark of respect. If there was ever a sign that Lynch was out of touch then this was it: the nation thrived on hunting, racing, rugby and golf, and no force on earth could change that. The theatres, pubs and cinemas continued to thrive. The longer-term effect of the executions can be gauged by the pattern of anti-Treaty activity which continued to diminish. Short of arms and with over 13,000 men and women in custody, the civil war was fizzling out. There would be no more executions for another month, but the trail of unofficial killings by National Army men continued, particularly in Kerry.

Apart from the seventeen prisoners killed in the landmine massacres, there were at least twelve other men killed in the custody of the National Army in March alone. It began with John Savage: shot dead by his escort. The list also includes John O'Sullivan, who was shot dead after capture, and Seamus Taylor, a prisoner on a National Army convoy who was taken off a lorry and shot near Tralee. Also, John Kevins, a wounded prisoner, bayoneted to death on the way to hospital. Frank O'Grady was shot in front of many prisoners by Captain Tiny Lyons of the Dublin Guard. Daniel Sugrue, the tailor, was killed for speaking out about torture at the Great Southern Hotel barracks.[30] Kerry was the last county where anti-Treaty fighters were putting up a co-ordinated fight, but there were other dynamics undermining their campaign. In remote townlands, famine had taken hold and for months National Army ran food convoys to the worst-affected areas. Some anti-Treaty fighters declined to ambush these convoys and, by degrees, organised resistance began to crumble.

In Dublin, the sense that it was all over had permeated into government circles. The spat between General Mulcahy and the Executive Council was patched up – whatever its immediate cause. A Supreme War Council was set up including O'Higgins, Cosgrave and General Mulcahy, and this may be seen as the start of the government taking back control from the army.[31] The anti-Treaty campaign had failed to bankrupt the government and now the financial crisis began to ease. Cosgrave announced that taxation receipts were up and that the budget deficit could be met without borrowing from abroad. This was the best sign that economic confidence was returning. There were others, including the end of the long-running milling strike: the management and the unions set up a joint industry council. The Agriculture Commission met to receive evidence on exporting eggs to Britain and everywhere there were signs that the war was all but over.

Chapter 15

April

Three themes emerge in April. First, the capture or killing of senior anti-Treaty fighters and the disintegration of their army. Second, there were a significant number of deaths in custody. Third, the executions would continue even after the war was actually over.

The End of the War

This was the moment the anti-Treaty faction began to sue for peace. At the beginning of the month the National Army announced the capture of 'practically the entire staff of what is known as the 3rd Southern Division'.[1] Tom Derrig was also captured and then Dan Breen along with many others. But it was the death of Chief of Staff Liam Lynch that most hastened the end. Lynch and his Executive were surprised during a conference that many hoped would bring the war to an end. They ran, and during the chase Lynch was wounded and died the same day: 10 April. The rest of his staff were pursued and scattered and were unable to reconvene for some time. Many of the senior officers in the anti-Treaty faction had favoured a negotiated peace – or any peace – and it had only been Lynch and a handful of his officers that had kept them fighting. Austin Stack was captured soon after; lying in a ditch, emaciated and too exhausted to offer any resistance. In his coat were found documents setting out the anti-Treaty Executive proposals for a ceasefire. The peace terms were published by the Free State government and derided in the press.[2]

The bulk of the anti-Treaty fighters were now in custody, in hiding or on the run. Many of these men represented a potent threat to the state and were bent on getting out and rejoining the fight. There were many failed breakouts, but some of the most determined anti-Treaty fighters had escaped. It had become one of the recurring features of the civil war: after the Four Courts siege, Ernie O'Malley had been held at Jameson's distillery but slipped out of a side entrance; Eamon MacCluskey walked out of Kilkenny gaol dressed as a women;[3] Patrick Mullaney from Mayo sawed his way through the bars of a window before forming a column that plagued the National Army for months. In Dundalk, the prison wall was blown out and Frank Aiken along with over 100 others made a run for the country. Ten more tunnelled their way out of prison in Sligo just after the proclamation announcing military courts. Tom Barry was sent to Gormanstown camp and crawled out under the wire, and in November, twenty-five more tunnelled their way out of Kilkenny gaol. At Mountjoy, Sean MacBride tried to get out in the garbage lorry but was found and returned to his cell in a 'disgusting state'.

As the war intensified, security tightened up. At Kilkenny gaol, John Edwards, a Belfast internee, was talking through his cell window to a friend in the street below. He was warned to stop but carried on and was then shot dead. At the Curragh, Richard Monks got under the wire but was mortally wounded as he scrambled out the other side. At Mountjoy, a prisoner and three gaolers were killed in an escape attempt in October. In December, Tom Behan from Kildare was shot dead trying to wriggle through a tiny window in the glasshouse at the Curragh.[4] In many gaols, prisoners with a capital charge against their name were noted in a register in red pen and passed their days not knowing when they might be called for a summary trial and execution. The trial register hints at barely contained chaos with a handful of prisoners escaping death because their papers had gone astray. Some, like Tom Heavey, held at Kilmainham, were released by accident after a short interview with the governor:

'Tom Heavey ...?'

'Yes.'

'I have your file and you are released.'

It was the wrong Tom Heavey, but he walked out of prison the same day.[5]

In Limerick gaol, the National Army tried to separate out the men interned without trial and move them up to the Curragh so that the prisoners held for trial could be more securely managed. One such prisoner was Jim Riordan from County Cork, who was awaiting trial for possession of rifles. A tunnel was being dug at Limerick by the prisoners, but there were problems getting Riordan through the tunnel because he was too big. The winter before he had been part of a group of Volunteers who came up to Dublin to pose for a painting by Seán Keating and in their spare time watch the Treaty debates at Mansion House. Keating's painting, *Men of the South*, became an iconic image in Munster. For decades, the portrait hung in the official residence of the President of Ireland although all the men in the picture had taken the anti-Treaty side in the civil war.[6]

By the spring of 1923, Riordan was in imminent danger of execution, but he managed to manoeuvre himself into a group of 'no charge' prisoners who were being moved off to the Curragh internment camps. There was a final inspection before the 'no charge' prisoners were moved out. Riordan found himself being inspected by a National Army officer: Denis Galvin. During the War of Independence Riordan and Galvin had been part of the same battalion, but Galvin had taken a commission with the National Army and Riordan with the anti-Treaty faction.

'What chance have I?' asked Riordan.

'A poor chance,' said Galvin, who had been the only man in his old unit to go with the Free State. Old loyalties died hard and Galvin said nothing.

Riordan was able to get away to one of the Curragh internment camps known as Tin Town: a barbed-wire compound surrounding hundreds of metal huts. Here he was swallowed up in the mass of prisoners. At Tin Town he would find lice, scabies, short rations, bad sanitation, casual brutality and home-brewed poteen. The prison guards would search repeatedly for Riordan and other missing death row prisoners. He was never found and survived the civil war.[7]

Michael Hassett, from Clarecastle, was convicted of possession of a revolver, but he was released in error. William Walshe from Cobh was tried and convicted in Cork for possession of a mills bomb and a Webley revolver. A legal difficulty resulted in an order that he be re-tried, but by the time the papers came back to Cork Command, he had already been sent up to Tin Town where he disappeared.

There was an organised campaign by prisoners to get men at risk of execution out of prison. This sometimes involved switching identities with internees.[8] Some men grew beards and wore their hair long and others cut their hair short and hoped they would not be recognised. Another ruse involved men under sentence of death signing the surrender document in the name of another prisoner to secure their release.[9] The pattern was repeated in most of the camps. Michael Mulvey from Galway was convicted of possession of bombs and detonating equipment. He escaped from Athlone before sentence of death was confirmed. Fourteen more prisoners under sentence of death escaped from Galway gaol.[10] Another escapee was Jeremiah O'Sullivan from Kerry, who had been convicted of possession of rifles and sentenced to death. O'Sullivan disappeared and it is not clear how, except, perhaps, the National Army had confused him with another Jeremiah O'Sullivan, a 'no charge' prisoner who was also from Kerry. This other prisoner was told that he had been sentenced to death and he may not have been a great deal happier to be told the sentence had been commuted to ten years. He was eventually released after the war by way of a writ of habeas corpus.[11]

Even in the late spring prisoners were still escaping. There was a series of tunnel escapes at the Tin Town internment camp. In April, seventy-one got out. News was later passed by the censors that in Limerick gaol thirty prisoners had escaped through a tunnel which had taken months to dig. One of them was Sean Darcy from Clare, who had been captured in January and brought into the prison gravely wounded. Two men captured with him had been executed, but Darcy had remained hidden in a clothes press until the tunnel was ready.[12] One other was Jim Cashman from Kiskeam, who had been wounded at Taur and nursed back to health to face a capital trial. For some of these men, escaping a death sentence would have been the driving factor, but for those who wanted to rejoin the fight, the reality was that their army had all but evaporated.

Deaths in Custody

A senior officer, Colonel Fred Henry from the Provosts Department, was sent down to Kerry to document cases of ill-treatment or shootings in custody. Despite this deterrent and Kerry being in the spotlight, there was still a trickle of deaths in custody that continued until the summer.[13] Even then there were a series of inquest verdicts coming in, which should have caused some disquiet in the National Army command.

In Kerry, an inquest jury convened to consider the death of Thomas Prendiville and found the prisoner was shot dead while under interrogation.[14] In the case of Thomas Conway, the jury found wilful murder of a prisoner in custody.[15] A review of these inquests shows General O'Daly always close at hand, sometimes giving evidence or shaping events into a favourable narrative. He had been doing this for months in the most brazen way. It may be surmised that he had discovered that Kerry was an isolated county: the last of the local newspapers had gone under the summer before, the national press could be managed and the inquest system manipulated. An example was the inquest into the killing of a local train driver at which O'Daly testified that this was the work of anti-Treaty fighters.[16] The killers were his own men. One of O'Daly's junior officers later wrote: 'I saw them leave the workhouse where I was stationed to carry out the crime, I also saw them return. They were not in uniform and they wore trench coats.'[17]

Killing prisoners continued sporadically elsewhere. At Kickham barracks in Clonmel, Jeremiah Lyons was shot dead while under interrogation.[18] Martin Moloney was shot in Clare after being captured at home unarmed.[19] At this point, there was a resurgence of extrajudicial killings in Dublin, which caused some to suggest that the 'Visiting Committee', if such an entity ever really existed, had left Kerry and was now back in Dublin. There were five instances of anti-Treaty men killed after capture in Dublin. The inquest evidence showed a pattern: these men were seized in daylight by men, sometimes in National Army uniform. The bodies were dumped in quiet locations. At the inquest into the death of Thomas O'Leary, the jury complained that 'the military did not give sufficient help to the inquiry'.[20]

One of the men killed was Bobby Bonfield, who had committed his share of killing in the anti-Treaty cause. Recognising the war was all but over he had returned to his dental studies at UCD. As he walked across Stephen's Green, he passed President Cosgrave and his bodyguard en route to mass. Bonfield was picked up. There is no evidence that Cosgrave knew what would happen next, but he must have guessed the truth when Bonfield's body turned up the next day riddled with bullets. Two more killings followed in which the inquest evidence suggested involvement of National Army men. Following these deaths, General Mulcahy issued a special order of the day condemning the killings. He called on any National Army soldiers with information to come forward and his order received wide publicity.[21] It was the first time any government minister had publicly repudiated what was being done, but the shootings continued and each killing was followed by an inquest which discovered nothing but the bare facts.

Another difficult issue for the government was the Kerry landmines affair which would not go away. Rumours abounded that the National Army had massacred prisoners and it had become widely known that there were survivors still in hiding. All of this prompted a question in the Dáil.[22] General Mulcahy ordered an army court of inquiry. It was later said that the Ballyseedy massacre 'had sparked an official military inquiry', but this misses the point.[23] An International Red Cross delegation was arriving in Ireland to investigate allegations of ill-treatment of prisoners. As is so often the case, the minutes of the Executive Council are silent on a crucial issue, but it may be surmised that General Mulcahy found it necessary to convene a military inquiry or face a series of difficult inquests or even an inquiry by the Red Cross.[24] Mulcahy placed Paddy O'Daly, the GOC in Kerry, in charge of the inquiry.

The shortcomings of the military court of inquiry deserve mention. O'Daly presided over the inquiry himself although the conduct of his own men was the sole issue. Even by the standards of the time there was a gross conflict of interest, but in this way O'Daly maintained control of the witnesses to be called and the questions asked. The other officers who sat on the inquiry included Colonel Jim McGuinness, who had been with O'Daly from the day the Dublin Guard landed at Fenit. McGuinness, according to contemporary sources, was honest but illiterate and was hardly the best choice for a searching inquiry. The third officer was General Eamon Price, a logistics officer from GHQ. The venue chosen for the hearing was not neutral: Ballymullen barracks was headquarters of the National Army in Kerry and it was widely known that prisoners were tortured there. In respect of the Ballyseedy massacre, some local people had been in earshot of what had taken place that night, but it would have taken a brave person to go to the barracks and give evidence. Unsurprisingly, the survivors from Ballyseedy (Fuller) and Countess Bridge (Coffey) never came before the inquiry and remained in hiding.[25] The press and public were not admitted to the inquiry and the families of the dead were not permitted to attend or even notified of the inquiry.[26]

A further issue related to the failure to carry out inquests. Where a person died in unexplained circumstances, the law required that a doctor examine the body to certify death and identify the cause of death. The doctor and any other witnesses would give sworn evidence before an inquest jury the next day at the nearest convenient location.[27] This practice was usually observed during the civil war but did not happen in respect of the prisoners killed in the landmine massacres. *The Cork Examiner* reported that the military had not even given notification of death to the coroner.[28] The findings of the Army inquiry were soon announced to the Dáil by General Mulcahy. In respect of Ballyseedy, Countess Bridge and Cahersiveen identical findings were reported: that the prisoners had lost their lives as a result of landmine explosions while removing barricades placed on the roads 'by Irregulars'.[29] Further, that 'no blame is attached to any officer or soldier engaged in the operations'. The report condemned 'the irregular propaganda submitted to the court' and praised the restraint and discipline of the National Army troops.

In the Dáil Mulcahy defended his army officers. 'The honour of the army is as deeply rooted in them as it is in any of us here at Headquarters.'[30] The International Red Cross Committee had arrived in Dublin the previous day and it was all a little opportune. Mulcahy declined to publish the evidence on which the military court of inquiry had acted. A request was made to provide the dossier to deputies alone, but this also was refused and no reasons were given.[31] Perhaps, had the actual evidence become public, the cursory nature of the inquiry and the close relationship between Major General O'Daly and the officers in charge of the prisoners would have become apparent. There were many unanswered questions building up about the necessity for night-time road clearance operations and the steps taken to avoid prisoner casualties. More fundamentally, some were asking why there were now two conflicting official accounts of what took place at Countess Bridge.[32] The landmine massacres would remain an unacknowledged scandal for decades.[33]

Executions

The Tuam executions

On 11 April, six men were executed at the old Tuam workhouse.[34] Five of the six had been part of an anti-Treaty column ambushed by a national patrol near Claremorris in Galway in late February. On a bitterly cold night with sleeting rain and a howling gale, a large National Army force moved to search a small hamlet at Cluid for a column of anti-Treaty fighters known to be in the area. They came upon the nineteen-strong anti-Treaty column just before dawn. The column was already up and on the move, but their guns were sheathed in rolls of cloth to protect against the heavy rain. They were fired on and scattered. Some took refuge in a barn. A mills bomb was thrown onto the roof and they soon put out a white flag and eight surrendered.

One anti-Treaty fighter was shot down running off into the night and the rest were rounded up. The captured equipment included rifles, revolvers, a landmine and a bag of mills bombs. Of the eighteen prisoners, one escaped a few days later.[35] All the others were tried and sentenced to death. Five were brought forward for execution. They included Francis Cunnane, the commanding officer, two junior officers and one man who held no rank. The sixth, O'Malley, was captured separately while resting up in the remote townland of Knocklahard. His rifle was found with him. The month before he had been part of a breakout at Galway. Fourteen men at risk of execution got over the wall, but one man fell and broke his leg. The commotion caused the guards to turn on the searchlights and open fire on the prisoners clustered around the rope ladder.[36] O'Malley had been left behind.

Questions arise as to why these executions took place and why so many. The answer lies with an anti-Treaty attack two nights previously on Headford barracks. There had not been much enthusiasm for the attack among local anti-Treaty fighters. The war was effectively over and most people knew it, but Liam Lynch was pressing for action and the orders from HQ were disseminated to local commanders. It was in these circumstances that men turned out and assembled at Oughterard on the edge of Lake Corrib. They crossed the lake by boat and made a night march to Headford where they joined with others in a pub opposite the barracks. Just before dawn, two men ran across the road and hung a mine on the barbed wire surrounding the wall of the barracks. The mine was detonated and a running gun battle ensued and lasted for hours. Two of the attackers were killed and two National Army men also. The attackers were eventually driven off by National Army troops arriving in a convoy of lorries.

The last letters of the condemned men show that on the evening of 10 April they were informed they were to be executed the next morning. They were moved from Galway prison to army HQ at the workhouse at Tuam that had become synonymous with famine and fever epidemics. The next morning, they were brought out in groups of three and shot against the Oratory wall.

A question arises as to why five of the men captured at Cluid suffered the death penalty and the rest did not. There is no direct evidence, but the likelihood is that the decision was driven by intelligence about the prisoners and the fact that four of the men were from the Headford area where the attack took place. As to the other executed man, James O'Malley, he was from Oughterard from where the attack on the barracks had been launched. In his last letter home, he remembered that in the struggle for independence he had been 'the first man in Oughterard to suffer imprisonment'. He would not now be remembered for that. Even before the executions went ahead, it was known that Liam Lynch had been killed crossing the Knockmealdown mountains and the civil war was over, but the executions went ahead and there were still a handful more to follow.

Clashmealcon Caves and the Tralee executions

The last area of significant resistance was Kerry. One of the few leaders still at large was John Cronin from Ballymacelligott. General O'Daly let it be known that there were three prisoners awaiting execution who would be shot if Cronin failed to turn himself in. Two of the prisoners were 'only sons' and Cronin turned himself in reluctantly.[37] There were now perhaps only two small columns left in the field.[38]

One column led by Tim Lyons was traced to a cave at Clashmealcon. Dunfort's cave was 100 feet below a 'precipitous' cliff face that overlooked the Atlantic. The National Army men could not get into the caves except one at a time, clinging to the edge on a steep, narrow cliff face path. One National Army soldier was killed in the attempt and another wounded.[39] Men who tried to rescue the wounded soldier were fired on from the cave and driven back and the soldier died of his wounds. An attempt was made to smoke the defenders out by dropping bales of hay and bedding soaked in oil into the cliff. Reinforcements were brought up and the cliff edge swarmed with soldiers carrying buckets of tar that were ignited and tipped over the edge. Mines were lowered on ropes and detonated as they reached the cave entrance, and later that night the glare of searchlights mixed with crimson flames stretched into the sky. Under cover of darkness, two of the men tried to creep along the cliff edge and drop into the Atlantic to swim around the headland, but they were swept out into the bay and drowned.[40]

The man still leading this column was Tim Lyons. A wiry man, Lyons had often escaped capture by just out-walking his pursuers, but now he was stuck in the cave and on the third day of the siege, he tried to negotiate a deal. Knowing that he faced execution, he offered to surrender with the guns if the others went free. Unsurprisingly, this offer was rejected by the National Army commander and eventually the men gave in through exhaustion and thirst. Lyons was pulled up on a rope, but as he neared the top, the rope was cut and he fell onto the rocks below. A machine gunner on the cliffs riddled his body with bullets. 'Cut the Rope' McCarthy was never brought to book.

Three prisoners were taken: Jim McEnery, Reginald Hathaway and Ned Greaney. This was the end of the Lyons column that had proved a thorn in the side of the National Army. They had burned out the Civic Guard station at Ballyheigue, robbed the post office at Ballyduff and sniped National Army forces whenever the chance arose. All three were tried and convicted on the day of their capture. A National Army press release suggested that Hathaway and McEnery said at their trial that they had gone back to war because Humphrey Murphy, one of the last anti-Treaty leaders at large, had threatened to have them shot if they did not fight. The press release was published to discredit the anti-Treaty cause and perhaps should be treated with caution.[41] There is no reliable evidence of what took place at the trials, simply that they were convicted. Sentences of death were confirmed. McEnery's last letter home expressed no remorse but asked that there be no reprisals: 'I am asking you one request; don't let anyone do anything.' The prisoners were shot at Ballymullen the next day, 25 April. The full story of Clashmealcon has never been told because all the men were killed, drowned or executed. All that is left is a fleeting reference by McEnery in his last letter home: 'It was just something awful.'

The main reason they were executed was that they had killed two National Army men during the course of armed resistance and each of them had been previously captured and released after signing the surrender note. They were the Irreconcilables, who continued to fight even after the death of Liam Lynch and when most others had given up the war. Jim McEnery was 30 years old. He was married with a baby son and kept a small farm overlooking Clashmealcon. He had been part of the Michael Pierce column that surrendered in February. Reginald Hathaway was English.[42] He had surrendered with Tom O'Driscoll's column some weeks before and was released on an undertaking not to bear arms against the state. After his release he had given up the fight, but his friend James Hanlon, who had not signed the surrender note, was brought forward for execution. After brooding a while, Hathaway rejoined the fight.[43] Ned Greaney, aged 21 from Ballyduff, was another man who had gone back on the undertaking to give up arms. Two days after the executions the anti-Treaty faction ordered a ceasefire.

The Ennis executions

At about 10.30 on the night of 21 April a two-man National Army patrol in Ennis town centre was carrying out searches. Private Stephen Canty was shot and killed. Canty, only 22 years old, had been due to return home to Kerry in a few weeks to marry. He was the last soldier to be killed in the civil war. The men who were later executed had been part of the anti-Treaty faction and were claimed by their own side, but there may be more to this affair. Clare had seen very little fighting during the war. In the summer before, Kilrush had been used to launch a seaborne landing against anti-Treaty forces in the west. But after that, Clare's remote setting meant that it enjoyed no strategic significance and the county had been quiet for many months.[44] Canty was the only National Army soldier to die in Clare during 1923 and it does not seem that his death had much to do with the war. In the furore after the shooting, many men were rounded up. Curiously, in local lore, the man who fired the fatal shot was Miko Casey, but he was never arrested or tried.

The inquest jury sat the following day. Two of the prisoners held in connection with the killing were present and took part: Mahoney and O'Leary. The jury found that Canty had been 'unlawfully shot in Carmody Street by some persons unknown'.

And: 'From the evidence we further find that neither the prisoners Mahoney and O'Leary could have fired the fatal shot.' The jury's narrative verdict might be seen as an attempt to rescue these two suspects from a death sentence.

Patrick Mahoney and O'Leary were tried by an army committee for possession of a partially loaded revolver and being involved in the attack on a National Army patrol. The word used in the official press release was that they were 'implicated' in the attack, which suggests they were not principals and were alleged to have some lesser involvement.[45] Both were convicted and sentenced to death. The sentence on O'Leary was commuted to ten years. Mahoney was executed and there was nothing in the official communiqué as to why one was shot and the other spared, but there is other evidence that Mahoney had previously been in custody and had signed the form to get out. At Mahoney's home a note was found: 'trust you got those rifles you asked for… and expect to hear something from you in the near future …' The note was dated 10 April just before the death of Lynch. There is no evidence that he took delivery of any rifles or that they were used or later recovered, but it is likely that this note resulted in the decision to execute him.[46] Patrick Mahoney was executed two days later at Home barracks in Ennis. The following day, the anti-Treaty forces published the order that had been widely expected by anyone who could read a newspaper: offensive operations were suspended.

Another prisoner tried was Bernard O'Regan, a GSWR railwayman. The army committee found that he was not directly implicated in the killing and O'Regan was sentenced to ten years.[47] Internal National Army records state that O'Regan was a member of an armed gang who had been planning a robbery on the night in question.

This was still not the end of the affair in Clare. Of the many men rounded up after the killing, two more were singled out for trial by military committee. They were William O'Shaughnessy and Christopher Quinn, both aged 18. They were tried by military tribunal on charges of possessing a loaded revolver and 'slaying' Private Canty. They were sentenced to death and executed.

Chapter 16

Summer and Autumn of 1923

May was the month of round-ups. Safehouses and dugouts were identified and raided, hundreds of prisoners were taken and large quantities of arms were seized. In the four weeks following the ceasefire there were seven cases of arson, five rail line blockings, seventeen attacks on the National Army and forty-five attacks on army posts: small-scale affairs carried out by diminishing columns of men hiding out in Cork, Carlow, Wicklow, Kerry and Sligo. There were six National Army casualties but no fatalities. There were also thirty-five armed robberies. The new chief of staff of the anti-Treaty faction issued the Dump Arms order on 24 May and after this attacks on the National Army diminished sharply again.[1]

There were 12,000 prisoners and the internment camps were heaving, but there were other pressing issues. The country was beset by agrarian crime and occasionally murder that was unconnected with the recent war. Despite all this, something approaching normality was returning. Newspapers were still censored but being published on time and interference with the mail became rare. Courthouses were still under armed guard, but district judges now sat in all the large towns, jury trial was being re-established and the Civic Guards were firmly in place.

The government and the church hierarchy represented the new status quo that snuffed out dissent wherever it arose. Actual hard power still resided in the army and its influence pervaded every area of life. A notable example of the new status quo might be the inquest into the death of Mick McGrath, from Tipperary.[2]

During the civil war, he went with the anti-Treaty faction, was wounded in a shoot-out in late April and was later seen by his family in hospital. The account later given by the National Army was that McGrath had had to be moved to the Curragh for an operation. Shortly afterwards, his family was called to the Camp where they were shown the body face down in a coffin with a bullet wound to the head. The family did not press for a coroner's inquiry at the Curragh for reasons which may be obvious and they took the body home.

Some days later, a coroner's court was convened in Powerstown at the national school. A National Army officer appeared in uniform – the Command legal officer – and pointed out that the Coroners Act required the inquest to be held in the place where the death occurred. In this he was correct. A juror intervened: 'We want to hear about the murder of McGrath.' No evidence had been called, the Command legal officer pointed out. Behind the Command legal officer sat another army officer jotting down the names of those not well disposed to the National Army. 'That matter is not ending here,' said the legal officer to the outspoken juror.

Solicitor for the family: 'You don't want the inquest held at all.'

Command legal officer: 'I want that down. Will you repeat that for me?'

Solicitor for the family: 'Certainly … Don't think you are going to intimidate me.'

Command legal officer to the coroner: 'A verdict recorded here this evening is not worth the paper it is written on … are we going to turn the law of the land into a hopeless farce?'

After some more hectoring about compliance with the law, the inquest was abandoned and the result was that no inquest ever took place into the death of Mick McGrath.[3] The army prevailed in this inquest by securing strict compliance with the letter of the law and there was more than a little irony in that. In the last months of the conflict the National Army had become prominent in inquests into deaths in custody and the honour of the army was jealously guarded.

Two trials in particular show the relationship of the military and civil authorities. In County Westmeath old Patrick Shally was robbed and shot dead at his home at Creagh. The robbers made off with a silver watch and very little else. The Civic Guard picked up three suspects who were brought before the District Court. In the ordinary course of events they would have been sent to the Assizes for trial, but some months previously all district judges had been given instructions to send such cases to the military for trial and, despite the war ending, the men were sent for trial by the army.[4] Unusually, preparations for trial were not swift but two other prisoners were not so fortunate.

On 30 May, Michael Murphy and Joseph O'Rourke were tried by military committee for robbing the Munster and Leinster Bank at Athenry a few days before. After the robbery, they had made off on foot and were captured a few hours later still holding short Webley revolvers and £700 in banknotes. No one had been hurt, their handguns had not been discharged and the money was recovered, but they were rushed to trial by military committee a few days later. At their trial they were not legally represented. They admitted the robbery and asserted that they had been coerced into crime by criminal elements involved in the 'land trouble'. They were sentenced to death.[5]

The prisoners were from the Athenry area: the sons of small farmers.[6] They wrote a joint letter for the newspapers saying that they were reconciled to death and wanted it to be known that their families were unaware that a robbery was planned. After writing this note, they were brought out into the barrack square at Tuam, each clutching the hand of the other. In the words of the local newspaper, they 'went unflinchingly to their doom'. Eight days had elapsed between the robbery and execution. These military tribunals would continue to function until the late summer when the army standing counsel advised that this practice could no longer be justified.[7]

At this time, there began a series of legal challenges to the internment without trial of anti-Treaty prisoners. In each case, counsel for the prisoner argued that a state of war no longer existed and, it followed, that martial law powers should fall away and prisoners be released. These legal actions were opposed by lawyers acting for the army.

The position of the government was more nuanced. It does not seem that Cosgrave's government were at all anxious to keep the prisons full: the cost was a considerable drain on the resources of the state. There was a growing realisation that legislation was needed to keep prisoners in custody. The penny had dropped slowly, but now there was a rush to bring in legislation before the courts upheld a writ of habeas corpus. This was the context of the habeas corpus action brought by Jock McPeake as the government pushed through the Public Safety (Emergency Powers) Bill, allowing internment without trial for persons thought to be a danger to the state.[8]

The McPeake case was settled by the government.[9] But with the ink on the new statute not yet dry there was one more application for a writ of habeas corpus brought by Nora Connolly-O'Brien.[10] The application was resisted by the army and the government on the grounds that there was a 'lull' in the fighting, but the war was not yet over. After hearing evidence by affidavit, the Court of Appeal ruled that a state of war no longer existed and directed that the prisoner be produced at court the next day with a view to release. The following day, the attorney general and the government legal team sought to make 'a return to the writ' by producing an internment order for Connolly-O'Brien that was dated that very day: the new Act having come into force just twenty-four hours before. Counsel for the prisoner pointed out that no Act could come into force immediately unless both the Dáil and Seanad had made a declaration that the Bill 'was necessary for the immediate preservation of the public peace or safety'. It was a technical argument, but for once the court seemed determined to take the side of the prisoner.

> The attorney general: 'I do not admit there was no declaration.'
> Chief Justice Molony: 'You will have to prove your declaration.'

No proof was forthcoming and an order was made for the release of the prisoner. There was no wide principle at stake here and there is more than a hint that the court was simply letting the government and the army know that the judiciary were back in control of law and legal process.

After the War

After the war the country became preoccupied with the impending general election.[11] The government won 39 per cent of the vote and the anti-Treaty candidates just over 27 per cent. Cosgrave and his team resumed the reins of power with the help of the minority parties although it was not quite the ringing endorsement he had hoped for. How the country faced the future was a critical issue. There were many now who hoped that old enmities could be settled, but this was not a general view and there were a number of prosecutions brought against anti-Treaty fighters for infractions of the criminal law during the war. Bob Lambert, the new TD for Wexford, was prosecuted for robbery and acquitted in the face of overwhelming evidence. Wexford had been one of the most divided counties, but there were many who were for putting the war behind them. In time, a general amnesty would be issued as part of the process of leaving the war behind.

The new Indemnity Act set in motion a process of releasing prisoners convicted by military courts. The new Board of Commissioners reviewed cases to decide which prisoners might have the unexpired portion of their sentence reduced or remitted. The review would take very many months although the policy of the government was generous. In broad terms, prisoners who had committed criminal offences had to serve out their sentences. Those who had committed offences in furtherance of the war had their sentences remitted. General Mulcahy issued an order that no applications for release should be opposed unless the case was one which the National Army 'could stand over'. The Board of Commissioners sent their reports to the Ministry of Justice and where the conclusion was favourable, the papers went to the governor general with an invitation to exercise the prerogative of mercy and to sign the order of release.[12]

As to untried prisoners, the Public Safety (Emergency Provisions) Act now provided a legal basis for people to be interned without trial and set up a committee to weed out prisoners who could safely be released, but it proved to be a very slow process. The continued detention of large numbers of prisoners would become a festering grievance which ended in a long and bitter hunger strike. It would also precipitate a major and ultimately unsuccessful legal challenge to the lawfulness of the internment legislation.[13] The number of prisoners diminished slowly, although there were still about 10,300 prisoners interned without trial. Those who were released faced a bleak future. For workers who had held government posts before the war there were no jobs, for the artisan class there were no government contracts and for the defeated there were few work opportunities and many emigrated.[14]

Amongst all these major issues, time was found to bring prosecutions against soldiers for killing prisoners. The Indemnity Act made it all but impossible to bring legal proceedings for acts done during the war, but it did allow the government a residual power to bring prosecutions.[15] As far as can be established, there were only two cases where prosecutions took place for killing prisoners. Lieutenant James Larkins was convicted of the manslaughter of Thomas Prendiville during interrogation. In this case, a prosecution was probably inevitable because the killing was carried out in barracks in front of witnesses and the body with gunshot wounds could not be explained away. A close examination of the evidence, however, suggested that Larkins was drunk and the circumstances resonated of gross negligence or unpremeditated murder. Larkins was sentenced to eight years' imprisonment.

At the old Green Street courthouse in Dublin, Sergeant Daniel Boyle was prosecuted for the murder of Nicholas Corcoran in Clare. The evidence showed that the prisoner was part of a work party assembled to clear a barricade in the road. The prisoners declined to work and the senior National Army officer fired a warning shot without any effect. The evidence showed Sergeant Boyle asked for and was given permission 'to put the wind up the prisoners'. He aimed his rifle at Corcoran and pulled the trigger and the prisoner was killed instantly. Sergeant Boyle, who had an otherwise exemplary character immediately asked to be made a prisoner and told his company commander that his rifle had a 'cut off' and that he had picked up the wrong rifle. The circumstances suggested negligence not intent and after a generous summing up by Chief Justice Molony, the jury acquitted the prisoner entirely. These men were prosecuted because they had killed openly in front of witnesses, but they were nothing like as culpable as those who carried out the premeditated and sometimes organised killing of prisoners. Such men were never brought to book, but the public conscience was salved and perhaps reassured, and all those ugly rumours about the war abated in the minds of many.

At this juncture the families of the prisoners killed in the Kerry landmine massacres applied for compensation from a government committee set up to help those affected by death or injury during the civil war.[16] They had the support of the commissioner of the Civic Guards and local officers. The dead men had been breadwinners and now their families were living in poverty. An attempt to secure compensation was blocked by the Executive Council on the grounds that there had been a full army investigation under Major General O'Daly and the system was not designed to pay out funds to the families of those who had been 'in default'. Somehow 'default' was equated with being a prisoner. General O'Daly and his officers would retire on government pensions, but the families of the dead were left to fend for themselves. It is in the nature of big institutions to obfuscate and deny culpability in times of crisis, and that reflex has been much in evidence in Irish life: the Ryan Commission and the Magdalene Laundries affair have shown that only too clearly. The inquiry into the Kerry Landmines Massacres was the first such cover-up in the new state and the denial of compensation to the widows and children of the dead was just another turn of the screw.

The country moved towards the end of 1923: impoverished and riven with bitterness. Control was maintained through censorship and special powers of arrest and internment of those thought to be a danger to the newly established order. The state was still just about in charge of the army but now in the pocket of the Catholic Church hierarchy. It was still not a nation that cherished all its citizens equally and would not be so for very many decades to come.

Chapter 17

Postscript

The trial regulations drafted by the judge advocate general in October 1922 ensured limited protections for those to be tried by military court: the opportunity to prepare a defence, cross-examine witnesses and call evidence, and access to a defence lawyer.[1] These safeguards lasted only a few weeks when four prisoners in the custody of the state were shot without trial at Mountjoy: a reprisal for the shooting of a TD. Immediately after this the Army Council brought in trial by army committee without seeking the sanction of the Dáil. These army committees were not bound by the laws of evidence or procedural fairness, such as the opportunity to cross-examine or free access to defence witnesses, and it is doubtful if any of the men tried had a lawyer. These committees sat in secret and the public and press were not admitted.[2] The convictions following trial by committee were not reviewed by the JAG and there was no appeal.[3]

The Army Council had originally intended that committees would deal with firearms cases where there was no apparent dispute about the facts, but it was, of course, the army lawyers who decided in advance of the trial whether there was a dispute about the facts. This Orwellian flaw was soon exacerbated, because within a few weeks the jurisdiction of military committees was extended to cover a wide range of contested cases and the number of capital charges also increased. Military committees quickly became the usual method of trial for anti-Treaty fighters and others who were just robbers or looters.

One of the most contentious policies was the suspended death sentence experiment tried out in Kerry and then apparently abandoned. Very quickly it became clear that the emerging policy was to amass a bank of prisoners under sentence of death: about 400 were under sentence of death at the end of the war.[4] All of these men were hostages for the good conduct of others. When attacks on the National Army took place, the Army Council searched around the bank of prisoners and fixed on those most closely connected with the attackers: executions followed.

The Executions

By the end of the war, eighty-three prisoners had been executed. Most of the executed prisoners were in their twenties or still teenagers. Most held low rank or no rank in the anti-Treaty faction. Apart from the Mountjoy executions only one other prisoner of high rank was executed.[5] Others, like Liam Deasy, were spared because they signed the form and encouraged others to give up the fight. Ernie O'Malley was spared because of his record, although it was said by some that he was so ill that an execution might have drawn unfavourable comparisons with the execution of James Connolly.[6] Pax Whelan, Michael Kilroy and many others of high rank were also spared.[7]

Similar considerations applied to TDs. A number were captured in arms but not executed.[8] Tom Maguire TD was one of the most senior and active anti-Treaty leaders until his capture and trial. In January 1923, he was due to be shot by firing squad with five others, but on the eve of his execution he was returned to his cell.[9] His younger brother John, aged 20, was a no-ranker who had been convicted of the same charge but was executed. The evidence suggests it was not considered politic to execute TDs or heroes of the War of Independence, and occasionally a prisoner with friends on the other side might avoid trial entirely.

The execution policy was justified by the government as an act of necessity. Whatever the arguments about the correctness and/or legitimacy of the policy in general, different considerations may apply to the executions which took place after the collapse of the anti-Treaty faction. There were six at Tuam on 11 April and three more at Ballymullen later that month. At the end of April, there were three more executions at Ennis and two at Tuam at the end of May. Even without the benefit that hindsight brings, the justification of necessity is questionable.

The anti-Treaty faction claimed most of the executed men as heroes – even some who had played no part or virtually no part in the civil war. This has obscured a fundamental issue. How many of these men committed the acts which resulted in conviction and execution?[10] The destruction of the trial records makes a proper inquiry impossible.

There are, however, a few straws in the wind, like the last letters written by men facing execution. These last letters home share extraordinary qualities of resignation and an absence of self-pity or any rancour or any desire for retribution. It has been argued that these letters were written to encourage the others still fighting, but a number of executed prisoners were not involved in the civil war and their last letters show precisely the same qualities. Every sentient being faced with the inevitability of death has a moment of complete honesty and the law has recognised this for centuries: 'no man dies with a lie on his lips'.[11] That concept may have some application to these letters written after confession and absolution at a time when these things mattered a great deal. In only two letters do prisoners assert their innocence. On the night of his execution, Patrick Hennessy scribbled away furiously: 'When arrested there was nothing on us, but afterwards the military found some stuff in a cock of hay and charged us with it, but we are innocent.'[12]

Many prisoners were captured unarmed. General Mulcahy had issued an edict in December making it clear that it was open to tribunals to infer possession of weapons found in the vicinity of the captured prisoner. This class of case was most open to error: Patrick Mahoney was convicted of 'being implicated' in the shooting a National Army soldier in Ennis. The case presented by the National Army was that the fatal shots were fired by others and Mahoney played a lesser but unspecified role. The inquest jury considering the death of the soldier found that Mahoney was not involved in the shooting, but the military court found the charge proved and a weapons charge also and he was sent for execution. In his last letter home, he wrote: 'I am innocent of the death of the poor soldier. I am sorry for his fate.'[13]

This is not quite the end of the issues touching on the shooting of prisoners. Many other prisoners were killed in custody and others suspected of being anti-Treaty men were kidnapped and murdered. It was never government policy, but what took place was not publicly disavowed by any minister until the war was all but won. Extra-judicial killings remain an awkward and uncomfortable part of the history of this war and the foundation of the new state.

Extrajudicial Killings

There were a large number of cases where suspects were kidnapped and taken off to some quiet spot to be murdered. The practice was mainly confined to Dublin and Kerry although there are a few documented incidents elsewhere.[14]

A review of inquests in the Dublin area shows that twenty-three men were detained and murdered during the civil war. The evidence suggests they were killed because they were anti-Treaty fighters or believed to be so. The consensus of academic opinion is that most were killed by the CID men from Oriel House and ex-Squad men and disaffected National Army intelligence officers.[15]

The killing of prisoners was strongly associated with the campaign in Kerry, but there were a small number of instances in west Cork, Clare, Sligo and Tipperary.[16] In Kerry, the First Westerns killed two prisoners after capture, but it was the Dublin Guard that was most culpable and increasingly out of control as the war progressed.[17] It should not be assumed, however, that most National Army soldiers approved of what was done in Kerry or elsewhere. The evidence shows that in the case of Jerry Buckley, local National Army soldiers were appalled and the same was true of the killing of Jack Galvin.[18]

Once brought into custody, most prisoners underwent interrogation, and ill-treatment was rife at places like Renmore barracks in Galway and routine at army bases in Kerry such as at Ballymullen, Hartnett's Hotel and the Great Southern Hotel in Killarney. The same was true in Dublin at Oriel House, Wellington barracks, the 'Knocking Shop' at Portobello and the basement at Mountjoy prison.[19] Ill-treatment occasionally spiralled out of all control. Three prisoners were shot dead under interrogation – killed by the handgun of the interrogator.[20] Two of these prisoners had nothing whatsoever to do with the civil war, they were just tragic victims of circumstance. In the inquest into the death of Jerry Lyons, the National Army intelligence officer told the jury the prisoner had tried to grab his gun and was killed in the fracas. It was usual, he said, to conduct questioning with a handgun because the questioner was both 'interrogator and guard'.[21] In the inquest into the death of Thomas Prendiville from Kerry, a similar scenario emerged, although in that case the interrogating officer was drunk and two of the military witnesses said he had fired on the prisoner without any reason.[22] In the last of the three cases, the National Army accepted that the officer conducting the interrogation had committed 'wilful murder', having become unhinged sometime previously.

The picture that emerges is more complex than might at first appear. The pattern here suggests a lack of supervision and regulation of junior officers in a chaotic environment where there were few safeguards in place.

In the space of a few months, thousands of anti-Treaty prisoners and those suspected of being so were interned without trial in makeshift prisons and camps. Many of the prisoners were bent on disruption and escape, and their National Army guards had no training for the role of gaoler. Conditions were primitive and chaotic, and ill-treatment of internees became routine in the civil war. At least five were shot dead during escape attempts and perhaps that is not surprising in a conflict such as this. Four more prisoners were shot dead in prison for infractions of prison rules where there was no suggestion of an attempt to escape or use force against their captors.[23] In addition, seventeen prisoners were killed in the Kerry landmine massacres.

Why it Happened

There is a connection here between killing prisoners in custody and official executions. Mulcahy himself told the Dáil in September of 1922 that unless powers to execute were granted to the state, then soldiers would take the law into their own hands because they did not regard internment as a sufficient response to attacks on National Army. This was, however, a much wider and more complicated phenomenon. Part of what took place occurred because the National Army was created in a hurry and some very unsuitable types were taken on in the frantic months that led to the fighting. Men may be given guns and uniforms, but it does not make them part of a disciplined army without much time and training.[24]

A contributory factor might be that very little attempt was made to discipline National Army soldiers for ill-treating or killing prisoners. This was raised with Mulcahy at an early stage of the war by anti-Treaty staff officer David Robinson, who wrote: 'You may imagine what the result will be if this goes on.' It does not seem that General Mulcahy welcomed this trend, but it has only been possible to identify two instances where a soldier was disciplined for injuring a prisoner.[25] Mulcahy never explained this aspect of his leadership, but it may be surmised that he believed that the rank and file might not stand for soldiers being court-martialled for ill-treating prisoners. Also, and perhaps more importantly, the cohesiveness of the new National Army depended to a considerable extent on ties that existed between men from the same village, town and county and also the personal loyalties to officers or between men that had been forged during the War of Independence. The tradition of loyalty to the new National Army itself had not been instilled. In these circumstances, prisoners were ill-treated without fear of the consequences.

Mulcahy did rather more about the Dublin murders. A clear-out of the intelligence department had been in prospect for some time. Liam Tobin's men were not suited to the new dispensation: truculent, not at all efficient or amenable to discipline. What was being done by Tobin and his men was an open secret in the National Army, and the Red Cow inquest probably accelerated the clear-out. Mulcahy put the issue on the Army Council agenda under a single word 'Clondalkin' (the inquest venue), but as was so often the case, the minutes do not record what was said. The bottom line was that three young men had been killed in the custody of army intelligence and the inquest revealed a conspiracy of silence that had become an embarrassment to the army. The intelligence crowd had developed into a clique that was perhaps too dangerous to remove from the National Army. Dalton, the chief suspect in the Red Cow killings, was shifted to a non-operational post as were Tobin and others. They were not relieved of their rank or their weapons, but for a few months the murders in Dublin tailed off.[26]

Mulcahy's approach can be contrasted to that of O'Higgins at Home Affairs who had responsibility for Oriel House and other para-military outfits: the Protective Corps and the Citizen Defence Force. It was O'Higgins who argued for the most extreme measures, such as the 'on the spot' shooting of men captured in arms. Another O'Higgins proposal was to 'suspend inquest juries'. These measures would have given the green light to Oriel House and all those other vigilante groups.[27] Both proposals were rejected by General Mulcahy and perhaps this is the best snapshot of how matters stood.

Note on Sources

Writing this book has presented certain challenges because of a dearth of reliable sources. There are many books on the civil war yet to be written and there are a few pointers which might assist. Just before de Valera came to power in 1932, the Ministry of Defence issued an order requiring the 'destruction by fire' of material which might lead to loss of life. This included Intelligence reports, Secret Service material and 'Proceedings of military courts and tribunals and reports on and details of executions 1922–23'. As a result, the trial records were destroyed along with most of the associated documents.

Other sources include the minutes of the Executive Council, but here the records are often so brief as to be of no value. Sensitive issues were only referred to obliquely, deliberately so. Most of the government ministers never spoke publicly about the events they had been involved in and the decisions that had been made.

The richest source of material is still the Mulcahy Papers, but a close scrutiny of these files suggests that the papers were winnowed to remove embarrassing material. Here too, sensitive discussions are referred to without any detail. By way of example, Army Council discussions about the notorious Red Cow affair and reorganisation of the army were simply marked 'Clondalkin'.

Then there is the Bureau of Military History (BMH). The men running the Bureau sought accounts of the struggle for independence, but with certain exceptions they did not encourage anyone to write about the civil war. Most of those who wrote statements abided by this rule. Here and there one sees a witness finish a long witness statement with a few guarded lines about the civil war but no more than that and there were sound reasons for reticence. Many of these men had taken part in the hardest fighting in the civil war and they did not trust the BMH to keep their accounts confidential. Some of these statements were taken by serving or retired army officers who had been part of the victorious National Army and one had been involved in some of the most shameful events in Kerry during the civil war. Even when the BMH was set up, the fear of retribution was still a live issue. This process of self-censorship has helped to bring about this gap in historical sources.

Another factor bearing on the available evidence is forced migration. After the war there was an exodus of young men who had been on the losing side and were excluded from mainstream economic and political life. Some of those who settled abroad later wrote accounts for the BMH, but many did not and quite a few who had a story to tell died abroad.

A significant constraint on research is censorship during the civil war. The press was heavily censored and the mainstream Irish press were pro-Treaty. Here again, censorship and self-censorship in the press have diminished what might otherwise have been an important contemporary source material. Even internal National Army documents are often suspect because officers occasionally repackaged what had taken place with an eye to forestalling criticism. Perhaps the only other remarkable source are the O'Malley notebooks which are valuable but suffer from the shortcomings of being the result of a one-man enterprise. These are the challenges facing any historian writing about this period.

Endnotes

KEY EVENTS AND MAIN PROTAGONISTS

1. For a masterly analysis of the election, see T.R. Dwyer, *Michael Collins and the Civil War* (Cork: Mercier Press, 2012), p. 231. The pro-Treaty margin of victory might have been greater. Dwyer points to compelling evidence that in some constituencies neutral candidates were put under pressure to withdraw and some did so, leaving the field clear for anti-Treaty candidates.

2. For an anti-Treaty perspective of the election, see E. Neeson, *The Civil War 1922–23* (Dublin: Poolbeg, 1989). See also N. O'Gadhra, *The Civil War in Connaught* (Cork: Mercier Press, 1999), p. 4. Afterwards, the anti-Treaty faction would allege the election was unfair. O'Gadhra points out that the electoral roll was out of date by some years and many of those who had fought in the Great War and in the War of Independence were not able to vote. Women between the ages of 21 and 30 were still excluded from voting. Finally, the draft constitution was not published until the day of the election and this meant that people outside Dublin had no opportunity to make a choice that was fully informed. It should be said, however, that the detail of the Treaty on which the draft constitution was based was well known. At the time, the election was regarded by both sides as a decisive vote in favour of the Treaty.

AUTHOR'S NOTE

1. J. Dorney, *The Civil War in Dublin: The Fight for the Irish Capital 1922–1924* (Dublin: Merrion Press, 2017).

CHAPTER 1

1. McPeake's own account was that he had known little about the war before signing up and had quickly become disillusioned with the pro-

Treaty cause. See E. O'Malley, *The Men Will Talk to Me: West Cork Interviews* (Cork: Mercier Press, 2015), p. 55.

2. Davitt's account has gained currency by repetition. See for instance, Duggan, J.P. *A History of the Irish Army* (Dublin: Gill & Macmillan, 1991), p. 128. For a reliable account of the theft of Slievenamon, see M. Ryan, *The Day Michael Collins Was Shot* (Dublin: Poolbeg, 1989) which relies heavily on primary sources.

3. The solicitor was William Mockler who had a small practice on the Mall in Cork City. Mockler had cut his teeth defending impecunious defendants in the police courts and before military courts convened by the British Army during the War of Independence.

4. Free State Captain Ned Somers had been the National Army officer in command at Callan, Kilkenny. In November 1922 he helped the anti-Treaty forces to take the barracks at Callan. He then deserted and joined the anti-Treaty forces taking many men with him. In the spring of 1923, Somers was tracked down to his hiding place in Tipperary. He and one other had been hiding in the ruins of Castleblake. Somers, perhaps recognising the likely outcome, declined to surrender and came out and exchanged fire with National Army troops. He and another man were killed along with a National Army officer.

5. This was the view of David Neligan, National Army Director of Intelligence, October 1923. IMA DOD/A//06842-0674. It was a view echoed by the chief justice who said of McPeake's conduct when he appeared for sentence: 'from the military point of view that would entitle him to be shot at sight.' *Irish Herald*, 2 November 1923.

6. The account of the habeas corpus proceedings is taken from contemporary press reports. The *Irish Times* and the *Cork Examiner* in particular. Also, from a memoir by James Comyn, a nephew of Michael Comyn.

7. Clause 8 of the *Irish Free State (Consequential Adaption of Enactments) Order* 1923 preserved the power under the *Indictable Offences Act* of 1848 to permit Irish warrants to be enforced in Scotland.

8. According to the trial register, the last recorded trials by military court took place in Athlone on 14 July 1923 when Terrence and Patrick Donoghue from Scramogue in Kerry were found not guilty of possession of firearms. It cannot be established when trials by army committee ceased, but it can be said with certainty that the National Army sought and received legal advice in early September that they could not continue to try civilians by military courts and committees.

See IMA, Judge Advocate General Files, Legal Advice of John O'Byrne, 3 September 1923.

9. None of the ministers concerned ever wrote about the resignation of General Mulcahy and his general staff, but Ernest Blythe later disclosed growing tensions at this time. BMH WS 939, Blythe. See also the minutes of the provisional government which show repeated requests by the cabinet to Mulcahy reminding him of his failure to deliver on his promise: 'to provide weekly reports', and also a terse request that he be present at each and every cabinet meeting. His conduct of the war and failure to carry out sufficient executions was also a source of criticism by ministers, particularly by O'Higgins. See *Mulcahy Papers*, P7/B/245–7.

10. See *ex parte O'Brien* [1923] 2 KB 361: where the British government had deported 110 prisoners from England to Ireland on suspicion of plotting against the Free State government. The House of Lords ruled they were unlawfully deported. In fairness to Cosgrave's government, they were returned as soon as a request was made by the British government. The prisoners were handsomely compensated by the Home Office.

11. See for instance, *R (O'Sullivan) v Military Governor of Hare Park Internment Camp* ILT 1924 63 – a case that revolved around confusion over the identity of the prisoner.

12. IMA: DOD/A//06842-0674. Records suggest he passed out of the hands of the military back into Western Road Prison in Cork on or about 17 July 1922.

13. IMA AFO 44/Legal/18. Costs in the sum of £48 3s & 11d.

14. J. Comyn, *Their Friends at Court* (London: Barry Rose, 1973), p. 56. D. Macardle, *The Irish Republic* (London: Corgi, 1969), p. 792 suggests that the trial was an example of the use of civil law to imprison known republicans where there was no other excuse to detain them. It is submitted that Macardle misunderstood the case. The McPeake affair was also misdescribed by Cahir Davitt. BMH WS 1751, p. 104. See also M. Ryan, *The Day Michael Collins Was Shot* (Dublin: Poolbeg, 1989), pp. 159–61. Meda Ryan gives a convincing and detailed account of the theft of Slievenamon. The legal aspects are outside the scope of that work.

15. J. Twohig, *The Dark Shadow of Beal na blath* (Cork: Tower Books, 1991), p. 226.

16. The jury found the army was implicated in the death of Lemass and called for a judicial inquiry which was refused by the government.

17. McPeake appeared before the Dublin City Commission on 1 November 1923. He was represented by Michael Comyn, KC, and James Comyn;

instructed by Sean Ó hUadhaigh. Prosecuting counsel was Michael Corrigan the state solicitor. It was later said by Comyn that a longer sentence was a safer option than a shorter one and he had done what he could to secure a long sentence. This account is quite fanciful at first blush, but it has to be said that Comyn's speech in mitigation before the chief justice was tactless and inflammatory and without any redeeming feature. When asked by the chief justice why McPeake had taken the car, Comyn replied: 'I don't know, maybe he wanted to take it for a drive.'

IMA files suggest that just before McPeake received his sentence, President Cosgrave tried to revive the question of desertion but was persuaded not to do so. According to Tim Pat Coogan, McPeake served his sentence at Portlaoise in circumstances of hardship. His parents died while he was inside. He went on hunger strike with republican prisoners and was disciplined for various infractions of prison regulations. McPeake finished his sentence in August 1928 and went back to Scotland. When de Valera came to power, McPeake got a secret service pension. Coogan argues persuasively that this should not be seen as evidence that McPeake had any involvement in the death of Collins. It was just a way of covering up government expenditure on those who had supported the anti-Treaty faction during the civil war. T.P. Coogan, *Michael Collins* (London: Hutchinson, 1990), p. 418. For years, the killing of Collins hung around McPeake's neck like a millstone. He eventually changed his name and emigrated to England. He died aged 84.

18. This figure includes the seventy-seven men claimed by the losers of the civil war. It includes four more who were executed for robbery. It also includes Jack Lawlor from Ballyheigue who was executed after a rudimentary and illegal trial on the night of his capture and Private Bernard Winsley, a National Army soldier who was executed for passing arms to anti-Treaty forces.

CHAPTER 2

1. BMH WS 939, Blythe, p. 149. Blythe's witness statement was made many years later without notes. It is very long and appears broadly reliable, although some errors of detail are apparent such as confusing Paddy O'Daly with W.R.E. Murphy who was, at the outset of the war, General Officer Commanding (GOC) in Kerry and was later replaced by O'Daly.

2. One of the last orders issued by Collins was a proclamation declaring

that licences to serve alcohol would be withdrawn from publicans selling alcohol to uniformed soldiers. Contemporary press report, 27 July 1922.

3. See for instance, *Mulcahy Papers*, P7/B/140. Report by Director of Intelligence, 8 January 1924.

4. K. Griffith and T. O'Grady, *Curious Journey* (London: Hutchinson, 1982), p. 300, quoting Tom Barry: 'The Munster Fusiliers, The Leinsters, The Dublins, The Connaught Rangers, all these regiments were disbanded at Oswestry in Wales, they were put into civvies and sent across from Holyhead to Ireland, where they were met by Free State lorries and brought to Beggars Bush barracks and put into green uniforms. Now some of these were probably decent men driven by hardship to join the British Army, but others were violently anti-Irish and some had left Ireland in very unfavourable conditions – they were driven out because of their having done things against the Republican movement.'

5. *Mulcahy Papers*, P7/B/114.

6. IMA Western Command CW/OPS/7. Report of 4 September.

7. *Mac Eoinn Papers*, UCDA. Drawn to my attention by D. Price, *The Flame and the Candle* (Cork: Collins Press, 2012), p. 240.

8. *Mulcahy Papers*, P7/B/40. Memo O'Duffy to General Mulcahy.

9. This account comes from BMH WS 1751, Davitt.

10. DOD/A/06861. After Collins was killed, Davitt wrote a memo to the Attorney General, 12 September 1922. He argued the case for the judge advocate general (JAG) to be a civilian, otherwise 'it would have all the appearance of an attempt by the military authorities to avoid all checks by civilian authority on the administration of military law'. His argument was accepted at that time.

11. The identification of the spy rests on the description of the case by the JAG in his memoir. Although the JAG did not name the prisoner, a local history in *The Tribune* (2 January 2008) suggests that James McGuinness was the man concerned. When de Valera came to power in 1932, McGuinness was given a government post and this was seen as confirmation that he had been passing information to the anti-Treaty faction.

12. BMH WS 939, Blythe.

13. For a Tipperary perspective, see S. Hogan, *The Black and Tans in North Tipperary 1913–22* (Dublin: Untold Stories Publishers, 2013), p. 413. For Sligo, see M. Farry, *The Aftermath of Revolution: Sligo 1921–23* (Dublin: Dublin University Press, 2000), p. 170. For the murder of ex-RIC men after the Treaty, see R. Abbott, *Police Casualties in Ireland* 1919–22

(Cork: Mercier Press, 2000). See also G. Clark, *Everyday Violence in the Irish Civil War* (Cambridge: Cambridge University Press, 2014).

14. Part of the judgment survives at Kilmainham gaol: 20 LG-3N15-05. It contains a useful legal analysis of the legal stance of the anti-Treaty faction.

15. It was not the first time that Judge Crowley had gone to prison for acting as a judge. During the War of Independence, the Dáil created its own courts which began to replace those that existed under British law. These Dáil courts were proclaimed as unlawful by the British administration and Crowley was caught presiding over such a court and he was sentenced to eighteen months. He served thirteen months of that sentence before the Truce came to pass. The full story of the Plunkett habeas corpus writ is that there were four judges of the Dáil Court. The other three were all unavailable at this time. Cahir Davitt maintains he was unwell and the other two were inexplicably absent. Crowley was obliged to sit alone on the case. Having granted the writ for the release of Plunkett, he made orders for the committal of the minister of defence (General Mulcahy) and the governor of Mountjoy for failure to comply with his order. However the law stood, his actions showed an unworldly naivety. Crowley's release was secured by Cahir Davitt. Davitt was pro-Treaty and had just been appointed JAG of the new National Army. He went to see General T. Mulcahy to plead the case for Crowley. See BMH WS 1751, Davitt.

16. *Dublin Gazette*, 1 August 1922.

17. The official cause of death was a brain haemorrhage although the symptoms were more indicative of poisoning. Curiously no autopsy or inquest was held.

18. See BMH WS 939, Blythe.

19. *The Irish Free State Constitution Act 1922*. 13 Geo. V., Ch. 1. By the end of the autumn, Cosgrave would assert that the settlement being thrashed out with Britain offered a degree of independence that was greater than that enjoyed by Canada and on a par with South Africa. In late October, the Dáil approved the draft constitution to be brought in when the Free State came into being. The Constitution guaranteed life, liberty, freedom of expression and conscience and due process.

20. Apart from Michael Collins, other notable casualties included Brigadier George Adamson shot down in the street without warning. Commandant Peter Doyle shot going into church and Commandants Collison and MacCurtain killed in ambush in Leix. It was not usual to hold inquests

on National Army soldiers killed in ambush, but a small number were held. At the old Maryborough Courthouse in Leix, the county coroner heard medical evidence that the wounds of Collison and MacCurtain had been caused by expanding bullets. 'Wilful murder' was the verdict of the jury who added a rider condemning the use of expanding bullets. Another inquest concerned Denis McCarthy from Barracks Street in Cork who was shot down outside his house as he was taking leave of his wife. An angry crowd chased but failed to catch the killers. The inquest jury returned a verdict of wilful murder. The same verdict was returned by the jury considering the assassination of Commandant Doyle.

21. August 1922: Bernard Daly, Alf Colley, Sean Coles. September 1922: J. J. Stephens, Pat Neville. December: Frank Lawlor. March 1923: Bobby Bonfield, Thomas O'Leary. April 1923: Chris Breslin, Joseph Kiernan, Martin Hogan. July 1923: Noel Lemass, Harry McEntee.

22. August 1922: Joe Hudson. September 1922: Sean McEvoy, Pat Mannion. October 1922: Brendan Holohan, Edwin Hughes, Joseph Rogers. November 1922: Jim Spain, Will Graham. 1922.

23. Brugha was the last anti-Treaty fighter killed in the aftermath of the Four Courts siege. Brugha and his men had fought a rearguard to allow others to escape and many did. His men eventually surrendered from a burning building and emerged hands up under a flag of truce. Brugha followed and it has never been disputed that he carried a revolver in hand. He was shot down and died in the Mater Hospital two days later.

Cathal Brugha was a household name and many wanted to know how he died. This was the first of a series of inquests into deaths in custody in which the anti-Treaty faction would pursue redress and propaganda through the courts on behalf of their own men killed by the National Army. As was the custom of the time, the inquest took place where the death took place: at the Mater Hospital. The city coroner, Louis Byrne, presided before a packed public gallery. The Brugha family were represented by Michael Comyn, KC.

The bare facts of any inquest required proof of the identity of the deceased and how he died. Brugha's identity was not in dispute and the medical evidence was quite clear: a single wound to the thigh that severed an artery. The house surgeon, Dr P.J. Smith, who tried to repair the artery, testified that the wound was probably caused by a revolver shot. A more senior colleague, Surgeon Blayney, testified the wound was caused by a rifle shot fired from a range of only 'a few yards'.

The coroner, Louis Byrne, abruptly announced he would permit no further evidence as to how Brugha died. Comyn, perhaps realising he had been outmanoeuvred, sought an adjournment to call three witnesses to the shooting to prove that Brugha had surrendered before being shot. The witnesses were in custody at Mountjoy and in the usual course of events would have been produced if counsel for the state made the request or the coroner wished it. Counsel for the state, perhaps realising the coroner was on his side, said nothing. The application was refused. Coroner Byrne ruled that it was his practice to 'rigidly exclude evidence but that which bore on the cause of death'.

A review of other cases heard by Coroner Byrne suggests he did not follow the same narrow approach in inquests where the National Army was not being criticised. Faced with the anger of the Brugha family and the dismay of Comyn, the coroner added this:

'These other matters could be investigated by a legal tribunal if the authorities deemed it necessary.'

The likelihood of the Free State setting up an inquiry into how anti-Treaty leaders were killed was remote to say the least. In any event, the coroner's view on law was far too narrow: where there was sufficient evidence it was perfectly usual for juries to find wilful murder or manslaughter as the facts indicated. Where an inquest jury found a person culpable, he would be committed to stand trial before the criminal courts. That was one of the functions of the coroner's court laid down by statute. *Coroners Act 1887* 50 & 51 Vic., Ch. 71. Faced with the medical evidence only, the jury of thirteen, one dissenting, found a bland verdict of death caused by shock and haemorrhage.

The result was that the only evidence the jury heard was that Brugha suffered a single wound to his leg which severed an artery and resulted in his death, but wider facts were suppressed by the coroner and this fuelled many lurid and essentially fictional accounts of Brugha's death. According to one account, 'riddled with bullets' (F. O'Donoghue, *No Other Law* (Dublin: The Irish Press, 1954), p. 274). There are many versions of his death: 'he walked towards his enemies with his revolver blazing, until he fell, mortally wounded' (T. Barry, *Guerilla Days in Ireland* (Dublin: Anvil Books, 1981), p. 188). Another one reads: 'A small smoke blackened figure, a revolver in each hand raised against the levelled rifles of the troops … Brugha darted forward, firing, and fell amid a volley of shots … Desperate wounds had been added to the fourteen scars of Easter week' (D. Macardle, *The Irish Republic* (London: Corgi, 1969), p. 686).

24. The background to this affair was that IRB had gone pro-Treaty, but Boland, who was very senior in the hierarchy, had been one of a few who voted against. In the aftermath of the Four Courts siege he feared for his life and hid out in the Grand Hotel in Skerries. The National Army was tipped off about his whereabouts and sent a raiding party from Dublin. There was no suggestion that Boland was armed, but a single bullet pierced the side of his chest and mortally wounded him. He lingered long enough to say the man who had shot him had been a fellow prisoner after the 1916 rebellion but would not give his name and asked that no retaliation take place. His death was either an assassination or a reckless act. It provided the anti-Treaty lawyers with another opportunity to continue this proxy war. Michael Comyn had learned something from the last inquest and persuaded the Boland family not to identify the body in order to force the coroner to call witnesses which would allow Comyn to explore the evidence.

Boland's inquest was held at St Vincent's Hospital a few days later. Louis Byrne presided again and much of Dublin's legal talent gathered to represent the state, the army, the police and the family.

Tim O'Sullivan, KC, appeared for the provisional government and declined to take any steps to bring the soldier who had shot Boland to give evidence. O'Sullivan hinted that there were fears for the life of the witness and that if an adjournment was ordered then it ought to be for some months to alleviate concerns for the witness.

Michael Comyn, KC, demanded the soldier who fired the fatal shot be called. Another man had been taken prisoner when Boland was shot and Comyn demanded this witness be called also.

O'Sullivan, counsel for the state, persuaded the coroner to hear the medical evidence and then rule on the application. The medical evidence was not in dispute; a bullet wound between the eighth and ninth ribs on the left side of the chest had caused the fatal injury. All that was lacking from the coroner's point of view was evidence of the identity of the dead man. A DMP officer gave evidence that the Boland family were in court but were refusing to identify the body. Coroner Byrne refused an adjournment and said as far as he was concerned the body had been 'sufficiently identified'. No further evidence was called.

Comyn declared this was murder and there followed a spat with O'Sullivan, counsel for the state, who dismissed the suggestion of murder as 'unfitting'. Comyn added: 'I will take no further part in this.'

He walked out, followed by the other lawyers representing the Boland family.

Faced with the absence of any evidence, the jury, with two dissenters, returned a bland verdict of death by 'shock and haemorrhage caused by a gunshot wound'. *Irish Times*, 12 August 1922.

25. Mannion was returning from Oriel House where a planned anti-Treaty attack had been called off. See E. O'Malley, *The Singing Flame* (Dublin: Anvil Books, 1978).

26. *Irish Times*, 20 September 1922.

27. The six in Sligo were Seamus Devins, Brian MacNeill, Patrick Carroll, Joseph Banks, Thomas Langham and Harry Benson. For an account of how they were killed, see IMA Contemporary Documents 333/66. See also J. McGowan, *In the Shadow of Benbulben* (Manorhamilton: Aeolus, 1993). Also, M. Farry, *The Aftermath of Revolution* (Dublin: Dublin University Press, 2000), p. 84. The circumstances of these killings remain controversial. M. Hopkinson, *Green Against Green: The Irish Civil War* (Dublin: Gill & Macmillan, 2004), p. 215 suggests that only four of the men were unlawfully killed. The three in Kerry included Sean Moriarty, Bertie Murphy and Jack Galvin. In Cork, Jerry Buckley at Macroom and Tim Kennefick at Coachford. Separately, Sean O'Donoghue was killed while in custody at Dublin's Hill on 28 September. Also, in Limerick, Michael Danford and in Tipperary, Con Hanly and in Mayo, Patrick Mulchrone.

28. The inquest was held by Coroner J. J. Horgan and a jury on 11 September 1922 at the Gilligan home in Coachford. The evidence showed Kennefick was a signalling officer with a local anti-Treaty brigade. He was taken into custody unharmed. His body showed facial injuries which were consistent with being beaten before the being shot.

29. *Dáil Debates*, 1 November 1922.

30. This proclamation was brought to my attention by Sean Boyne in his biography *Emmet Dalton: Somme Soldier Irish General Film Pioneer* (Dublin: Merrion Press, 2016).

31. The attack took place on 11 September on the bridge at Carrigapookha. National Army Commandant Tom Keogh and six soldiers were killed and others were wounded.

32. BMH WS 1674, T. Buckley.

33. *Mulcahy Papers*, P7/B/82.

34. Emmet Dalton returned all the officers to Dublin with the exception of one Sean O'Connell. It is likely that the other officers were redeployed and there is certainly no evidence they were the subject of discipline.

35. David Robinson DSO was formerly a British Army officer with the Marine Artillery unit. He lost an eye and suffered serious leg wounds during the Great War. He later took part in the War of Independence in Wicklow. When the civil war came he took the anti-Treaty side and was later captured in the company of Erskine Childers, his cousin. He was interned. He became a senator in 1932.

36. *Mulcahy Papers*, P7/B/86.

37. See for instance, D. Macardle, *Tragedies of Kerry 1922–23* (Dublin: Irish Freedom Press, 2004). An avowedly anti-Treaty text, but the author's factual research cannot usually be faulted. See also T. Doyle, *The Civil War in Kerry* (Cork: Mercier Press, 2007), p. 186.

38. The 1911 census shows Julia Murphy with three young children. She records herself as married for six years. By 1922 she was widowed.

39. See *Cork Examiner*, 2 October 1922. This inquest was adjourned for a few days at the request of Mrs Murphy, but it is not possible to trace a record of what then took place. Such evidence as there is suggests the killer was David Neligan, the director of intelligence in Kerry. See BMH WS 938, D. Mulvihill.

40. See for instance, the Dan Daly Inquest in Tralee. Dan Daly was a railway driver who was shot down near Tralee railway station by men in trench coats and hats; his friend was wounded. The incident took place in January of 1923 and it seemed on the face of it that he had been killed as part of the anti-Treaty campaign against the railways system.

   The inquest convened two days later and quickly took an astonishing turn. See *Irish Times*, 27 January 1923 for instance. The new GOC of the National Army in Kerry, Major General Paddy O'Daly, took the stand. He told the court that sensitive papers had been found only hours earlier and asked the coroner and the jury not to ask to look at these documents for fear of putting others in danger. To this suggestion the jury readily agreed. Major General O'Daly then told the jury that the documents showed that Dan Daly had been asked to take part in a plan to disable trains, kidnap a Free State officer and ambush troops. The plan had been due to be put into operation some days before and since it had not come off the implication was that Dan Daly had declined and been murdered by anti-Treaty men. General O'Daly's evidence at the inquest diverted blame for what his own men had done onto the dead man's associates.

   One of the flaws in General O'Daly's account was that there is reliable evidence that just before the murder the killers had been seen by a young

National Army officer leaving the army barracks and returning after the killing. See N. Harrington, *Kerry Landing* (Dublin: Anvil Books, 1992), p. 147: 'Without knowing their intent, I saw them leave the workhouse where I was stationed, to carry out the crime, I also saw them return. They were not in uniform and they wore trench coats.' The young officer was Niall Harrington and there is good reason for believing his account because he was until then one of General O'Daly's staunchest admirers. General O'Daly had been one of Collins' squad of assassins during the Tan War and it is most unlikely that he was unaware that his men had left his own HQ and killed Dan Daly on their own initiative. There is also compelling evidence that officers of the Dublin Guard frequently killed suspected anti-Treaty fighters in Kerry and O'Daly was usually there at the inquest explaining, justifying or limiting the fall out. In April, he took this to a new level when he presided over the army inquiry into the Landmines Massacres carried out by his own men.

41. W.R.E. Murphy to C in C, 1 October 1922. IMA. Murphy did not dispute the killing of a prisoner but simply related that Galvin had signed a letter of surrender and had been released but took up arms again and on a later occasion shot Captain Burke. Later accounts of the war suggest neither of these assertions were true, but they seemed to make the killing of Galvin rather more palatable to W.R.E. Murphy and provided a reason to do nothing.

42. T. Horgan, *Dying for the Cause* (Cork: Mercier Press, 2015). For an account of the Inquest see Cork *Examiner*, 24 January 1923.

43. A description used by P. Yeates in his excellent history *A City in Civil War: Dublin 1921–24* (Dublin: Gill & Macmillan, 2015), p. 259.

44. See BMH WS 434, Dalton.

45. Dr J.P. Brennan.

CHAPTER 3

1. T.P. Coogan, *Michael Collins* (London: Hutchinson, 1990), p. 398.

2. As quoted by Coogan in *Michael Collins*.

3. *Mulcahy Papers*, P7/B/29.

4. *Mulcahy Papers*, P7/B/29 et seq.

5. This was the sentence awarded to Walter Cullen of Ballymaghary at Downpatrick Assizes in the summer of 1922. The offences were possession of a fully loaded Webley, four rounds of ammunition and a bomb for an unlawful purpose. The available sentences included death.

Cullen was given seven years' penal servitude and fifteen strokes of the cat. See *Irish Times*, 2 August 1922. The sentence was not uncommon in the North at this time.

6. The Leix Ambush, as it was known, took place on 29 July. Also killed was Volunteer Grace. Brigadier Grey and another officer were wounded. The inquest was conducted by the county coroner Dr Higgins, father of Kevin O'Higgins.

7. *Mulcahy Papers,* P7/B/71, Dalton to Mulcahy, 2 September 1922.

8. In the President's address to the Dáil on 11 September, Cosgrave specifically alludes to the arson campaign as a means of 'driving of the wealthy classes out of the country with consequent loss of revenue ...'

9. Churchill to Collins, 12 April 1922.

10. This is evidenced by the creation of the Irish Distress Committee in England in May 1922. This organisation was created to deal with the flood of refugees from Ireland. See also E. Delaney, *Demography, State and Society: Irish Migration to Britain 1921–1971* (Liverpool: Liverpool University Press, 2000), who suggests a 5 per cent decrease in the population of southern Ireland between 1911–31. Delaney argues this figure is in part explained by the turbulent events of 1914–23: the deaths of Irish soldiers in the Great War (of which there were at least 27,405), and those who simply never returned. Also, the departure of crown officials and their families after the War of Independence (34,000) and many RIC men. The precise scale of emigration abroad cannot be ascertained, but what may be most relevant is the perception of the government and the church that this was a serious problem affecting the new state.

11. *Ex parte Sean Beaumont, Irish Law Times and Solicitors' Journal,* September 1922.

12. *Irish Times,* 8 October 1922.

13. See, for instance, the Dáil in Committee 27 March 1923, speech by O'Higgins. In the financial year 23/24 expenditure on the army would rise to over £10 million.

14. For the list of published claims, see *Irish Times* 4 October 1922.

15. Hitherto such claims had been dealt with by the British government under *The Malicious Damage Act*. The Dáil acting by resolution on 1 November announced a procedure for such claims to be filed 'in respect of damage to or destruction of property committed by persons acting for or purporting to act on behalf of any organisation engaged in armed resistance to the provisional or Free State government ...' This was

subsequently ratified by legislation in 1923 by *The Damage to Property (Compensation) Act 1923.*

16. See for instance, T. Doyle, *The Civil War in Kerry* (Cork: Mercier Press, 2008), p. 192.

17. So described by P. Ó Ruairc, in *Blood on the Banner* (Cork: Mercier Press, 2009), p. 313.

18. P. Yeates, *A City in Civil War Dublin 1921–24* (Dublin: Gill & Macmillan, 2015), p. 152 which reads: 'The Army Emergency Powers Act never reached the statute book.' It was never intended to be a statute.

19. B. Kissane, *The Politics of the Irish Civil War* (Oxford: Oxford University Press, 2005), p. 88.

20. This was so because the *Irish Free State (Agreement) Act 1922* was in force and permitted legislation.

21. My thanks to Gerard Hogan whose analysis pointed the way. See G. Hogan, 'Hugh Kennedy, The Childers Habeas Corpus Application and the Return to the Four Courts' in C. Costello (ed.), *The Four Courts* (Dublin: The Incorporated Council of Law Reporting for Ireland, 1996).

22. P7/B/245/30. The order was issued on 30 August. Under the terms of the order these deputies would no longer be permitted to enter the Dáil.

23. Laurence Ginnell had been expelled in September for allegedly disruptive behaviour.

24. *Dixieme Conference internationale de la Croix Rouge tenue a Geneve du 30 Mars au 7 Avril 1921, Compte Rendu, ICRC, Geneva, 1921.* Resolution XIV.

25. These were laid before the Dáil in early October and became known as the *General Regulations as to the Trial of Civilians by Military Courts 1922.*

26. P7/B/245/86, 4 October 1922.

27. *Iris Oifigiuil*, 31 October 1922.

28. P. Murray, *Oracles of God* (Dublin: University College Press, 2000).

29. *General Regulations as to the Trial of Civilians by Military Courts 1922.* The full list of specified offences included: attacking National Army forces or aiding and abetting that offence; possession without proper authority of arms, ammunition, dynamite, gelignite or any explosives or bombs of any description; also looting, arson, destruction and seizure of property; and any breach of any general regulation or order made by the Army Council. The available penalties included death, penal servitude, imprisonment, deportation, internment and/or a fine. Military courts were to be convened by the general officer commanding the area in

which the offence was believed to have been committed. The court would include a president – an officer with the rank of not less than commandant – and a legal officer certified by the attorney general to be a person of legal knowledge and experience. The military courts were bound by the laws of evidence and, so far as practicable, to have regard to the regulations laid down for trial of National Army soldiers which were more generous to prisoners. See *The General Regulations as to Discipline, 1922.*

30. A review of cases during the civil war suggests that district judges released such cases to the military courts. It is also evident from a review of the Executive Council minutes that in some cases with no political dimension the criminal courts were permitted to try suspects. The decision seems to have been made by the minister of home affairs on a case to case basis and later ratified by the Executive Council.

CHAPTER 4

1. Colonel Commandant Michael Hogan of the First Western Division had arrived in Kerry in August. He had led a force of 240 men by ferry from Kilrush to Tarbert and fought their way down the coast to Tralee where the hardest fighting would soon begin.

2. For other accounts see T. Horgan, *Dying for the Cause* (Cork: Mercier Press, 2015), p. 103. Also D. Macardle, *Tragedies of Kerry* (Dublin: Irish Freedom Press, 2004). The other man who escaped was Thade Paddy Reidy who provided an account of much of what took place.

3. The regulations prohibited any trial until forty-eight hours after capture and entitled an accused to an opportunity to prepare a defence and also to legal representation if practicable. The verdict and sentence also required confirmation from the Army Council which, in the time frame in which these events took place, was not possible.

4. T. Doyle, *The Civil War in Kerry* (Cork: Mercier Press, 2008), p. 206. Doyle recounts that a raid on the home of Pierce Godley at Ballyheigue took place on 20 October, resulting in the arms find. The IMA trial register shows the trial took place on 3 November.

5. *Dáil Debates*, 15 November 1922. Mulcahy answering a question from Darrell Figgis TD.

6. BMH WS 829, McGleenan, p. 35.

7. The army press release, *Irish Independent*, 18 November 1922 tends to suggest that Cassidy and Gaffney were dealt with separately the day after the other two in respect of an arrest on a different occasion. The JAG's memoir implies that they were all dealt with on the same date. BMH WS 1751, Davitt.

8. BMH WS 1751, Davitt.

9. Minutes of provisional government meeting 31 October 1922. Brought to my attention by C. Campbell, *Emergency Law in Ireland*. See P7/B/245/142 'arrange for the immediate trial of the men arrested in connection with the attack on Oriel House'. See also IMA DOD/A/07577.

10. A memoir by Joe O'Connor who had organised the attack implied that Fisher, Gaffney, Twohig and Cassidy had taken part in one of the Oriel House raids and were captured in the round up that followed. BMH WS 554.

11. Sean Mac Mahon. Statement to the Army Inquiry 1924. *Mulcahy Papers*, UCD.

12. E. O'Malley, *The Singing Flame* (Dublin: Anvil Books, 1978), p. 212. O'Malley's account was plainly second-hand and the reliability of his account on this issue is questionable. Although, it should be acknowledged that his histories were usually factually accurate.

13. Death certificate courtesy of Sharon Kelly.

14. A request for the families of executed men to be informed before execution was considered and refused. P7/B/245/172. Requests for last visits were also refused. See *Dáil Debates*, 30 January 1923.

15. The undertaking was given by General Mulcahy in answer to questions from back benchers. *Dáil Debates*, 28 September 1922. It has not been possible to trace any record of the state making provision for lawyers at state expense.

16. *Irish Times*, 21 November 1922.

17. The date of capture was 8 November. The other men captured were Sean Whelan from Dungarvan and Eddie Spratt from Mount Odell. Three revolvers were found together with ammunition and despatches. So far as can be established, these men were never tried. *Mulcahy Papers*, P7/B/64. Waterford Command Report, 11 December 1922. See also T. Mooney, *The Deise Divided* (Dungarven: de Paor, 2014) p. 134.

CHAPTER 5

1. 7 August 1922, Collins to National Army director of intelligence.

2. The incident was witnessed by David Robinson (later senator). Robinson was himself armed but was able to slip away and hide his gun before also being arrested and interned. From the David Robinson Papers cited in A. Boyle, *The Riddle of Erskine Childers* (London: Hutchinson, 1977).

3. *Irish Times*, 9, 10 November 1922. The young men were Edwin Hughes, Brendan Holohan, Joseph Rogers. All teenagers, the youngest was sixteen.

4. R. Brennan, *Allegiance* (Dublin: The Richview Press, 1950).

5. J. Comyn, *Their Friends at Court* (London: Barry Rose, 1973), p. 76.

6. *In re Clifford and Sullivan*, 1921, 2 AC 570.

7. And Conor Maguire, then junior counsel, later chief justice. Childers solicitor was Sean Ó hUadhaigh. The State was represented by Hugh Kennedy, Michael Corrigan and John O'Byrne as junior counsel.

8. *The Firearms Act* 10 & 11 Geo. V., Ch. 43.

9. Much of the legal argument that followed would turn on the analysis of recent case law. *Egan v Macready* [1921] 1 IR 265.

10. One final point of importance arose out of the embryonic international law that was developing in response to the Great War and the ethnic conflicts which were sweeping Europe. It was submitted that during the International Red Cross Conference of 1921 certain standards had been accorded recognition. One was that prisoners taken in civil war were entitled to be accorded the status of prisoners of war. This point was accorded no weight either before the military court or the High Court, but here we see the beginnings of international human rights jurisprudence.

11. BMH WS 939, Blythe.

12. The Dáil courts were established by a decree of the Dáil. The decree abolishing the Dáil courts in Dublin on 29 July 1922 was issued by the home affairs minister of the provisional government, ostensibly with the concurrence of the Dáil cabinet. In fact, the Dáil cabinet did not meet at this time, but it was politic to order the decree in the name of the Dáil.

13. See M. Kotsonouros, *Retreat from Revolution* (Dublin: Irish Academic Press, 1994), p. 15. Where it is persuasively argued that this determination to assert control of the judiciary resulted in the *Courts of Justice Act 1924* being delayed for many months as deputies and senators resisted government efforts to control the new judicial system.

14. *The King (Childers) v The Officer Commanding the Troops, Portobello*

Barracks in the County of Dublin and the Adjutant General of the Forces of the Irish Provisional Government [1923] 1 IR 5.

15. *Irish Times*, 24 November 1922.

16. For an analysis of the legal issues, see G. Hogan, 'Hugh Kennedy, the Childers Habeas Corpus Application and the Return to the Four Courts' in C. Costello (ed.), *The Four Courts* (Dublin: The Incorporated Council of Law Reporting for Ireland, 1996). See also R. Keane, *The Will of the General, Irish Jurist*, 151 (1990–92); C. Campbell, *Emergency Law in Ireland 1918–25* (Oxford: Oxford University Press, 1994).

17. Although in this case a new and clever argument had been developed by Henry Hanna KC for the prisoners. Hanna argued the National Army had not been constituted under Article 8 of the Treaty between Britain and Ireland: the provisional government was entitled to legislate to raise an army, but no such legislation had been passed. The only other legal regime that claimed jurisdiction over Ireland was the Dáil, but the army constituted by the Dáil was still out in the field fighting against the provisional government. Therefore, the argument ran, the National Army had no legal standing.

18. See *The King (Johnstone v The Officer Commanding Adaravan House Barracks. Johnstone v O'Sullivan and Others* IR [1923] [Vol. II] 13.

19. J. Bowman (ed.), *Ireland: The Autobiography: Eyewitness Accounts of Irish Life Since 1916* (Dublin: Penguin 2016).

20. *Irish Times*, 25 November 1922.

21. BMH WS 1751, Davitt rewriting a line from *After the Battle* by Thomas Moore which recounted the night following the battle of Aughrim, in which two regiments of the defeated Irish declined to try and flee into the night and waited to be slaughtered when the sun rose. None were spared.

22. *Irish News*, 18 November 2002. Brought to my attention by M. O'Dwyer, *Seventy-Seven of Mine Said Ireland* (Cork: Deshaoirse, 2006).

23. His primary role in the Irish War of Independence was as a propagandist for the insurgents. He had also been a director of the Land Bank and a justice of the Dáil courts in south Dublin. He was elected a member of the Second Dáil. He was later secretary to the Irish delegation charged with negotiating a treaty with Britain. He argued against accepting the Treaty terms and would later repudiate the agreement and soon became involved with the anti-Treaty cause.

24. It is submitted there is little evidence for the proposition that Childers was coming up to Dublin for this reason. His role in the anti-Treaty

ranks had been that of a non-combatant although he was ready to take on a more active role and would probably have jumped at a chance of an air raid on Leinster House. There is nothing in his papers or that of his companion, David Robinson, which suggests he had Baldonnel in mind. See for instance, A. Boyle, *The Riddle of Erskine Childers* (London: Hutchinson, 1977). The probability is that he was coming up to assist de Valera with the setting up of a counter state. This analysis receives some support from E. O'Malley, *The Singing Flame* (Dublin: Anvil Books, 1978), p. 194.

25. It has been suggested that the decision to execute while an appeal was pending was made by the provisional government and it was 'almost certainly' the case that the attorney general advised that the execution could go ahead. G. Hogan, 'Hugh Kennedy, the Childers Habeas Corpus Application and the Return to the Four Courts' in C. Costello (ed.), *The Four Courts* (Dublin: The Incorporated Council of Law Reporting for Ireland, 1996), p. 198. There is no actual evidence that this was so. However, the attorney and the government stood in the relationship of client and lawyer and it is inconceivable that the attorney was not asked after the Master of the Rolls gave his judgment about what the options were. One view would have been that the National Army had won the Childers case and the case of the widow Johnstone and the judgments had been delivered by the two most senior judges in the country. Second, there was no longer any judicial 'stay' operating to prevent execution. Nor was there any undertaking not to execute in force. The contrary argument was that the provisional government had submitted to the jurisdiction of the court and should therefore have let the case run its course.

26. J.P. Duggan, 'Poltergeist Pistol', *History Ireland* 3 (1995).

27. J. Comyn, *Their Friends at Court* (London: Barry Rose, 1973), p. 75.

28. Griffith's dislike of Childers is well documented and appears to stem from his anti-Treaty stance which began during the Treaty negotiations in London and also during the Treaty debates in Dublin. Matters came to a head in early 1922, see *Dáil Debates*, 10 January 1922. The occasion was the inaugural address of the new President Griffith who may have been acutely conscious that the pro-Treaty faction was in danger of being seen as too cosy with the British administration. Faced with a difficult question from Childers he declined to answer and then said: 'I will not answer to any damned Englishman in this house.' Childers replied in measured terms that his entitlement to ask questions arose from the

fact that he was an elected TD. The debate dissolved into an unseemly squabble that was unworthy of Griffith. Childers sought re-election in the summer of 1922 but was resoundingly defeated. He returned to England and arrived back in Ireland soon after to take the anti-Treaty side. After Griffith died in August 1922, the anti-Childers sentiment in government grew. O'Higgins seems to have believed Childers enjoyed high rank in the anti-Treaty faction. This was probably on account of erroneous reports by the *Times* and the *Irish Times* also. O'Higgins singled him out for especially vitriolic abuse during the debates on the Army (Special Powers) Resolution.

29. A point well made in Tim Breen-Murphy's excellent study. See T. Breen-Murphy, *The Government's Executions Policy During the Irish Civil War 1922–23* (Maynooth: NUI, 2010). See also E. O'Malley, *The Men Will Talk to Me: Kerry Interviews* (Cork: Mercier Press, 2012) where Childers emerges as an isolated figure without responsibility. The same picture emerges in O'Malley's *West Cork Interviews* (Cork: Mercier Press, 2015) and see M. Hopkinson, *Green Against Green: The Irish Civil War* (Dublin: Gill & Macmillan, 2004), p. 132.

30. *General Regulations as to the Trial of Civilians by Military Courts*, 2 October 1922, regulation 21 & 22.

31. An example of this collaborative approach was the replacement of a three-man Army Council with the five-man Army Council in September 1922. Another example might be the Mountjoy executions where Mulcahy went to the cabinet to seek agreement for his proposal to execute prisoners by way of reprisal for the murder of Sean Hales. He took a similar approach to the decision to utilise suspended death sentences in Kerry. The initial decision to suspend death sentences was made by the Army Council, but Mulcahy put it before the Executive Council of the government and sought and obtained consent to this course of action. See minutes of the Executive Council, 12 December 1922.

32. It was later insinuated that the first four executions (Fisher, Gaffney, Twohig and Cassidy) had been carried out to provide the government with a more palatable context in which their main target, Childers, could be executed. The timing of events is against this: Childers was not captured until after the men had been tried by the special directive of the government. For those young men only one outcome was ever likely. It is not impossible, however, that political considerations dictated the order of executions.

33. The weapons and equipment which were the subject of the charges had

been found in the grounds of their spacious home. Some evidence has since emerged that their home was used by others who were actively anti-Treaty. See L. O'Duibhir, *Donegal and the Civil War* (Cork: Mercier Press, 2011). O'Duibhir suggests these prisoners were released as a result of the hearing before the Court of Appeal, but there is no doubt the prisoners lost their case. There is no record of Mrs Johnstone and her daughter undergoing trial and the probability is that after the judgment of the Court of Appeal, National Army lawyers reviewed the case against the two ladies and decided not to go to trial.

34. James Mallin, Joseph O'Toole, Henry Casey and Daniel Regan.

35. Michael Geraghty was acquitted of possessing a rifle. Patrick Keily from Clonmee in County Longford was sentenced to eighteen months imprisonment.

36. Hoolan was later replaced by Liam Fraher and he too resisted the execution policy.

37. *Mulcahy Papers,* P7/B/135. Dalton's letter cannot be traced in the *Mulcahy Papers* and it rather looks like it has been winnowed out. It is referred to in some detail in a memo to the JAG dated 2 December 1922 by a command legal officer.

38. A few senior officers discreetly turned a blind eye to the fact that prisoners were captured with arms. See P. McConway, 'Offaly and the Civil War Executions', *Offaly Heritage*, 5 (2008).

39. William Richard English Murphy, DSO, MC. Born in Wexford in 1890, died in 1975. Joined the army as an officer cadet in 1915. He was wounded at the battle of Loos and fought at the Somme and Delville Wood. He left the army in 1918 with the rank of lieutenant colonel. He returned to Ireland and became a school inspector in Derry. He was headhunted by Michael Collins to join the new National Army in 1922. He fought at Limerick and Kilmallock. He was appointed GOC in Kerry, a post he held until January 1923 when he was recalled to Dublin and given a training post before being appointed commissioner of the DMP. There is more than a suspicion that he was replaced in Kerry because he had failed to implement the execution policy. He was the commissioner of the DMP from the spring of 1923 until it merged with Garda Síochána. He was then deputy commissioner of the Gardaí until he retired in 1955.

40. T. Doyle, *The Civil War in Kerry* (Cork: Mercier Press, 2008), p. 206. Doyle recounts that a raid on the home of Pierce Godley at Ballyheigue took place on 20 October resulting in the arms find.

41. The Army Council now consisted of the C in C (Richard Mulcahy), chief

of staff (Sean Mac Mahon), the adjutant general (Gearóid O'Sullivan), director of intelligence (Diarmuid O'Hegarty) and one other.

CHAPTER 6

1. BMH WS 1751. Davitt was then JAG and advised the Army Council as to whether the convictions could be confirmed.
2. The family connection is asserted by the JAG. BMH WS 1751. In the trial record his name is shown as Mallon, but his address is given at Mount Brown in Dublin and the 1911 census shows that Michael Mallin had a son James who was aged 12 in 1916.
3. Michael Burke from Windgap. See E. Walsh, *Kilkenny: In Times of Revolution* (Dublin: Merrion Press, 2018), p. 245. Burke survived the war but died in 1934 owing to ill-treatment at Mountjoy during a hunger strike.
4. The trial register at the IMA has faded to such an extent that the term of years cannot be discerned.
5. Michael Hearty and Gerald Mulhern were tried for using force against the National Army and possession of a revolver. In respect of these prisoners, the court did not convict but made an order under Reg 26 – a recommendation for two years' hard labour. The regulations permitted a recommendation for detention, but the recommendation for hard labour was ultra vires. See 20LG-1C35-22 Kilmainham Gaol Museum. John McGuill from Dundalk was convicted of the possession of a pistol and sentenced to seven years' penal servitude. Patrick Clark from Knockbride was convicted of the possession of a revolver and sentenced to six years' imprisonment.
6. Two prisoners from Shankill village in Dublin were dealt with for attacking National Army forces and possessing arms. One, Andrew O'Rourke was given six years and the other, James Farrell, five years. Arthur Waters (22) from Loughlinstown, County Dublin was convicted of using force against National Army forces and possession of arms and a bomb. He was sentenced to six years' penal servitude. John Richmond from Carrickmines was convicted of the possession of a rifle and a bomb and attacking National Army forces. He was sentenced to six years' penal servitude.
7. *Dáil Debates*, 30 November 1922.
8. *O'Malley Papers*, UCDA.
9. Operation Order, No. 11: Enemy Murder Bill. Dated 30 November 1922. *O'Malley Papers*, UCDA.

CHAPTER 7

1. For an analysis of the personalities and tensions, see J.M. Regan, *The Irish Counter Revolution 1921–36* (Dublin: Gill & Macmillan, 1999), p. 85 et seq.

2. Related by Sean Caffrey, believed to have been an intelligence officer for the anti-Treaty forces at that time. Caffrey maintained that there was no specific order issued which gave rise to this killing, just the general 'shoot at sight' order issued by Lynch.

3. A great deal of print was later devoted to the question of whether Mellows was reconciled with the church before execution. According to Canon Pigott, he made his peace with the church minutes before his death and received Viaticum. J. Pigott (Canon), 'Executions Recalled', *Athenry Journal*, 8 (1997).

4. The account relied on here was written by Father Pigott, who attended the prisoners at their execution. See J. Pigott (Canon), 'Executions Recalled', *The Athenry Journal*, 8 (1997).

5. From an account by Sean MacBride. See U. MacEoin, *Survivors* (Dublin: Argenta, 1980).

6. *Constitution of the Irish Free State (Saorstat Eireann) Act 1922*, Article 70.

7. S. Darcy, 'The Evolution of the Law of Belligerent Reprisals Military Law Review', *Military Law Review*, 175, (March 2003) 184. Under the embryonic international law that then existed, the principle of belligerent reprisals had no application to internal conflicts. This branch of international law has been in development. It is submitted by way of example that the American bombing of Syria in 2017 to deter the Syrian government from using chemical attacks on civilians has been recognised as a proper development of this doctrine.

8. P. Murray, *Oracles of God* (Dublin: University College Dublin Press, 2000), p. 87.

9. N. O'Gadhra, *The Civil War in Connaught* (Cork: Mercier Press, 1999).

10. An examination of the Dáil reports shows that Hales had not voted for the Army (Special Powers) Resolution. His companion, Ó Máille, the deputy speaker, had voted for the resolution.

CHAPTER 8

1. This letter is referred to in BMH WS 1751, Davitt. The original cannot now be traced.

2. Proclamation, 7 December 1922. Irish National Archive, DOD/A/07266.
3. It has been suggested by one commentator that the Committee system was ancillary to the military courts system. See P. Yeates, *A City in Civil War: Dublin 1921–24* (Dublin: Gill & Macmillan, 2015), p. 258. In fact, most trials after mid-December took place under the committee system. The trial system had simply been degraded. This was the view expressed by C. Campbell, *Emergency Law in Ireland 1918–25* (Oxford: Oxford University Press, 1994).
4. The trial of Tom Maguire was brought to my attention by D. Price, *The Flame and the Candle* (Cork: Collins Press), p. 232.

CHAPTER 9

1. Stephen White, Kildare (labourer), aged 18. Jack Johnston, Kildare (labourer), aged 18. Patrick Mangan, Kildare (railway worker), aged 22. Patrick Nolan, Kildare (railway worker), aged 34. Bryan Moore (labourer), aged 28. James O'Connor, Bansha Tipperary (railway worker), aged 24. Patrick Bagnall, Kildare (railway worker), aged 19. Patrick Moore, Thomas Behan and James White.
2. BMH WS 1571, J. Dunne, p. 20.
3. J. Durney, 'The Curragh Internees 1921–24. From Defiance to Defeat.' Kildarearchsoc.ie 2015/11.
4. *Leinster Leader*, 23 December 1922.
5. See for instance, M. O'Dwyer, *Seventy-Seven of Mine Said Ireland* (Cork: Deshaoirse, 2006).
6. The National Army press release describes the men as part of 'a column of ten which operated against railways, goods trains and shops…'
7. See for instance, E. O'Malley, *The Men Will Talk to Me: West Cork Interviews* (Cork: Mercier Press, 2015), p. 159.
8. *Freeman's Journal*, 20 December 1922 and also *Irish Times*, 23 December 1922.
9. Annie Moore spent twelve months in custody and was released after an eighteen-day hunger strike. Annie and her mother later made a dependant's pension claim in respect of Bryan Moore. Annie, who was hardly unbiased, related that the raiding party were 'an unruly mob'. They were in occupation for two days and 'ate and drank everything in the house' which they wrecked and stole everything they could carry away. With the bread winners in custody Mrs Moore and her 77-year-old husband sold off two acres to pay the bills. The old man died soon

after and his widow struggled on until a pension award was made in 1934. BMH Pension Records DP7504.

CHAPTER 10

1. BMH WS 1571, J. Dunne, p. 17.
2. James Dunne was intimately concerned in the planning for this raid. See BMH WS 1571. He does not suggest that Childers was involved. It is submitted there is no reliable evidence for the proposition that Childers was coming up to Dublin for the Baldonnel raid. His role in the anti-Treaty ranks had been entirely non-combatant although he was ready to take on a more active role. There is nothing in his papers or that of his companion, David Robinson, which suggest he had Baldonnel in mind. See for instance, A. Boyle, *The Riddle of Erskine Childers* (London: Hutchinson, 1977).
3. A. Pinkman, *In the Legion of the Vanguard* (Cork: Mercier Press, 1998), pp. 94–5.
4. The men were Patrick Mullaney from Mayo. From Dublin: Charles Kelly, William Wyse, Francis Brennan and Bertie Hawney. From Celbridge in Kildare: Thomas Cardwell, James Dempsey, John O'Connor. From Maynooth: Tim Tyrell. From Leixlip: Michael O'Neill, Patrick Nolan and John Gaynor. From Drogheda: Thomas McCann. From Glasgow: James Kelly. From Cavan: Thomas O'Brien. Also, John Curley. (The names of these sixteen are set out in the trial register at IMA. Charlie O'Connor from Celbridge was too badly wounded to be tried.)
5. BMH WS 1751, Davitt, p. 60.
6. *The General Regulations as to the Trial of Civilians by Military Courts* required the court to have regard as far as practicable to *The General Regulations as to Discipline* which governed the trial of National Army soldiers. Regulations 53 & 54 of those regulations stipulated that it was for the accused to enter his plea personally. This was regarded a significant protection for the accused.
7. This assessment might have been generous to Swayne who was not a subtle advocate but had some experience of fighting lost causes. The year before under British rule, he had been counsel for five prisoners captured in arms. They had been caught by a lorry load of Auxiliaries laying an ambush at Drumcondra bridge. Outnumbered and out-gunned they had run. One had been shot and mortally wounded and the Auxiliary unit had followed the others into a cul-de-sac where they

surrendered their arms. Swayne appeared for the prisoners and did all he could to derail the trial by taking legal points. In that case, four of the five prisoners were hanged for levying war against the King. History was about to repeat itself for Swayne. The Leixlip prisoners had no defence, but he did what any experienced counsel would try to do: throw a legal spanner in the works.

8. IMA DOD/2/68520. Letter JAG to C in C, February 1923.

CHAPTER 11

1. *Mulcahy Papers*, P7/B/72 (6–7).
2. *Irish Times*, 23 December 1922.
3. E. O'Malley, *The Singing Flame* (Dublin: Anvil Books, 1978), p. 297.
4. Murphy was from Bennettsbridge. Phelan was from Thomastown in Kilkenny.
5. Letter JAG to C in C, 1 February 1923. DOD/2/68520.
6. BMH WS 1751, Davitt.
7. Mooney resigned at the end of January 1923 and his resignation was accepted. A few weeks later, he wrote to General Mulcahy asking to be reinstated and listing his complaints. He was not taken back on.
8. Carrrick on Suir, Callan and Mullinavat were captured and a significant number of National Army soldiers deserted and went over to the anti-Treaty side.
9. BMH WS 939, Blythe.
10. E. Walsh, *Kilkenny: In Times of Revolution* (Dublin: Merrion Press, 2018), p. 222, citing M. Hopkinson, *Green Against Green: The Irish Civil War* (Dublin: Gill & Macmillan, 2004). It does not actually seem as though that point was ever made in *Green Against Green*. General John Prout emerges as a steady and thoughtful officer. His family had emigrated from Tipperary to America when he was young and he became a career soldier in the US Army serving in the 69th regiment which was largely Irish. He fought in France in 1917–18 and came back to Ireland and fought in the War of Independence and later joined the National Army. He was not a brilliant commander, but he had some significant successes in the summer offensive in 1922 and in the closing stages of the war his men were responsible for shooting Dinny Lacey and the break up and capture of his column. His men also tracked down and shot Liam

Lynch in April, an event that brought about the end of the war. It is noticeable that there were only a few instances of killing prisoners or cases of excessive force in his command area during the war. Exceptions include John Edwards who was shot dead in Waterford gaol by an overly zealous sentry and John Walsh from Kilmacthomas who was also shot in gaol in circumstances which were disquieting. A review of the war in Kilkenny and Waterford does not suggest in any way that Prout was an ambitious officer without scruples.

11. The decision to execute prisoners convicted by military court lay with the five-man Army Council in Dublin. This was the effect of *The General Regulations as to the Trial of Civilians by Military Courts*. All the available evidence suggests that the Army Council reserved the decision to execute to itself.

12. January 1, 1923. Contemporary press reports.

13. E. O'Malley, *The Singing Flame* (Dublin: Anvil Books, 1978). O'Malley's observation related to Dublin in particular. There is not a great deal of contemporary evidence about the attitude of non-combatants during the civil war. Although a significant strand of evidence relates to inquest juries. These showed no sympathy for the anti-Treaty cause. What evidence there is suggests that in most counties the public were weary of the fighting.

14. See BMH WS 1751, Davitt, p. 63 et seq. Other arson attacks on the prominent pro-Treaty supporters included an attack on business premises belonging to J.J. Walsh and Denis McCullough and the homes of many of the old ascendency.

15. *Irish Times*, 1 March 1923. Report of Sir William Goulding, the chairman of the Great Southern and Western Railway Company.

16. Contemporary press reports. The men were John Talty from Lisdeen, County Clare and Henry McLoughnan from Buncrana, County Donegal.

17. U. MacEoin, *Survivors* (Dublin: Argenta, 1980), p. 378, quoting Susan Casey, wife of Con Casey, one of the men under sentence of death.

CHAPTER 12

1. *Mulcahy Papers*, P7/B. O'Higgins wrote: 'It is probable that when half a dozen judiciously selected cases have been dealt with in each county, there will be very little trouble with the remainder.'

2. *Mulcahy Papers*, P7/B/245, O'Higgins to Mulcahy. It has not been possible to trace minutes of the planning meeting.

3. The trial record at the Irish Military Archives shows Mullaney's sentence of seven years' penal servitude for an armed attack on national forces and possession of arms taking effect as 28 April 1923. The entries for the other men are recorded in identical form. IE/MA/CW/P/02/02/23. The significance of the date 28 April is that the prisoners were under sentence of death until that point and were, like many others, hostages to secure the good conduct of others until the war was won.

4. When the split came about half of the Carlow Volunteers remained neutral and the rest divided evenly between pro-Treaty and anti-Treaty. The military barracks at Carlow remained in the hands of what became the National Army and most of the anti-Treaty men were rounded up in the summer of 1922. A small number of men led by former Volunteers Tom O'Connell and Larry O'Neill evaded capture and kept fighting. Although the terrain favoured guerrilla fighting, these men faced other difficulties: the proximity of National Army barracks at Carlow and the fact that most of the local population favoured the government side. Finding safe houses was increasingly hard (see BMH WS 1572, Kane). The column led by O'Neill and O'Connell scored no big victories, but they surprised and disarmed national soldiers, destroyed bridges and railway engines.

   In October 1922, anti-Treaty fighters carried out an ambush on the Baltinglass road at Graney Cross by the river. A lorry containing eight National Army men had gone out to Castledermot. The passage of the lorry had been noted and about twenty anti-Treaty fighters gathered at Graney Cross to ambush the lorry on the return journey. Below the ruins of the castle where the road bends as it comes to the bridge, they waited until the lorry approached the Cross and fire was opened from a cottage wounding the driver. The lorry spun off the road and into a ditch where it came to rest on its side. A few grenades were thrown and the ambush was over. The anti-Treaty men left loaded down with captured weapons.

   They left behind three dead National Army men: James Murphy from Baltinglass, Patrick Allison from Carlow and Edward Byrne from Hacketstown. The driver of the lorry was 18-year-old James Hunt from Ballyconnell who was grievously wounded. Although his commanding officer got him to hospital, he died a few days later. A number of other National Army men were wounded.

A few weeks later, James Lillis and Richard Coburn turned up at Knocksguire, a remote hamlet that was close enough to walk to Muine Bheag, where they could see their families. On 14 November they were captured there. Lillis and Coburn were sent up to Kilmainham, where they were put on a line-up of the survivors of the ambush. Lillis was tried for taking part in the ambush at Graney and possessing a rifle and was convicted on both charges. Coburn got ten years for possessing a rifle.

The trial register suggests there were a significant number of trials by military court in Carlow in early December which appear to arise from a big push by the National Army. Michael Carr from Tullow and Edward Keegan from Rathvilly were each tried for possession of a rifle. The court made no determination and recommended imprisonment for one year under Regulation 26. John Delaney from Fighting Cocks was given five years' penal servitude for possession of a rifle. John McDonald from Tinduff, Joseph Mara from Grangefort and Dennis Nolan from Connaberry were each sentenced to five years' penal servitude for possession of a rifle. James Lillis from Killincarrick (not to be confused with James Lillis from Muine Bheag) was convicted of possessing two rifles and was sentenced to ten years' penal servitude. Michael Keating from New Ross, Wexford was tried and convicted of possessing a rifle and was sentenced to five years' penal servitude. Christopher Lamon from Blackparks, Athy in Kildare was tried and convicted of taking part in a raid and possession of a gun. He was sentenced to five years' penal servitude.

There were no more executions in Carlow and the death of James Lillis effectively marked the end of the civil war in that county.

5. Last letter home to his sister Teresa. I express my thanks to Ellen D. Murphy for making available Patrick Hennessy's last letters.

6. Vincent McMahon was 23; the younger of the two brothers. It is not possible to discern a reason why he was not tried and the only inference is that it was not considered expedient to execute two men from the same family. That seems to have been the rule of thumb used by the Army Council.

7. Patrick McNamara. The Trial Record suggests his home was Killary, Derrycastle, Nenagh. The probability is that he was from Killary, Ballina.

8. *Irish Times*, 3 March 1923.

9. Michael Walsh from Derrymore, Hubert Collins from Headford and Martin Burke and Stephen Joyce both from Caherlistrane.

10. Thomas Hughes from Bogginfin, Athlone.

11. *Dáil Debates*, Vol. 2, No. 22, 30 January 1923.

12. The anti-Treaty campaign against the railway network would reach its zenith in the third week of January 1923 in the Liscahane train disaster. A party of anti-Treaty fighters laid plans to intercept a troop train. They kidnapped the linesman who was watching the junction and tore up the sleepers on a culvert. By mischance the troop train was delayed and a goods train came in its place. The ambushers led by Tom O'Driscoll from Kilmoyley tried to warn the engine driver by firing shots, but the train driver, perhaps fearing a hijack, pressed on and the train travelling at about 30 miles an hour, slid off the track and down the embankment. The guard who was at the back of the train was unhurt and going forward found the fireman Daniel Crowley badly scalded and mortally injured. He was the sole breadwinner for his mother, widowed sister and her five children. Perhaps realising that his injuries were fatal, he called to the guard to rescue the driver: 'Save Paddy.' The guard then went forward and found the engine driver Paddy Ó Ríordán crushed under his engine; only his legs were visible. Ó Ríordán left a widow and five children. The engine was wrecked and with it twenty-eight wagons were scattered around the embankment. *Irish Times*, 20 January 1923. For a full account of the war on the railways see B. Share, *In Time of Civil War – The Conflict on the Irish Railways 1922–23* (Cork: The Collins Press, 2006).

13. O'Daly to Mulcahy, 19 January 1923. IMA Ops Kerry 16/10.

14. *Irish Times*, 2 January 1923.

15. It has not been possible to trace a record of any request by O'Daly to execute Hanlon or any order authorising this step. That does not necessarily mean the formalities were not complied with.

16. From an account by Bill Bailey a Free State soldier based at Ballymullen. E. O'Malley, *The Men Will Talk to Me: Kerry Interviews* (Cork: Mercier Press, 2012), p. 106.

17. Fitzgerald was from South Main Street, Youghal. O'Reilly was from the Coastguard Station in Youghal.

18. This theory was expounded by Pax Whelan amongst others. It should be added that it suited the anti-Treaty faction to portray the government of the Irish Free State as being in the pocket of the British government and it may be that is why this story was promoted. It may also have diverted attention from an unpalatable truth: that men like Pax Whelan bore a heavy responsibility for leading others into civil war.

19. Sentence of death was passed on two other Waterford prisoners tried for arms offences. Patrick Murphy from Windgap near Carrick on Suir had his death sentence commuted. Patrick Cuddihy from Tramore was tried and in his case the file reads 'Proceedings not returned by confirming authority', which simply means lost. This prisoner's name is recorded in the trial register as Patrick Cuddihy although he is also named as Peter Cuddihy in P. McCarthy, *The Irish Revolution 1912–23 Waterford* (Dublin: Four Courts, 2015), p. 115.

20. O'Malley Notebooks UCDA P17b/104. Drawn to my attention by Philip McConway, 'Offaly and the Civil War Executions', *Offaly Heritage*, 5 (2008).

21. BMH Pension File 3916.

22. This contention has been persuasively argued by Philip McConway, 'Offaly and the Civil War Executions', *Offaly Heritage*, 5 (2008).

23. E. Gaynor, *Memoirs of a Tipperary Family – The Gaynors of Tyone* (Geography Publications, 2003), p. 206.

24. The voting was 41–13 against the motion that Dáil Éireann disapproves of the General Order of the Army Council dated 8 January 1923. As far as can be ascertained, no prisoners were convicted of offences created by the stand clear order.

25. Proclamation published on 2 February 1923.

26. Internal National Army order signed by Mulcahy and dated 27 January 1923, Irish Military Archives.

27. Operation Order, No. 16: Senators. Dated 26 January 1923.

28. Cicero, *De Legibus*, III. 8.

29. Major General Dan Hogan from Tipperary. His brother was Michael Hogan after whom the Hogan Stand at Croke Park was named to remember the events of Bloody Sunday in 1920. Dan Hogan was typical of many senior Free State Army officers. The son of a farmer he went to work as a railway clerk. A career in lower middle management seemed likely until the War of Independence when he proved to be an inspirational leader in Monaghan. After the split, he sided with the provisional government. In 1923, he was just 28, a big, athletic and charismatic man. Some years after the civil war, he became chief of staff of the Free State Army. He was forced to resign after punching Desmond Fitzgerald, the minister of defence in an argument over the pay of army officers. Most army officers thought Fitzgerald got what he deserved and the army lost an able chief of staff. He emigrated to America and some years afterwards walked out of the family home and disappeared without trace.

30. According to one memoir, groups of four prisoners from each county

were drafted into Mountjoy to provide sufficient numbers for executions if more TDs were shot or some other emergency arose. See BMH WS 938, Daniel Mulvihill.

31. BMH WS 939, Blythe.

32. Senator Eamonn Mansfield resigned immediately after the Hales shooting and Sir Horace Plunkett stayed on until his family home was burned out.

33. *Mulcahy Papers*, P7/B/177.

34. *Mulcahy Papers*, P7/B/101/19, 1 February 1923.

CHAPTER 13

1. L. Deasy, *Brother against Brother* (Cork: Mercier Press, 1998), p. 110.

2. Ernie O'Malley wrote: 'I told him what I thought of his conduct.' E. O'Malley, *The Singing Flame* (Dublin: Anvil Books, 1978), p. 229. O'Malley and Lynch seemed to regard Deasy's conduct as an act of indiscipline.

3. E. O'Malley, *The Men Will Talk to Me: West Cork Interviews* (Cork: Mercier Press, 2015), p. 197.

4. See by way of example, the *Cork Examiner*, 13 October 1922 for the surrender notes of Patrick Barry and Andrew Ahern from Cork.

5. E. O'Malley, *The Singing Flame* (Dublin: Anvil Books, 1978), p. 224.

6. *Mulcahy Papers*, Army Council Minutes, 14 February 1923.

7. *Mulcahy Papers*, P7/B/284.

8. J. Dorney, *The Civil War in Dublin* (Dublin: Merrion Press, 2017), p. 253.

9. The memo was written by O'Higgins. *Mulcahy Papers*, P7/B/101/19, 1 February 1923. It is uncertain if Mulcahy really envisaged putting this proposal into effect or whether he hoped that the Army Council would not support it, thereby isolating O'Higgins.

10. Army Council Decisions, 12 February 1923, *Mulcahy Papers*, P7/B/178.

11. Memo No. 10: Enemy Peace Moves, dated 10 February 1923, *O'Donoghue Papers*.

12. General Order, No. 17, 8 March 1923, *Mulcahy Papers*, UCDA.

13. General Order, No. 16, 19 February 1923, UCDA.

14. Constitution of Saorstat Éireann 1922, Article 70.

15. 'No military tribunals are exercising jurisdiction over the civil population in any area in which all the civil courts are open or capable of being held in respect of charges which may suitably be tried by them.' Statement to the Dáil in answer to a question by Gavan Duffy, February 1923.

16. A full list is set out in the Irish Military Archives and makes remarkable reading. IMA IE/MA/CW/P. Athlone, Beggars Bush, Hare Park, the Curragh, Carlow, Athy, Carrick on Shannon, Cork, Dundalk, Gormanstown, Kilmainham, Kilkenny, Limerick, Maryborough, Mountjoy, Mullingar, Naas, Navan, Newbridge, North Dublin Union, Portobello, Sligo, Tipperary, Thurles, Templemore, Trim, Tralee, Wellington, Waterford and Westport.

17. Martin Byrne from Fallowbeg, Luggacurren, Queen's County. The eldest son of widow Bridget Byrne (farmer). The established view is that no one was charged with this murder. See J.P. McCarthy, *Kevin O'Higgins: Builder of the Irish State* (Dublin: Irish Academic Press, 2006), p. 97. The records at the IMA suggest otherwise. See the list of prisoners tried and also BMH WS 1751, C. Davitt for an account of the proceedings.

18. Proclamation, 20 January 1923. Published in the *Dublin Gazette*, 2 February 1923. Also on 27 January, detailed orders were issued by General Mulcahy for the conduct of army committees.

19. Theodore C. Kingsmill-Moore, 1893–1979. Irish High Court 1947–51 and of the Supreme Court 1951–66. He was for a time a member of Seanad Éireann. He was an accomplished author on fly fishing – *A Man May Fish*.

20. BMH WS 1751, Davitt, p. 69.

21. BMH WS 1751, Davitt, p. 70.

22. Bogtown Lane, Cloneygowan which was then in King's County now Offaly. He was 25 years old, the eldest son of Michael and Anne.

23. *Cork Examiner*, 27 February 1923.

24. Last letter home by the prisoner.

CHAPTER 14

1. For an account by a National Army officer who was stationed in Kerry at the time, see N. Harrington, *Kerry Landing* (Dublin: Anvil Books, 1992). For a later assessment, see T. Doyle, *The Civil War in Kerry* (Cork: Mercier Press, 2008), p. 279. Also from an account by a National Army soldier based at the barracks: Bill Bailey in E. O'Malley, *The Men Will Talk to Me: Kerry Interviews* (Cork: Mercier Press, 2012), p. 102. See also T.R. Dwyer, *Tans Terror and Troubles* (Cork: Mercier Press, 2001), p. 369. National Army reports can be found in IMA. The Harrington Papers can be found at NLI.

2. Captain Michael Dunne from Malahide. Edward Stapleton from

Lower Gloucester Street, Dublin. Lieutenant Patrick O'Connor from Castleisland. Privates Michael Gallivan from Killarney and Laurence O'Connor from Causeway in Kerry. Private Joseph O'Byrne from North Wall, Dublin was grievously wounded and lost his legs.

3. Reference to this incident comes in a captured anti-Treaty despatch dated 10 March 1923. It contains the very first written report on what took place at Ballyseedy and Countess Bridge. It also asserts that four prisoners were removed from barracks to clear an obstruction on the Castleisland to Scartaglin road on the same night as the Ballyseedy affair. The account about Ballyseedy and Countess Bridge has since been substantiated and in the circumstances there is no reason to doubt the rest of the account.

4. N. Harrington, *Kerry Landing* (Dublin: Anvil Books, 1992), p. 148.

5. The time of the Countess Bridge is not apparent from a reading of internal army reports. However, in his account to the Dáil, General Mulcahy fixed the time of the approach to Countess Bridge as approximately 3 a.m. *Dáil Debates*, 17 April 1923, column 134.

6. The dead were John Daly, George O'Shea, Tim Twomey, Patrick Hartnett, James Walsh, Patrick Buckley, John O'Connor and Michael O'Connell.

7. D. Macardle, *Tragedies of Kerry* (Dublin: Irish Freedom Press, 2004).

8. IMA CW/OPS/08/03, Box No. 023.

9. The despatch was dated 10 March and written by Humphrey Murphy leader of the anti-Treaty fighters in Kerry. According to this despatch the prisoner who was 'practically demented' was Coffey who had escaped the Countess Bridge massacre. In his despatches to GHQ General O'Daly appears to have thought it related to the prisoner who had escaped from the Ballyseedy massacre.

10. The dead at Countess Bridge were Jeremiah Donoghue, Stephen Buckley, Tim Murphy and Daniel Donoghue. Tadhg Coffey survived.

11. A partial account of the inquiry can be found in the National Archive, Department of Justice, File H 197/52. The dead men were all from Waterville. Eugene Dwyer, William Riordan, Daniel Shea, John Sugrue and Michael Courtney. The officer in charge of the National Army soldiers was Commandant J. J. Delaney. His second in command is recorded as Lieutenant P. Kavanagh. For the lead to the Justice Ministry file, I acknowledge the research of Deaglán de Bréadún, *Irish Times*, December 31 2008. The earliest written accounts of the Bahaghs massacre comes from D. Macardle, *Tragedies of Kerry* (Dublin: Irish Freedom Press, 2004). Macardle was a partisan historian, but her factual research

has proved reliable. Macardle records that three of the five bodies were unrecognisable and all of the dead had suffered non-fatal bullet wounds. This latter point cannot now be verified in the absence of an inquest.

12. The Cahersiveen massacre spawned a widespread belief that these young men had been done to death by the 'Visiting Committee' of the National Army. Such evidence as there is points to a small circle of officers in the Dublin Guard including O'Daly. See in particular, N. Harrington, *Kerry Landing* (Dublin: Anvil Books, 1992).

13. The Army Council Minutes for 13 March contain a fleeting reference to the 'Daly letter' with no detail as to what was discussed or decided. The minutes for the following day refer to a complaint regarding the 'treatment of Kerry prisoners' which was referred to the GOC in Kerry (O'Daly) for a response.

14. Notice of execution, *Cork Examiner*, 16 March 1923.

15. IMA IE/MA/HS/A0770. The two other men captured were Murt Walsh and William Parle, the younger of the two Parle brothers. It is not clear why these two men were not executed save that when faced with two brothers convicted of a capital offence, General Mulcahy always refrained from executing both.

16. James O'Rourke was then aged 19. He was from Dublin. Pension records show he had worked as a sales clerk.

17. John Dorney relates that they held junior officer rank in the anti-Treaty faction. They stated that they had been pressured into continuing the fight by senior officers who had made dire threats. They were willing to repudiate the actions of their leaders publicly. J. Dorney, *The Civil War in Dublin.* (Dublin: Merrion, 2017), p. 244, citing IMA CW/P/02/02/02.

18. In the 1930s the families of the dead men were refused a pension by the Pension Board in respect of their executions. Both families received pensions for pre-Truce service and there is some evidence that both were involved on the anti-Treaty side in the early stages of the civil war. The ground of refusal was that they had not been on active service at the time of capture; the implication being that this raid was not authorised.

19. This analysis is supported by the fact that the witness statements that would form the case against them were taken on 30 December 1922. See Abstract of Evidence against Daniel Enright. 20LG IB43-13. Courtesy of Kilmainham Gaol Museum.

20. T. Horgan, *Dying for the Cause* (Cork: Mercier Press, 2015), p. 411.

21. IMA CW/OPS/06/12, Box No. 018.

22. L. O'Duibhir, *Donegal and the Civil War* (Cork: Mercier Press, 2011), p. 225.

23. K. Griffith and T. O'Grady, *Curious Journey* (London: Hutchinson, 1982), p. 305. Other works have cited *Curious Journey* for the proposition that Sweeney was present, conducted the executions and personally administered the coup de grace to his old friend Daly. See T. Doyle, *The Civil War in Kerry* (Cork: Mercier Press, 2008), p. 280. Sweeney's account quoted in *Curious Journey* does not say that he administered the coup de grace or even that he was present.

24. The remaining prisoners of this group – James Donaghy, James Lane, Frank Ward and Dan Coyle – did sign a letter which was published in the press in which surrender was not mentioned, but they repeated the sentiments expressed by Deasy in his letter calling for an end to the war. They also railed against the policy of keeping prisoners hostage to ensure the good conduct of others: 'We think it not fair to us to hold us responsible for the actions of those we disclaim.' See *Cork Examiner* and *Irish Times*, 24 March 1923.

25. *Mulcahy Papers*, P7/B/101. Cosgrave to Mulcahy, 25 January 1923.

26. J. Dorney, *The Civil War in Dublin* (Dublin, Merrion Press, 2017), p. 245. John Dorney argues that the executions were resumed at the insistence of O'Higgins because of the Kerry Mine massacres. This he presents as undisputed fact: 'As a remedy, he insisted that the official executions, suspended since February 1923, be resumed so that troops would not resort to unofficial reprisals.' There is no record of such a conversation taking place.

27. BMH 939, Blythe, p. 178. There are no other contemporaneous sources. The Executive Council minutes of this period are too brief to provide any detailed information and there is a dearth of other evidence. O'Higgins did not survive long after the civil war to tell his story and Mulcahy kept his silence. Cosgrave and Blythe made statements to the BMH but neither touch on this issue in any way.

28. Tension between Mulcahy and the cabinet had been evident for many months. A particular bone of contention for the cabinet was Mulcahy's failure to keep the cabinet informed of the progress of the war. As early as the previous autumn, Mulcahy was rebuked by the cabinet for failing to attend Executive Council meetings. P7/B/245/152: 'It is the wish of the cabinet that you be in attendance at all cabinet meetings in future.' On other occasions he was rebuked for failing to provide weekly reports on the progress of the war. See *Mulcahy Papers*, P7/B/245/70.

29. P. Murray, *Oracles of God* (Dublin: University College Dublin Press, 2000), p. 86.
30. For the deaths in custody in Kerry, I acknowledge the research of Dr Tim Horgan.
31. Minutes of the Executive Council suggest the resignations were seen and rejected on 9 April. *Mulcahy Papers*, P7/B/247. Other sources suggest that these events were resolved at the end of March and the beginning of April.

CHAPTER 15

1. *Cork Examiner*, 30 March 1923.
2. For an account of the disintegration of the anti-Treaty forces, see F. O'Donoghue, *No Other Law* (Dublin: Irish Press Limited, 1954), p. 289 et seq.
3. Brought to my attention by E. Walsh, *Kilkenny: In Times of Revolution* (Dublin: Merrion Press, 2018), p. 185.
4. See Chapter 9, The Rathbride Prisoners.
5. MacEoin, *Survivors* (Dublin: Argenta, 1980), p. 454. As a matter of detail, Heavey made his escape towards the end of 1923.
6. In *Men of the South*, Riordan is shown in the back row on the far right of three men holding a rifle. A version of this picture can be seen at the Crawford Gallery in Cork.
7. Denis Galvin died in a training accident only a few weeks later.
8. See for instance, E. O'Malley, *The Singing Flame* (Dublin: Anvil Books, 1978), p. 217. See also E. O'Malley, *The Men Will Talk to Me: Kerry Interviews* (Cork: Mercier Press, 2012), p. 53. An example is given of a 'no charge' prisoner impersonating a man who had been marked down for execution by the National Army. The impersonator later received news from the gaolers that a baby had been born to the wife of the man he was impersonating and this gave rise to a dilemma. The mother wanted to know what name the baby should be given.
9. E. O'Malley, *The Singing Flame* (Dublin: Anvil Books, 1978).
10. N. O'Gadhra, *The Civil War in Connaught* (Cork: Mercier Press, 1999), p. 80.
11. *R (O'Sullivan) v Military Governor of Hare Park Internment Camp*, ILT 1924 63. The prisoner was represented by Michael Comyn, KC and Gavan Duffy. It cannot now be known for certain if this was a genuine

mix up or if the prisoner had colluded in an identity swap to free another man at risk of execution. In any event, this Jeremiah O'Sullivan was not released until late March 1924.

12. Not much more is known about Darcy. He was from Cooraclare. His brother Michael fought in the War of Independence. In a shoot-out with the British Army in 1920, he was shot and fell into the river and drowned. Another brother, Patrick, was a national school teacher in Doonbeg. He was shot as a spy by the IRA. It was suggested that he had passed the whereabouts of wanted men to the RIC. See for instance, BMH WS 1226, M. Russell.

13. On 6 April William O'Connor and George Nagle were killed after capture. See T. Horgan, *Dying for the Cause* (Dublin: Mercier Press, 2015), p. 333. Also on 29 May Jeremiah O'Leary was killed in custody. He was taken prisoner after the end of hostilities and removed to National Army headquarters at Harnett's Hotel in Castleisland and held overnight. In the morning, he was taken to the yard and told to shut the gate. As he did so he was shot down by three officers of the Dublin Guard – Lieutenant Patrick McGinn, Captain Michael Nolan and Patrick Byrne. See T. Horgan, *Dying for the Cause* (Dublin: Mercier Press, 2015), p. 219. Also T. Doyle, *The Civil War in Kerry* (Cork: Mercier Press, 2008).

14. The inquest jury censored the National Army and noted that Lieutenant Larkin had been under the influence of drink when he fired the fatal shot and recommended the state pay compensation to the widow and her four children. See *Cork Examiner*, 7 April 1923.

15. See *Cork Examiner*, 7 April. The inquest into the death of Thomas Conway on 23 February at the Workhouse in Tralee. The official National Army report recorded that Conway had been killed trying to escape. General O'Daly came forward and told the jury that this was now found to be incorrect. He had been killed by Captain James Byrne without any good cause. The jury found Byrne had been unhinged and unfit to carry a firearm for some time and found wilful murder. O'Daly gave evidence that an internal army inquiry had found that Byrne had killed this prisoner and gave a character reference for Byrne who was described as suffering from something like what we now know as PTS disorder.

16. *Irish Times*, 27 January 1923.

17. See N. Harrington, *Kerry Landing* (Dublin: Anvil Books, 1992). Lieutenant Niall Harrington was a junior officer who had been part of

the seaborne invasion of Kerry the previous summer. He had been an ardent admirer of O'Daly at the start of the Kerry campaign.

18. This incident occurred the same day that the bodies of two National Army officers were found and the prisoner was probably being questioned in that regard when he was killed. See Breen, BMH WS 1763, p. 180. The dead National Army officers were Lieutenants James Kennedy and George Cruise. They had been missing for months and it has been said that they had been unarmed when kidnapped and later murdered by the anti-Treaty faction.

19. Inquest report *Cork Examiner*, 12 April 1923. Martin Moloney was fatally wounded after capture. He pointed out and named the man who shot him as Collins who was present. Collins did not dispute that the prisoner had been shot in custody, but he accused another soldier (Foody) of shooting the unfortunate man. Foody denied firing the shot.

20. *Irish Times*, 28 March 1923. Brought to my attention by J. Dorney, *The Civil War in Dublin* (Dublin: Merrion Press, 2017).

21. *Irish Times*, 10 April 1923.

22. *Dáil Debates*, 27 March 1923. The question was asked by Thomas Johnson the leader of the Labour Party.

23. M. Valiulis, *Portrait of a Revolutionary: General Richard Mulcahy* (Dublin: Irish Academic Press, 1992), p. 190.

24. A transcript of the Ballyseedy inquiry and the Cahersiveen inquiry survive. It has not been possible to trace a record of the Countess Bridge inquiry.

25. The survivor of the Countess Bridge affair was Tadhg Coffey who later described being marched from the barracks to the barricade in the road and how they were fired on by their captors before the mine was detonated. As the smoke cleared, he saw three of the others gravely wounded. He and Jeremiah Donoghue crawled away as the National Army unit finished off the dying by lobbing grenades and firing into the smoke. Donoghue was mortally wounded and Coffey was wounded in the leg but escaped and went into hiding.

The survivor at Ballyseedy was Stephen Fuller. In later years, Fuller became a TD. He was a reserved man who spoke with no rancour about the civil war or the events that had made him famous. He had been part of a group of prisoners undergoing interrogation. One prisoner had a broken arm, one had spinal injuries and a third a broken wrist, the result of torture with a hammer. The men had been in the custody of Colonel Commandant Neligan who was in charge of intelligence. The prisoners had been removed from the barracks in a lorry and some feared they would be subject to a mock execution or that they might be shot under the pretext of trying to escape.

At Ballyseedy, the prisoners were tied together around the mine. Their shoelaces were tied together to stop them running. The captain in charge of the National Army unit offered the men a cigarette and told them in a matter of fact way that they were to be blown up for what had been done at Knocknagoshel. They were given a few minutes to say their prayers and as they were saying goodbye to each other the mine was detonated.

Fuller was blown clear into a ditch and heard the National Army men firing. Grievously wounded and in great pain he crawled away and took shelter in a nearby house and was later moved to a dugout on the mountain side where a local doctor, Edmond Shanahan, was brought out to treat him: 'All his back was burned with gunpowder and dozens of small pieces of grit embedded in the skin.'

26. A copy of the Ballyseedy and Cahersiveen inquiries survive. Author's collection.

27. There are a handful of examples in the civil war where in different parts of the country military officers convened military courts to inquire into the deaths of prisoners: it was convenient and it kept the army in control of the inquiry, but it was not lawful.

28. *Cork Examiner*, 12 March 1923.

29. A point relied on by National Army spokesmen was that in respect of each of the landmine explosions, National Army soldiers were injured and therefore, ran the argument, the fatalities were just an accident. Fuller's account showed that some National Army men had to stand sufficiently close to ensure that no one escaped and in this way three National Army men sustained injuries. Fuller recalled that the National Army men were close at hand to machine gun the survivors after the explosion. This difficulty was circumvented at Countess Bridge and Cahersiveen by machine gunning the prisoners before detonating the charge. In this way National Army soldiers avoided the risk of injury.

30. General Mulcahy issued an order that no more night-time road clearances were to take place. Second, that an inspection of barricades should take place before prisoners were put to work and that prisoners should be supplied with grappling hooks which would lessen the risks from explosions. This was as close as General Mulcahy ever came to admitting that something untoward had taken place.

31. *Dáil Debates*, 17 April 1923, column 190.

32. The official account given by General Mulcahy to the Dáil was that: 'As part of a sweeping operation involving the areas of Killarney, Beaufort, Killorglin, Barraduff an officer and twenty-five men left Killarney at 3 a.m. to go in the direction of Kilgarvan. In order to get out of Killarney without attracting attention, they left barracks by the East Avenue Gate, and on reaching Countess Bridge found a barricade of stones on the road near the bridge. The officer was sent back at once for prisoners to remove it. Five prisoners were brought back and ordered to remove the obstruction. When they had been working for a few minutes, there was a loud explosion followed by several smaller ones. The military party had, meantime, been ordered to stand clear while the work of removing the barricade was going on. On approaching the barricade after the explosion they found four of the prisoners dead. The fifth prisoner was missing.'

The official account published by the senior National Army officer at Killarney on the day of the explosion read: 'Information was received last night that there was a barricade of stones across the road at Countess Bridge. I sent out a party of men under Lieutenant Golden to investigate. He reported back and told me it was a fact that there was a barricade of stones there.

I sent him out again at six this morning with five prisoners to clear the obstacle, when the prisoners removed a stone, with the result that there was a heavy explosion.

Simultaneously, there was machine gun and rifle fire directed on the troops and barracks, and it was some time before we could attend to the wounded prisoners, who were dead when the doctor arrived.' *Cork Examiner*, 9 March 1923.

33. The National Army officers involved at Ballyseedy, Killarney and Countess Bridge have always held their silence and until recently so too did all their fellow officers. O'Daly, Neligan and Joe Dolan all made BMH witness statements but were conspicuously silent about events in Kerry during the civil war. Many years later, one of those National Army soldiers spoke out. Niall Harrington had been one of the Dublin Guard that took part in the seaborne landing at Fenit in August of 1922: he was then a young man very much in awe of the legendary Paddy O'Daly and served with the Dublin Guard at Ballymullen. Harrington wrote that the massacres in Kerry had been 'planned by a clique of influential Dublin Guard officers in Ballymullen' and the mine used at Ballyseedy was

'constructed under the supervision of two senior Dublin Guard officers'. These men were later named as Captains Ed Flood and Jim Clarke of the Dublin Guard. These men were not publicly named by Niall Harrington in *Kerry Landing*, but after his death the names were given in a 1997 RTÉ documentary produced by Pat Butler.

34. Irish Military Archives, 1E/MA/HS/A/0770. See also *Irish Independent*, 12 April 1923. The men were James O'Malley, Francis Cunnane, Michael Monaghan, James Newell, John Maguire, Martin Moylan.

35. John Francis Rattigan from Caherlistrane.

36. IMA CW/OPS/03/1.

37. *Irish Times*, 4 April 1923. Also see E. O'Malley, *The Men Will Talk to Me: Kerry Interviews* (Cork: Mercier Press, 2012), p. 210.

38. One small column was led by Bertie Scully: E. O'Malley, *The Men Will Talk to Me: Kerry Interviews* (Cork: Mercier Press, 2012), p. 161. Interview with Bertie Scully: 'it was no good carrying out any operations as our men in gaols would be taken out and shot.' Also still at liberty was Humphrey Murphy who was ill and the Lyon's column in north Kerry.

39. Private O'Neill from Granville Street Dublin was killed and Lieutenant Pierson an engineer was gravely wounded and later died of his injuries.

40. Thomas McGrath and Patrick O'Shea.

41. Propaganda had become part of the war effort and there is some evidence that O'Daly had a particular hatred for Humphrey Murphy.

42. His name appears in the trial record as Richard, but this seems to be an error. In any event, his real name was believed to be Walter Stenning. He was from Slough in Berkshire. He deserted from the East Lancashire Regiment which was based in Tralee in the latter stages of the War of Independence. After the Truce, he joined the National Army, but when civil war threatened he deserted. When he was later captured at Clashmealcon, he was portrayed as an unscrupulous man: a deserter twice over. There is a more complex picture of a man who had found himself in the British Army by force of circumstances but joined the Volunteers to fight against Britain out of choice. After the Truce, he joined the National Army for employment, but when civil war beckoned, he walked out of barracks at Tralee with his rifle and walked up the north coast of Kerry to join his old companions.

43. E. O'Malley, *The Men Will Talk to Me: Kerry Interviews* (Cork: Mercier Press, 2012).

44. A review of anti-Treaty military action in Clare in the spring of 1923 shows evidence of destruction of bridges and the rail infrastructure. The most notable incidents include an ambush of National Army soldiers at Corkscrew Hill near Lisdoonvarna which inflicted no casualties. There was also an attack on National Army engineers who were rebuilding a bridge near Cooraclare. In this engagement an anti-Treaty fighter was killed and one wounded. In March at Mountscott, a National Army patrol raiding a dugout was sniped at without casualties. Also, near Miltown Malbay National Army troops were sniped at, but no casualties were caused. This analysis derives some support from the trial register which shows only three trials by military court. All took place in February 1923 and none were for attacking the National Army. Michael Hassett from Clarecastle was convicted of the possession of a revolver. He seems to have been released in error. Thomas Murphy from Clarecastle was acquitted of the possession of a shotgun. James Pierce, also of Clarecastle, was convicted of unlawful possession of property. There is no record of any other prisoners from Clare being tried by military court. There may have been some tried by committee but it has not been possible to identify any.

45. IMA IE/MA/HS/A/0770. The communiqué was published in the *Freeman's Journal*, 27 April 1923.

46. The full text of the note is as follows:

HQ 1st W/D 10/4/23
Dear Paddy
Herewith – I enclose £2. I received your message regarding the price of petrol for those jobs. The other £1 you may have for personal expenses. I was disappointed to learn that you were unsuccessful in burning up that show the other night. Better luck next time. Try and finish it off as soon as possible again. I trust you got those rifles you asked for and expect to hear something from you in the very near future. I am sure there are many handy jobs in town and many golden opportunities for carrying off same. I would be glad if you would intensify the campaign in that town. It needs something in that way and of course you are the only one we expect anything from in that way.

The note was written the day Liam Lynch was killed with the consequent collapse of the anti-Treaty forces. The rifles, if they ever arrived, were never used and never found.

47. O'Regan's case was one of many that was later reviewed by Judges Doyle and Dromgoole and he was released in 1924.

CHAPTER 16

1. Between 9 June and 13 July there were six attacks on the National Army but no casualties. There were four cases of arson and four of wire destruction. There were also fifteen robberies, two shootings and three escapes from custody. The affidavit of Adjutant General of the National Army Gearóid O'Sullivan. *The King (O'Brien) v the Military Governor of the Military Internment Camp, North Dublin Union, and the Minister for Defence.*

2. McGrath was from Powerstown in Tipperary where he was a 'ganger' working on the roads. During the War of Independence his skills had been used to trench roads in Tipperary. Nothing else is known about him.

3. *Clonmel Chronicle*, 19 May 1923.

4. *Irish Times*, 21 May 1923.

5. There has been confusion about the dates of execution and other details about these two prisoners. Davitt suggests they were the last men to be executed. BMH WS 1571. Campbell points out they do not appear in Macardle's list in the *Irish Republic* or National Army press releases, but there is no doubt that they were executed.

6. Both were from Ardrahan in Galway.

7. JAG files, IMA. Advice by John O'Byrne, 3 September 1923.

8. *The Public Safety (Emergency Powers) Act, No. 28 of 1923.*

9. For an analysis of the McPeake case see Chapter 1.

10. *The King (O'Brien) v the Military Governor of the Military Internment Camp, North Dublin Union, and the Minister for Defence.*

11. For an analysis of the 1923 election, see M. Hopkinson, *Green Against Green: The Irish Civil War* (Dublin: Gill & Macmillan, 2004), p. 262.

12. The Board of Commissioners consisted of Judges Dromgoole and Doyle about whom little is known.

13. The challenge came in 1924 in *The King (O'Connell) v The Military Governor of Hare Park Camp.* IR [1924 104]. Counsel for the prisoner were Michael Comyn KC and Gavan Duffy. For the government: Tim Sullivan KC leading John Costello. The prisoner was John Daniel O'Connell from Lismore House near Tralee who was reckoned to be a

senior anti-Treaty figure in Kerry. The basis of the challenge was that the Act permitting internment without trial was incompatible with the Constitution which did not permit such a course of action. The court ruled it was a temporary measure to meet an abnormal situation and was therefore lawful.

14. See for instance, R. Foster, *The Irish Civil War and Society: Politics Class and Conflict* (Dublin: Macmillan, 2014).

15. *The Indemnity Act*, No. 31 of 1923.

16. *Dáil Debates*, 18 May 1923. See *The Damage to Property (Compensation) Act*, No. 15 of 1923. See also The Compensation (Personal Injuries) Committee set up by the Act.

CHAPTER 17

1. Prisoners who were represented by a lawyer include Childers, Michael Kilroy and Martin Byrne who were all tried by military court. Most prisoners were not represented. Before the end of November 1922, this was usually because anti-Treaty prisoners were under orders not to recognise the court and to take no part in the proceedings. After the introduction of committees in December, it does not seem that any prisoners were represented by lawyers before these tribunals.

2. See C. Campbell, *Emergency Law in Ireland* (Oxford: Oxford University Press, 1994), who argues that after the summer of 1923, trials by committee continued and 'some claimed they did not even know they had been tried'. See p. 219.

3. It has been pointed out that these committees acquitted slightly more prisoners than were convicted. See P. Yeates, *A City in Civil War: Dublin 1921–24* (Dublin: Gill & Macmillan, 2015). This is hardly a ringing endorsement, since there were no charging standards. Prisoners were swept up in raids and trials followed swiftly in the circumstances that were sometimes haphazard and chaotic. The available evidence suggests that prisoners were not always charged because there was an evidential case against them but on account of intelligence about the prisoner.

4. 'We were marched over to Harepark and lodged there. As far as I knew they were emptying the other jails and lodging what remained there. There were about three or four hundred who had got the death sentence.' U. MacEoin, *Survivors* (Dublin: Argenta, 1980) p. 481. The files of the JAG at the IMA are incomplete and do not provide figures for death sentence passed.

5. Charles Daly at Drumboe Castle in March.

6. O'Malley's record was decisive according to the then JAG. BMH WS 1751, Davitt. There is other evidence that the prison doctor declined to sign off the prisoner as fit for trial. Until that certificate was forthcoming the regulations did not permit trial.

7. There are many other examples of anti-Treaty officers captured in arms but spared execution. One was James Keena, a high-ranking anti-Treaty officer from Offaly who was captured with a loaded gun in March 1923, see P. McConway, 'Offaly and the Civil War Executions', *Offaly Heritage*, 5 (2008). Others included Ned Bofin from Sligo whose men had sacked Castleconnell in February and were captured the following month. In Mayo, Joe Baker and his column were captured in March, but no executions followed. Also in this category was Paddy Lacken and Sean Gaynor from Tipperary. One of the more remarkable instances concerned Jeremiah Foley from Limerick. In April, Foley was hiding out at a farmhouse near Abbeyfeale when a National Army patrol burst in while he was eating dinner. Foley grabbed his gun and ran out into the yard where he shot dead one soldier and wounded another before being wounded and captured. Inquest report, *Cork Examiner*, 16 April 1923.

8. Austin Stack, Michael Kilroy, Dan Breen, Tom Derrig, P.J. Ruttledge and Tom Maguire.

9. *Survivors* (Dublin: Argenta, 1980), p. 294.

10. An example of prisoners who were not involved in the civil war include Cunningham, Conroy and Kelly who were executed at Birr in January 1923. It was the view of the priest who attended these youths that they had committed robbery which had nothing to do with the war. E. Gaynor, *Memoirs of a Tipperary Family – The Gaynors of Tyone* (Geography Publications, 2006), p. 206.

11. *Nemo moriturus praesumitur mentiri.* Not simply a Latin adage. A dying declaration or a declaration made under a settled expectation of death has been admissible in evidence for centuries because it was recognised as being credible. See for instance, *R v Johns* (1790), East P. C. 357. The principle has been recognised widely: 'Truth forever on the scaffold' (Lowell) or 'Truth sits upon the lips of dying men' (Arnold).

12. Last letter home to his sister Teresa. I express my thanks to Ellen D. Murphy for making available Patrick Hennessy's last letters.

13. M. O'Dwyer, *Seventy-Seven of Mine Said Ireland* (Cork: Deshaoirse, 2006), p. 375.

14. In Limerick, Michael Danford was taken from his home in September

1922 by a group of National Army officers. His body was found riddled with bullets the next day.

15. CID at Oriel House were nominally under the control of the minister for home affairs, Kevin O'Higgins. The Protective Corps and the Citizens' Defence Force were set up at his instigation. The Protective Corps was responsible for protecting government ministers, TDs and Senators. They were armed and not uniformed. The Citizens' Defence Force, which provided intelligence, was also operating in Dublin. They were also armed and without uniform.

16. Notably Jerry Buckley and Tim Kennefick in west Cork. In Clare, Martin Moloney was killed after capture. He had surrendered and there was no suggestion at the inquest that he was armed. The vexed issue at the inquest was which soldier had fired the shot. In mid-March, Nicholas Corcoran was also shot during a road clearance operation although the evidence at the trial of the soldier suggested gross negligence not malice.

17. Killing prisoners was a phenomenon strongly associated with Kerry and some analysis of local considerations is necessary. The fighting in Kerry was harder and more protracted than in any other part of Ireland. Ten National Army soldiers died in the battle for Tralee in August 1922. Some casualties had an especially painful quality: Private Patrick Harding, a stretcher bearer, was shot dead on the outskirts of Tralee. Some days later, Private Lydon was shot dead while cycling near the old Mill at Blennerville: his Red Cross armlet on plain view.

In Kenmare, local Free State Commander Tom Scarteen O'Connor and his brother were dragged from their beds by men disguised as National Army officers and shot dead. This was precursor to a conventional assault on Kenmare.

All three senior army national officers who took part in the landing at Fenit were wounded in the campaign that followed. By the late spring, sixty-nine National Army soldiers had been killed and 157 wounded: some of the casualties had been sustained in delivering food to outlying parts of Kerry.

In February, an opportunity had been allowed for men to surrender and three local columns had taken up this opportunity. Those who continued to fight were few in number but utterly determined to go on even with no prospect of victory. It was in these circumstances that the mine trap laid at Knocknagoshel was triggered, setting in motion the reprisals which resulted in seventeen prisoners being killed.

There may have been a more personal dynamic at work, one that involved Michael Collins and two senior National Army officers in Kerry: General O'Daly and Colonel David Neligan. Collins was killed on 22 August and the first serious ill-treatment of a prisoner took place at Ballymullen barracks the following day. Ballymullen barracks would become a centre for torture.

Paddy O'Daly had headed up the Squad set up by Collins and carried on a campaign of assassination from the spring of 1920 until the Truce in the summer of 1921. When the Treaty was signed and the National Army was formed, O'Daly became brigadier of the new Dublin Guard and many of the Squad joined up under his command. Collins was the man who had directed them and controlled them and suddenly he was dead.

The other person in this complex trio was Colonel David Neligan who was in charge of intelligence gathering in Kerry: the interrogation of prisoners was one of his primary duties. Neligan had been one of Collins' spies in Dublin Castle during the War of Independence. Neligan had no prior republican sympathies before being recruited by Collins and his loyalty seems personal rather than ideological. Both had been in constant danger of discovery and the bond must have been a strong one.

In the autumn of 1922, O'Daly and Neligan were under the command of W.R.E. Murphy who was an old-fashioned disciplinarian, a professional soldier, and it may be that his presence acted as a partial brake, but after he was recalled to Dublin at the end of December 1922, the gloves were off. The new GOC was the freshly promoted Major General O'Daly.

Neligan's interrogation techniques are now infamous. They resulted in intelligence which Paddy O'Daly's men used to effect captures and seizures. Ultimately, torture became endemic at National Army headquarters at Ballymullen and at the Great Southern Hotel at Killarney. From torture it was perhaps a short step to killing prisoners.

It is reasonable to surmise that for O'Daly the penny was beginning to drop: Kerry was an isolated county where the Civic Guard was still yet to be firmly established. The last of the local newspapers had gone under the summer before; the national press could be managed and the inquest system manipulated or occasionally disregarded.

18. See Chapter 2 of this volume.

19. See for instance, K. O'Malley, *No Surrender Here!* (Dublin: The Lilliput Press, 2008), pp. 356–66.

20. Thomas Prendiville and Thomas Conway in Kerry. Also Jerry Lyons in Clonmel.

21. Inquest into the death of Jeremiah Lyons, aged 23 (grocers assistant). *Clonmel Chronicle*, 7 April 1923. The jury 'strongly condemned' the practice of brandishing a gun while conducting an interrogation.

22. Inquest into the death of Thomas Prendiville from Kerry, 7 April 1923. The inquest jury condemned what had taken place and stipulated that the government should pay compensation to the dead man's family. The officer James Larkins was later prosecuted for manslaughter and sentenced to eight years' imprisonment.

23. Tony Mulrennan a prisoner in Custume barracks was shot down by a National Army officer while sitting on a refuse bin. One of many accounts of this incident can be found in *Survivors* (Dublin: Argenta, 1980). In this case, the inquest proceedings were repeatedly adjourned and obstructed by lawyers acting for the state. John Edwards an internee in Kilkenny gaol was speaking from his cell window to a friend in the street outside the prison when he was shot dead by a guard after refusing to desist. The inquest jury decided that the soldier was acting in the course of his duty. John Walsh was shot in Kilkenny gaol. In this case, only an account by other prisoners survives and corroboration from National Army records has proved impossible to trace. Contemporary press reports have proved elusive. Michael Buckley was shot dead in November 1922 in Limerick prison. The inquest evidence suggested that he had been signalling prisoners in the main section of the prison and that he was shot for that reason. See *Cork Examiner*, 8 November 1922. In this day and age, the use of force by servants of the state is much more nuanced. But even applying the standards of the time it was hardly a proportionate use of force.

24. A point made by Chief of Staff of the National Army General Sean Mac Mahon in a different context: Statement of Evidence to the Army Inquiry 1924: 'built in a hurry without the necessary training, and which had no time or means of fostering discipline.'

25. Company Sergeant O'Shaughnessey was tried by Field General Courts Martial in Cork for assaulting a prisoner. He was sentenced to three months hard labour. See *Cork Examiner*, 5 November 1922. Most unusually, this prosecution was personally initiated by the GOC in Cork. Another case concerned the capture of half a dozen internees who had

escaped from Tintown in April. Also swept up in these arrests was Leo Cardwell. When the dust settled, he gave his age as 13 and a half. He was held overnight and whilst awaiting release he sustained 'a slight neck wound' in circumstances which seem very curious but were not publicly disclosed. See Dáil Reports, 3 May 1923. A soldier was held for court martial, but it has not been possible to trace the detail of the case or the result.

26. For this point I am indebted to John Dorney's analysis. See *The Civil War in Dublin* (Dublin: Merrion Press, 2017), p. 236. John Dorney argues the effect of this strategy was to limit the influence and activities of these men and it went some way to resolving the problem in the short term. But Mulcahy's concerns about the reaction of these men was well founded. They became a cadre of angry and vengeful officers who would form their own secret society and in due course provide the impetus for the Army Mutiny in 1924.

27. O'Higgins to Mulcahy, 1 February 1923, *Mulcahy Papers*, P7/B/101/19.

Select Bibliography

National Library of Ireland

Gavan Duffy Papers.
Harrington Papers.
O'Donoghue Papers.

UCDA

Mulcahy Papers.

Irish Military Archives

BMH Witness Statements.
Pension Records.
List of Prisoners Tried By Military Court IE/MA/CW/P/02/02/23.
Executions 1922–3 IE/MA/HS/A0770.
Proclamations by the Army Council:
  3 October 1922.
  10 October 1922.
  15 October 1922.
  7 December 1922.
  27 January 1923.

National Army Publications

General Regulations as to the Trial of Civilians by Military Courts 1922.
General Regulations as to Discipline 1922.

Statutes (Westminster)

The Coroners Act 1887, 50 & 51 Vic., Ch. 71.
The Irish Free State Agreement Act, 12 Geo. V., Ch. 4.
The Irish Free State Constitution Act 1922, 13. Geo. V., Ch. 1.

The Irish Free State (Consequential Provisions) Act 1922, 13. Geo. V., Ch. 2.

The Restoration of Order in Ireland Act 1920, 10 & 11 Geo. V., Ch. 31.

Statutes (Irish Free State)

The Constitution of the Irish Free State (Saorstat Éireann) Act 1922 (No. 1 of 1922).

The Indemnity Act, No. 31 of 1923.

The Public Safety (Emergency Powers) Act 1923, No. 28 of 1923.

The Defence Forces (Temporary Provisions) Act 1923.

Case Law

Egan v Macready [1921] 1 IR 265.

Ex Parte Beaumont ILT & SJ September 1922.

Ex Parte O'Brien [1922] 2 KB 361.

Johnstone v O'Sullivan and Others [1923] IR [Vol. II] 13.

R (Childers) v Adjutant General of the Provisional Forces [1923] 1 IR 5.

R (Murphy) v The Military Governor of Mountjoy Prison [1924] ILTR 1.

R (O'Brien) v Military Governor NDU [1924] IR 32.

R (O'Connell) v Military Governor of Hare Park Camp [1924] 2 IR 104.

R (O'Sullivan) v Military Governor of Hare Park Internment Camp [1924] 58 ILTR 62.

R v (Cooney) v Clinton [1924] 2 IR 104.

Secondary Sources

Abbott, R., *Police Casualties in Ireland 1919–22* (Cork: Mercier Press, 2000).

Boyle, A., *The Riddle of Erskine Childers* (Hutchinson: London, 1977).

Campbell, C., *Emergency Law in Ireland 1918–25* (Oxford: Oxford University Press, 1994).

Clark, G., *Everyday Violence in the Irish Civil War* (Cambridge: Cambridge University Press, 2014).

Comyn, J., *Their Friends at Court* (London: Barry Rose, 1973).

Coogan, T.P., *The IRA* (Glasgow: Fontana, 1980).

Delaney, E., *Demography, State and Society: Irish Migration to Britain 1921–1971* (Liverpool: Liverpool University Press, 2000).

Ferguson, K., *King's Inn Barristers, 1868–2004* (Dublin: The Honourable Society of King's Inn, in association with the Irish Legal History Society, Irish Academic Press, 2005).

Foster, R., *The Irish Civil War and Society: Politics Class and Conflict* (Dublin: Macmillan, 2014).

Garvin, T., *1922: The Birth of Irish Democracy* (Dublin: Gill & Macmillan, 2006).

Griffith, K. and O'Grady, T., *Curious Journey* (London: Hutchinson, 1982).

Hart, P., *The IRA at War 1916–23* (Oxford: Oxford University Press, 2003).

Hopkinson, M., *Green Against Green: The Irish Civil War* (Dublin: Gill & Macmillan, 2004).

Kissane, B., *The Politics of the Irish Civil War* (Oxford: Oxford University Press, 2005).

Litton, H., *The Irish Civil War – An Illustrated History* (Dublin: Wolfhound Press, 2006).

Macardle, D., *The Irish Republic* (London: Corgi, 1969).

MacEoin, U., *Survivors* (Dublin: Argenta, 1980).

Murray, P., *Oracles of God: The Roman Catholic Church and Irish Politics, 1922–37* (Dublin: University College Press, 2000).

Neeson, E., *The Civil War 1922–23* (Dublin: Poolbeg, 1989).

O'Donoghue, F., *No Other Law* (Dublin: Irish Press Limited, 1954).

O'Dwyer, M., *Seventy-Seven of Mine Said Ireland* (Cork: Deshaoirse, 2006).

O'Malley, K., *No Surrender Here! The Civil War Papers of Ernie O'Malley* (Dublin: The Lilliput Press, 2008).

Ó Ruairc, P., *Revolution – A Photographic History of Revolutionary Ireland* (Cork: Mercier Press, 2014).

Regan, J.M., *The Irish Counter Revolution 1921–36* (Dublin: Gill & Macmillan, 1999).

Ryan, M., *Tom Barry IRA Freedom Fighter* (Cork: Mercier Press, 2003).

Share, B., *In Time of Civil War – The Conflict on the Irish Railways 1922–23* (Cork: The Collins Press, 2006).

Valiulis, M., *Portrait of a Revolutionary: General Mulcahy and the Founding of the Irish Free State* (Dublin: Irish Academic Press, 1992).

Walsh, T., *Ireland in a Revolutionary World 1918–23* (London: Faber and Faber, 2016).

Memoirs

Augusteijn, J., *The Memoirs of John M. Regan. A Catholic Officer in the RIC and RUC 1909–48* (Dublin: Four Courts Press, 2007).

Brennan, R., *Allegiance* (Dublin: The Richview Press, 1950).

Deasy, L., *Brother Against Brother* (Cork: Mercier Press, 1997).

O'Donnell, P., *The Gates Flew Open* (Cork: Mercier Press, 2013).

O'Malley, E., *The Singing Flame* (Dublin: Anvil Books, 1978).

Biographies

Coogan, T.P., *Michael Collins* (London: Hutchinson, 1990).

Dwyer, R.T., *Michael Collins and the Civil War* (Cork: Mercier Press, 2012).

Laffan, M., *Judging W.T. Cosgrave* (Dublin: Royal Irish Academy, 2014).

Longford, Earl and O'Neill, T.P., *Eamon De Valera* (London: Hutchinson & Co., 1970).

McCarthy, J.P., *Kevin O'Higgins: Builder of the Irish State* (Dublin: Irish Academic Press, 2006).

Tierney, M., *Eoin MacNeill: Scholar and Man of Action, 1867–1945* (Oxford: Clarendon Press, 1980).

Essays and Dissertations

Breen-Murphy, T., 'The Government's Executions Policy during the Irish Civil War 1922–23' (NUI: Maynooth, 2010).

Darcy, S., 'The Evolution of the Law of Belligerent Reprisals Military Law Review', *Military Law Review*, 175 (March 2003) 184.

Durney, J., 'The Curragh Internees 1921–24. From Defiance to Defeat.' Kildarearchsoc.ie 2015/11.

Hogan, G., 'Hugh Kennedy, the Childers Habeas Corpus Application and the Return to the Four Courts' in C. Costello (ed.), *The Four Courts* (Dublin: The Incorporated Council of Law Reporting for Ireland, 1996), pp. 177–219.

Hopkinson, M., 'The Civil War from the Pro-Treaty Perspective', *The Irish Sword*, 20, 82, 287 (1996–7).

Keane, R., 'The Will of the General: Martial Law in Ireland 1535–1924', *Irish Jurist*, 151 (1990–2).

McConway, P., 'The Civil War in Offaly', *Offaly Tribune*, January 2008.

McConway, P., 'Offaly and the Civil War Executions', *Offaly Heritage*, 5 (2008).

Pigott (Canon), J., 'Executions Recalled', *The Athenry Journal*, 8 (1997).

Shortall, L., 'Sources for the Study of the Revolutionary Period in King's County/Offaly 1912–1923', *Offaly Heritage*, 9 (Tullamore: Esker Press, 2016).

Local Histories

Athlone

Burke, J., *Athlone 1900–1923: Politics, Revolution and Civil War* (Stroud: The History Press, 2015).

Clare

Ó Ruairc, P., *Blood On the Banner* (Cork: Mercier Press, 2009).

O'Malley, E., *The Men Will Talk to Me: Clare Interviews* (Ó Ruairc, P. & O'Malley, Cormac K.H., eds) (Cork: Mercier Press, 2016).

Cork

Hart, P., *The IRA & Its Enemies: Violence and Community in Cork 1916–23* (Oxford: Clarendon, 1998).

Ó Ríordáin, J.J., *Kiskeam Versus the Empire* (Tralee: The Kerryman, 1985).

Ryan, M., *The Day Michael Collins Was Shot* (Dublin: Poolbeg Press, 1989).

O'Malley, E., *The Men Will Talk to Me: West Cork Interviews* (Cork: Mercier Press, 2015).

Donegal

O'Duibhir, L., *Donegal and the Civil War* (Cork: Mercier Press, 2011).

Dublin

Dorney, J., *The Civil War in Dublin: The Fight for the Irish Capital 1922–1924* (Dublin: Merrion Press, 2017).

Yeates, P., *A City in Civil War: Dublin 1921–24* (Dublin: Gill & Macmillan, 2015).

Galway

McNamara, C., *War and Revolution in the West of Ireland: Galway 1913–22* (Dublin: Irish Academic Press, 2018).

O'Comhrai, C., *Sa Bhearna Bhaoil Ghaillimh 1913–23* (Chonnacht: Clo Iar, 2015).

O'Gadhra, N., *Civil War in Connaught* (Cork: Mercier Press, 1999).

O'Malley, E. (O'Malley, C. & O'Comhrai, C., eds), *The Men Will Talk to Me: Galway Interviews* (Cork: Mercier Press, 2013).

Kerry

Doyle, T., *The Civil War in Kerry* (Cork: Mercier Press, 2008).

Dwyer, T.R., *Tans, Terror and Troubles* (Cork: Mercier Press, 2001).

Harrington, N., *Kerry Landing* (Dublin: Anvil Books, 1992).

Horgan, T., *Dying for the Cause* (Cork: Mercier Press, 2015).

Macardle, D., *Tragedies of Kerry* (Dublin: Irish Freedom Press, 2004).

O'Malley, C.K.H. and Horgan, T. (eds), *The Men Will Talk to Me: Kerry Interviews* (Cork: Mercier Press, 2012).

Kildare

Durney, J., *The Civil War in Kildare* (Cork: Mercier Press, 2011).

Kilkenny

Walsh, E., *Kilkenny: In Times of Revolution* (Dublin: Merrion Press, 2018).

Limerick

O'Callaghan, J., *Revolutionary Limerick* (Dublin: Irish Academic Press, 2010).

Ó Ruairc, P., *Battle for Limerick City* (Cork: Mercier Press, 2010).

Toomey, T., *The War of Independence in Limerick* (Limerick: privately published, 2010).

Louth

Maguire, M. and Hall, D., *County Louth and the Irish Revolution 1912–23* (Dublin: Irish Academic Press, 2017).

Mayo

Price, D., *The Flame and the Candle: War in Mayo 1919–1924* (Cork: Collins Press, 2012).

O'Malley, E. (O'Malley, C. & Keane, V., eds), *The Men Will Talk to Me: Mayo Interviews* (Cork: Mercier Press, 2014).

Meath

Coogan, O., *Politics and War in County Meath 1913–23* (Dublin: privately published, 1983).

Monaghan

Dooley, T., *The Irish Revolution, 1912–23* (Dublin: Four Courts Press, 2017).

Sligo

Farry, M., *The Aftermath of Revolution: Sligo 1921–23* (Dublin: Dublin University Press, 2000).

McGowan, J., *In the Shadow of Benbulben* (Manorhamilton: Aeolus, 1993).

Tipperary

Hogan, S., *The Black and Tans in North Tipperary 1913–22* (Dublin: Untold Stories Publishers, 2013).

Gaynor, E., *Memoirs of a Tipperary Family – The Gaynors of Tyone* (Geography Publications, undated, 2006).

Waterford

McCarthy, P., *The Irish Revolution, 1912–23 Waterford* (Dublin: Four Courts Press, 2015).

Mooney, T., *The Deise Divided* (Dungarven: de Paor, 2014).

Westmeath

The Journal of the Old Athlone Society, 2, 10 (2015).

Wexford

Mac Suain, S., *County Wexford's Civil War* (Ireland: privately published, 1995).

Newspapers and Periodicals

Irish Independent
The Clare Champion
The Cork Examiner
The Derry Journal
The Freeman's Journal
The Irish Law Times and Solicitors Journal
The Irish Times
The Killarney Echo
The Mayo News
The Manchester Guardian
The New York Times
The Sligo Champion
The Times
The Waterford News

Index